The Prymer
or
Lay Folks' Prayer Book.

Early English Text Society.
Original Series, No. 105.
1895.

BERLIN: ASHER & CO., 13, UNTER DEN LINDEN.
NEW YORK: C. SCRIBNER & CO.; LEYPOLDT & HOLT.
PHILADELPHIA: J. B. LIPPINCOTT & CO.

FACSIMILE OF THE FLY LEAF OF A MANUSCRIPT PRYMER.

LATIN VERSION, BRITISH MUSEUM, SLOANE 2633.

The Prymer

or

Lay Folks' Prayer Book.

(WITH SEVERAL FACSIMILES.)

EDITED BY

HENRY LITTLEHALES

FROM THE MS. Dd. 11, 82, ab. 1420-30 A.D., IN THE LIBRARY
OF THE UNIVERSITY OF CAMBRIDGE.

LONDON:
PUBLISHED FOR THE EARLY ENGLISH TEXT SOCIETY
BY KEGAN PAUL, TRENCH, TRÜBNER & CO., LIMITED,
PATERNOSTER HOUSE, CHARING CROSS ROAD, W.C.
1895.

UNIVERSITY PRESS

Great Clarendon Street, Oxford OX2 6DP
United Kingdom

Oxford University Press is a department of the University of Oxford.
It furthers the University's objective of excellence in research, scholarship,
and education by publishing worldwide. Oxford is a registered trade mark of
Oxford University Press in the UK and in certain other countries

© The Early English Text Society 1895

The moral rights of the authors have been asserted

Database right Oxford University Press (maker)

First Edition published in 1895

All rights reserved. No part of this publication may be reproduced,
stored in a retrieval system, or transmitted, in any form or by any means,
without the prior permission in writing of Oxford University Press,
or as expressly permitted by law, or under terms agreed with the appropriate
reprographics rights organization. Enquiries concerning reproduction
outside the scope of the above should be sent to the Rights Department,
Oxford University Press, at the address above

You must not circulate this book in any other form
and you must impose this same condition on any acquirer

Published in the United States of America by Oxford University Press
198 Madison Avenue, New York, NY 10016, United States of America

British Library Cataloguing in Publication Data
Data available

Library of Congress Cataloging in Publication Data
Data available

Original Series, 105

ISBN 978-1-84-384002-2

TO

DR. F. J. FURNIVALL,

TO WHOM ENGLISH STUDENTS ARE GREATLY INDEBTED,

THIS WORK IS INSCRIBED.

PREFACE.

SECTION I of the present volume, the Essay on the Origin of the Prymer, is from the pen of Mr. Edmund Bishop, to whom the grateful thanks of our Society are due. For all other matter I am wholly responsible.

Our thanks are also due to Mrs. Willett of Haywards Heath, for the kind loan of her valuable MS. York Prymer; to Dr. Furnivall, who has punctuated the present volume; to the Rev. Canon Christopher Wordsworth for his care in reading the proofs, and to many officials of various libraries, especially all those of the Department of MSS. in the British Museum, to whom for ever-ready aid in obscure readings, and unstinted labour in procuring frequently very many MSS. for examination at a time, for some years past, I am personally very greatly indebted.

Of works dealing with the subject of the Mediæval Prayer Book, I may specify the third volume of Maskell's *Monumenta Ritualia;* the volumes issued by and the property of Messrs. Longman, under the title of *The Prymer;* a little book by Mr. Athelstan Riley, restricted to the Hours of the Blessed Virgin, and two separate forthcoming works, respectively by the Rev. C. H. Evelyn-White and the Rev. Edgar Hoskins.

In the present volume I have endeavoured to *add* something to our knowledge of the subject, and to repeat as far as possible nothing hitherto published; and it will be noticed that I have attempted to treat only of the earlier or MS. copies of the Prymer.

H. L.

Bexley Heath.

CONTENTS.

		PAGE
I.	On the Origin of the Prymer	xi
II.	Some Historical Notes	xxxix
III.	The Distribution of the Psalms of the Prymer	liii
IV.	An Attempt to define the Structure of the Prymer according to the Uses of Sarum and York	lv
V.	The Structure of the Prymer Secundum Usum or Consuetudinem Angliæ	lxxiii
VI.	The Structure of two Eleventh-Century Versions of the Hours of the Blessed Virgin Mary	lxxv
VII.	The Structure of the Durham Prymer (Brit. Mus. MS., Harl. 1804)	lxxxv
VIII.	Table showing the Reading of Six Sarum Prymers	xci

CONTENTS.

		PAGE
I.	THE HOURS OF THE BLESSED VIRGIN MARY:	
	1. MATINS	1
	2. LAUDS	7
	3. PRIME	16
	4. TIERCE	20
	5. SEXT	23
	6. NONE	25
	7. EVENSONG	28
	8. COMPLINE	31
II.	THE 7 PENITENTIAL PSALMS	37
III.	THE 15 GRADUAL PSALMS	44
IV.	THE LITANY	47
V.	THE OFFICE FOR THE DEAD:	
	1. PLACEBO (VESPERS)	52
	2. DIRIGE (MATINS)	56
	3. DIRIGE (LAUDS)	70
VI.	THE COMMENDATIONS	79

INTRODUCTION.

I.

On the Origin of the Prymer.

BY EDMUND BISHOP.

THE late Henry Bradshaw has given the following account of the origin of the Prymer:

"It is known that the layman's prayer-book (the *primarium* or *primer*, as it was called in England) consists, in its earliest form, of the Psalter and Litany, to which the Vigils of the Dead are commonly added. By the end of the 13th century, we find it consisting not of the whole psalter, but of the seven penitential psalms only, with the Litany and the Vigils of the Dead, and having prefixed to it what are known as the Hours of the Blessed Virgin (*Horae Beatae Mariae Virginis*). These hours seem to me to have originated in a special commemorative service to be used during Advent in connection with devotion to the Incarnation; just as, still later, we find the Hours of the Passion (*Horae de sancta Cruce*) and the Hours of the Holy Ghost (*Horae de sancto Spiritu*) drawn up, apparently, as special commemorative services for use at Passiontide and Whitsuntide. As time went on, the constant public use of the full daily hour-service in church, at which all were expected to attend, fell off; while the clergy, being bound in any case to say their hours, were allowed to repeat them privately. The laity were relieved from the use of the full hour-service of the Breviary, and these shorter commemorative services were then made of general application, instead of being supplementary devotions to be used merely during the season of the year to which they were especially appropriate. They thus came to be more constantly found in the layman's prayer-book. With the growth of the devotion to the Mother of our Lord, the *Advent*

Hours of the *Incarnation* took the form, or rather the name, of Hours of the *Blessed Virgin*, used constantly *throughout the year;* and they thenceforward became the leading or principal element in these layman's prayer-books, and eventually, in later times, gathered round them a mass of miscellaneous devotions, which varied to an almost unlimited extent in different localities. Such are the conclusions which a careful study of the books themselves has led me to adopt" (*The early Collection of Canons known as the Hibernensis*, Cambridge, 1893, pp. 55-56).

This account has in more than one quarter been cited with approval. The means whereby Mr. Bradshaw reached his conclusions was, he says, "a careful study of the books themselves." It is unnecessary to delay the inquirer here with any criticism of the details of this theory of the origin of the *Prymer*, on which one or two remarks will be made at the close of this discussion. The questions which present themselves for examination are:

(1) What was the relation of this favourite layfolks' prayer-book, called the *Prymer*, to the authorized and official service-books used in the public worship of the Church? Or, as Dr. Furnivall writes: "The point I want to know is—if a man took the *Prymer* to church, would he hear the same service or set of services in Latin? Is the *Prymer* a translation of a public service-book, or one of private devotion, or partly of both?"

(2) Since the *Prymer* presents certain practically unvarying elements—viz. the Office of the Blessed Virgin, the Office of the Dead, the Penitential and Gradual Psalms, the Litany, and Commendations—which may be considered as substantially *the* Prymer— how came precisely these elements to be brought together? Is there any historical reason which accounts for this particular selection? I think that there is; and that the case will be found plain enough if we proceed by the simple method of a historical inquiry into the origin and use of each item of which the *Prymer* is made up. This point of origins in detail once elucidated, the relation of the *Prymer* as a whole to the public services of the Church can be seen without difficulty. It may seem a far cry from the English *Prymer* to St. Benedict of Aniane,—from a book the product of the 14th century to the practice of the close of the 8th or beginning of the 9th; but to begin at the beginning will save trouble in the end; and it is only thus that a clear understanding of the whole question can be arrived at.

St. Benedict of Aniane[1] was of Gothic race, but the son of a firm and distinguished adherent of the royal house of the Franks, which had absorbed into its dominions the old Gothic kingdom of Aquitaine. He was born in the middle of the 8th century in that quarter of France which borders on the Mediterranean and the Spanish frontier. In early manhood he became a monk far from his home at the monastery of Saint-Seine near Dijon, and soon made himself remarked for his austerities: though professing the Rule of St. Benedict, it was a common and almost contemptuous saying with him that such a Rule was fit for the tyro and the weakling only, and he turned with special satisfaction to the more rigid or fervent monastic teaching of the East, the words of St. Basil, the discipline of St. Pachomius.[2] After some years he returned to the country of his birth, and gathering around him some kindred spirits, adopted a mode of life resembling in many respects the first Cistercian austerity of later times. He would have no chalice but of wood, later of glass, then tin; nor tolerate mass vestments of silk.[3] As time went on, he mitigated his severity, and, in building and fitting the church of the abbey of Aniane which he had founded, he admitted all the splendour and costliness then usually shown in edifices of this kind.[4] But his singularity appears in a point of detail: anticipating a devotion which spread in the later Middle Ages, but was alien to the mind and feeling of those earlier times, he dedicated his church, not under the title of a saint, but under that of the Holy Trinity.[5] It is unnecessary to follow the spread of his reputation, his foundation of new monasteries, and reform of older houses. In this work he before long came under the personal notice of Lewis, son of Charles the Great, constituted by his father King of Aquitaine, over whom Benedict soon acquired an ascendancy which only grew stronger as years went on. Lewis committed to him the visitation of all the monasteries of Aquitaine. On succeeding to the empire in 814, Lewis summoned Benedict to his palace, and from that time forward Benedict was, till his death in 821, the most influential person at the court of the new Emperor. But he was no mere minister or courtier; he remained, first and before all, a monk.

---

[1] The following is from his life by his friend Ardo, in *Mon. Germ. hist.*, *Script.* t. XIII.
[2] "Regulam quoque beati Benedicti tironibus seu infirmis positam fore contestans, ad beati Basilii dicta necnon et beati Pacomii regulam scandere nitens, quamvis exiguis possibilia gereret, iugiter impossibilia rimabat" (p. 202).
[3] p. 204.   [4] p. 207.   [5] p. 206.

One of Lewis's first measures was to build a monastery for thirty monks close to his own palace at Aachen, with a double object; first, that he might have Benedict as counsellor always at hand; secondly, this monastery of Inde or Cornelimünster was to serve as a model according to which others were to be reformed. And to compass the desired end, Lewis now gave him those general powers over the monasteries of his Frankish dominions which as king he had granted him for the reform of those of his realm of Aquitaine. The general scheme was this: all houses were to be reduced to an absolute uniformity of discipline, observance, even of habit, according to the pattern of Inde[1]; visitors were to be appointed to see that the constitutions were strictly observed. The new scheme was to be launched at a meeting of all abbats to be held at Aachen in 817. But to plan is one thing, to carry into effect another. It is clear that, in the general assembly of abbats, Benedict, backed as he was by the Emperor, had to give up for the sake of peace, and in order to carry through substantial reforms, many details of observance by which he set great store. His biographer and friend Ardo, too, who knew everything by personal observation and at first hand, in a roundabout way and darkly gives this to be understood.[2] But the decrees of this meeting of Aachen, of which Benedict was as well the author as the life and soul, were a turning-point in the history of the order, forming the basis of later legislation and practice. After the great founder himself, Benedict of Nursia, no man has more widely affected Western monachism than did the second Benedict, he of Aniane.

We may now turn to the points which are of direct interest for the history of the *Prymer*. And first it is well to advert to a broad fact of general experience which may be said to constitute a law in the development of devotional forms and practices: the source of new forms of private devotion which become by and by popularized is in the religious orders. This holds good in regard to the monks of earlier days, the mendicants of the high tide of the Middle Ages, or the various institutes of clerks regular of modern times. Mr. Bradshaw very rightly says that the *Prymer* is the outcome not of the Divine Office, in its strict sense, but what he calls "supplementary devotions." It will be readily conceived that such devotional additions and accretions will not easily have found their origin with the secular clergy engaged in the active duties of the ministry, and

[1] pp. 215, 216, 217.   [2] p. 216.

generally dispersed, or at most but loosely organized; whilst, on the other hand, such additions to the prescribed divine service almost inevitably must ensue upon the decrease of manual labour in the monasteries, such as had already taken place by the 9th century; and any revival or reform of monastic discipline would in such circumstances be naturally accompanied, as a dictate of piety, by the adoption of novel and extraordinary devotional practices in addition to the traditional Office. And this was, in fact, the case with St. Benedict of Aniane in settling the practice of his pattern monastery of Inde. His biographer Ardo gives a detailed account of these additions. On going to the church for matins, he prescribed that the brethren should first visit all the altars, saying the Lord's Prayer and Creed at each altar; and then, going to their places in the choir, each should privately recite fifteen psalms, divided into three sets of five, each set to be followed by a short prayer or collect relative to the intention for which the five preceding psalms had been said; the first five for all the faithful living; the second five for all the faithful dead; the third five for all recently deceased. And then only, on the arrival of the officiant or hebdomadar, were matins to begin. He prescribed a second visit to the altars before prime, and a third after complin. At these two latter visits, the brethren were free to say either the Lord's Prayer or to make acts of contrition.[1]

The devotional recital of the fifteen psalms before the Church office of matins, thus introduced, obtained a permanent footing in monasteries, and in the following century—the 10th—it was of universal observance among monks. The biographer of Benedict does not say in express words that these fifteen psalms were the fifteen gradual psalms (119 to 133; or 120 to 134 according to the Authorized Version), but in view of the invariable later practice, from the very first occurrence of definite statements on the subject, there can be no doubt that these were the fifteen actually prescribed, and said at Inde from the first institution of the devotion.

It is to be understood that what now follows has reference exclusively to practice in monasteries, and among monks. By the second half of the 10th century, as has been observed, the testimony of monastic custom-books is uniform, that the recitation of the fifteen gradual psalms before matins obtained everywhere. By what steps this uniformity was brought about there is, however, no evidence to show. But it seems certain that as late as the middle of the 9th

[1] p. 216; and p. 217, "Hic tribus per diem vicibus," &c.

century, two distinct and sharply antagonistic schools existed, the one favouring, the other opposed to, Benedict's innovation in this point. These schools are represented by two commentators on "the Rule" of "the Great Benedict" of Nursia, Smaragdus and Hildemar. The divergence between the two writers, and their different tendencies, come out clearly in their observations on the apparently simple direction of the eighth chapter of the Rule, that the monks "in winter should rise at the eighth hour." The case is not so simple as it at first sight might appear to us who are accustomed all the year round to "hours" of equal length, and fixed as to time, both night and day; whilst the length of the "hour" in the Rule varied continually throughout the year, according to the Roman reckoning, as the nights or days were longer or shorter. But this difficulty was not the point which divided Smaragdus and Hildemar; the discussion was only the opportunity for the former to make room for the new practice, and by a little prudent manipulation of terms to enable him to show that "eight" may conveniently mean "half-past seven."[1] Hildemar, whose book is a series of notes of lectures on the text of the Rule rather than a formal commentary, comes down on this artificial method with the sledge-hammer of common sense: "*Rise at eight o'clock of the night.* What is it, *rise at eight o'clock?* It is as if he said, 'neither before eight, nor after eight, but at eight precisely.'"[2] But, for all that, the party represented by Smaragdus carried the day; a devotional current had set in which was to flow in increasing volume in the immediately succeeding centuries.

There is ground for supposing that the visits to the altars and the fifteen psalms were not the only additions which Benedict of Aniane had adopted and had desired to impose generally, although

---

[1] Migne, *Patr. Lat.*, 102, 829, 830.
[2] *Vita et Regula SS. P. Benedicti*, ed. Mittermüller (Ratisbonae, 1880), pp. 277, 278. The differences between the two schools were by no means confined to this point. A much more important matter, the partial substitution of the office of the clergy for the office prescribed by the Rule, seems to have been evidently favoured in practice by Benedict of Aniane. See Herrgott, *Vetus disciplina monastica* (Parisiis, 1726), p. xxxvi, *seqq*. Hildemar, as might be expected, took the conservative view, and enforced it with no little vigour (p. 310, *seqq.*). The commentary which has been printed under the name of Paul Warnefrid, an earlier writer, but which is probably of a somewhat later date (*Bibliotheca Cassinensis*, t. IV, *Florilegium*, p. 94), runs on the same lines. These two writers represent the Italian conservative ideas, as opposed to Ultramontane innovations, taking up just the position of Monte Cassino towards Cluny a century or two later. The *Memoriale qualiter in Monasterio conversari debemus* represents the same conservative party, and it is not easy to see how it can have St. Benedict of Aniane for its author (as is assumed in the *Winchester Obedientiaries' Rolls*, p. 196).

in face of opposition he was unable to carry out his design. It seems not improbable that among the additions thus dropped was the regular recital of the office for the dead, which forms so important a part of the *Prymer*. The origins of this office are obscure; a recent writer has declared it to be purely Roman, and a creation of the beginning of the 8th century. Extant testimonies by no means warrant so confident a tone.[1] A document seemingly of the second half of the 8th century, detailing the observances of Monte Cassino, states that on the burial of a monk, the brethren after vespers (of the day, that is) recited for him the seven penitential psalms and the litany.[2] A document of the year 811 or 812, drawn up by the monks of Fulda and presented to Charles the Great, gives the following account of the offices for the dead as said in that monastery: (1) for deceased brethren, a commemoration twice a day, after lauds and vespers, consisting of the antiphon *Requiem eternam*, the "first part" of the psalm *Te decet hymnus Deus* (lxiv), a verse and collect; (2) on the first day of every month for the first abbat, Sturm, and the founders of the house, "a vigil and fifty psalms"; (3) on the anniversary of Abbat Sturm, "a vigil and the whole psalter."[3] As the object of this petition of the Fulda monks to the Emperor was the maintenance of the discipline introduced by the first abbat, and he had drawn the observance prescribed by him from the monasteries of Rome and the neighbourhood, including the recently reestablished Monte Cassino,[4] it is probable that these offices of the dead, at least in a general way, represent practices prevailing in Italian monasteries also; although it is open to question what is here precisely meant by the word "vigil."

But it is certain that Benedict of Aniane had determined to intro-

---

[1] Batiffol, *Hist. du Bréviaire romain*, pp. 188-190. The author's best argument appears to lie in his personal and subjective appreciation of what the Roman office must have been, "dans son état le plus pur" when "dégagé de toute influence monastique." The reference "Amalar., *De ord. antiph.*, 65 et 79" settles nothing. So far as mere testimonies are concerned, it would not be difficult to make out a stronger case in favour of non-Roman than in favour of Roman origin. This is not the place to discuss the question; it is necessary, however, only too frequently to warn the reader against the positive tone of this writer on matters as to which either nothing is known or the evidence is of a doubtful and uncertain character.

[2] "Cum frater ad exitum propinquaverit, omnis congregatio ante eum psalmos decantet; illoque sepulto, post vesperum septem psalmos cum litaniis omni corpore in terram prostrati decantent" (Hergott, *Vet. disc. mon.*, p. 3).

[3] J. G. Eccard, *De rebus Franciae Orientalis*, II, 72.

[4] See the tenth article of the petition (p. 73), compared with Eigil's Life of Sturm (*Mon. Germ. hist., Script.*, II, 371).

duce uniformity (a matter on which he laid the strongest stress)[1] in this detail also of the office of the dead, or the mode of its recital. On the accession of Lewis the Pious to the empire, it was very soon understood on all hands that Benedict would now have a free field and full powers for carrying out generally his own long-cherished plans. One abbat at least, though distant from the seat of government, the Abbat of Reichenau, an island on the Lake of Constance, had the wisdom to take time by the forelock, and set his house in order before the measures which he saw would be taken were promulgated, and the great scheme launched; lest the monastic visitors coming from Benedict with imperial command to settle the houses on the new model should find him unprepared. He accordingly sent two of his monks to Inde, to stay there, ascertain by practical experience the custom of that monastery, and report to him the chief points of observance that were to be insisted on, and changed in the old foundations. Their report[2] was drawn up certainly before 817, perhaps a year or so earlier. Of the twelve points of practice given in their report, there is one describing "how the vigil of the dead is celebrated" by St. Benedict of Aniane and his monks in the pattern monastery. "As soon as vespers of the day are over" (runs the document), "they immediately say vespers of the dead, with antiphons; and after complin, matins of the dead with antiphons and responsories, sung with full and sonorous voice and with great sweetness (*plenissime atque suavissime*); next morning, after matins of the day, lauds of the dead."[3] Martene, without any ado, takes it for

[1] Ardo repeatedly returns to this point: "Ut autem sicut una omnium erat professio fieret quoque omnium monasteriorum salubris una consuetudo" (*M. G. SS.*, xiii. 215). "Perfectum itaque prosperatumque est opus [the Council of Aachen] . . . et una cunctis generaliter posita observatur regula, cunctaque monasteria ita ad formam unitatis redacta sunt, acsi ab uno magistro et in uno imbuerentur loco. Uniformis mensura in potu, in cibo, in vigiliis, in modulationibus cunctis observanda est tradita" (*ibid.*). "In abitu quoque dissimiles fecerat multorum consuetudo. . . . Quam ob rem vir Dei uniformem cunctis tenendum monachis instituit modum," etc. (p. 217). The "Goths" had been "the outs" in the time of Charles the Great; they had their day gloriously under his son, and for the time were masters all along the line.

[2] Printed in Herrgott, pp. 19-21.

[3] "Undecimo, ut defunctorum vigilia hoc modo eis celebratur. Vespera solito finita, statim vesperam cum antiphonis celebrant pro defunctis, et post completorium vigiliam cum antiphonis vel responsoriis plenissime ac suavissime canunt; et post nocturnos intervallo matutinos pro mortuis faciunt. Facto autem primo mane . . . missam celebrant pro defunctis publicam. . . Qua percelebrata statim cantant primam, si fuerit tempus, aut certe tertiam" (p. 21). On "intervallo" Herrgott remarks: "that is, in the interval between matins and lauds of the day." As to this "interval," see the *Disciplina Farfensis* (Herrgott, p. 49-50), and the English *Concordia regularis* (in Reyner, *Apostolatus*, Pt. III, p. 81, l. 8). But this interpretation seems by no means sure;

granted that this means a daily recital of the office of the dead, after the regular Divine office;[1] reading the document as a whole, the general terms in which it is couched make this interpretation a possible one. And it is to be remembered that these monks of Reichenau are reporting to their abbat points of importance in which observance usual amongst them is to be altered. Still, the words as they stand by no means require such general interpretation to be put upon them; it is possible, for instance, that the novelty consisted in the mode of recitation. But if the devotional addition of the office of the dead daily was any part of Benedict's programme, it is certainly one of the items insistence on which he saw fit to give up when he met his brother abbats in general assembly at the great meeting held by order of the Emperor at Aachen in 817. This assembly passed some eighty resolutions, which were confirmed by imperial authority, prescribing points of discipline to be inviolably observed in all monasteries. It is worthy of note that more than one seems to be aimed at novelties favoured by Benedict. The fiftieth resolution relates to prayer for the dead, and is couched in these curiously impatient terms: "that, doing away with piecings up of the Psalter, the *psalmi speciales* be said for benefactors and the dead."[2] The "psalmi speciales" here mentioned are nothing else than the seven penitential psalms, which, it will be remembered, are specified in the Monte Cassino observance a few decades earlier. Another resolution of the meeting evidently contemplates the recital of some "office of the dead" after complin; it may be matins, as specified in the report of the two monks of Reichenau; but this recital is here certainly contemplated as only an occasional occurrence.[3]

A few years later, Amalar, a writer deeply concerned in the then fashionable liturgical movement, and admitted into the Emperor's confidence in this matter, tells us that the office of the dead was

---

it might be the interval between lauds of the day and prime (see *Capitula monachorum Sangallensium*, cap. xxxi, in Herrgott, p. 36); or, if we may judge from a later practice, both, according to the season of the year, as will be explained below.

[1] *De ant. Mon. rit.*, lib. I, c. 2, § 19, and c. 10, § 28.

[2] "De specialibus psalmis pro eleemosynariis et defunctis cantandis. Ut praetermissis partitionibus psalterii, psalmi speciales pro eleemosynariis et defunctis cantentur" (Herrgott, p. 29). *Speciales psalmi* are the seven penitential psalms; besides Ducange, see *Concordia regularis* (in Reyner, III, p. 84, 1. 24); and the Verdun St. Vannes customs in Martene, *De ant. Mon. rit.* (ed. Antv. 1764), 297 b, 1. 20.

[3] "Ut si necessitas poposcerit ob operis laborem, post refectionem vespertinam, etiam et in quadragesima pari modo, et quando officium mortuorum celebratur, priusquam lectio completorii legatur, bibant" (Herrgott, p. 25).

recited on the third, seventh, and thirtieth days after decease, but explains that different practices were followed in different places: (1) in some places, a commemoration was made for the dead at lauds and vespers, except in Eastertide and on feast-days; he evidently here has in view the practice explained in the Fulda memorial; (2) elsewhere there was a daily mass for the dead; (3) in some places, at the beginning of the month, "nine psalms and nine lessons and as many responsories are said for them."[1] Here nothing is said of either lauds or vespers of the dead, although he mentions them elsewhere;[2] nor does he apparently know, or at least think fit to mention, any addition daily of the devotional office of the dead to the traditional Divine Office of the day. Of course it will be understood that this office of the dead, which afterwards came to form part of the *Prymer*, is not a *Burial Service*; as indeed may sufficiently appear from what has been already said, and will be said in the sequel, as to its use. It is what its name calls it, an office of the dead and nothing more.

In spite of the silence on this point of documents, it is, after all, not improbable that Benedict of Aniane may actually have introduced and practised the devotion of a daily recital of the office of the dead; and for this reason. Some hundred and twenty or thirty years later, all extant testimony goes to show that the daily recital of the office of the dead as a supplement to the Divine Office was universally admitted among Benedictine monks; and there seems to be no other reasonable way of accounting for such a general observance, except on the assumption that it was in fact recommended by the example of a person of most widely reaching influence and authority (and no such person but the greatly-revered Benedict of Aniane occurs in that age); and that it was introduced in several and widely distant quarters simultaneously, so that it could spread gradually from many centres, as might well have happened after the Aachen meeting in 817.

But certain it is that the idea of these devotional accretions to the daily Divine Office started by Benedict of Aniane took deep root, and became imitatively expressed in ways of which he could have

---

[1] Amalar, *De ecclesiasticis observationibus*, lib. IV, c. 42 (in Hittorp, *De divin. eccl. offic.*, ed. 1610, col. 499, 500). Any obscurity of expression in this passage is cleared up by lib. II, c. 44 (*ibid.* c. 439). Amalar is of opinion that the office of the dead is framed on the pattern of the office of the last days of Holy Week (*i. e.* of the office of our Lord's passion and death).

[2] *De eccl. offic.*, lib. III, c. 4 (Hittorp, c. 452 D).

had no anticipation. It is not uncommon in a vague and general fashion to attribute the origin and spread of such accretions to the example of Cluny, the great prestige attaching to that name being doubtless a sort of convenient and handy means of solving any difficulty of the kind.[1] But in the present case this is to attribute to Cluny an influence which it obtained only at a later date; the practices are too widely observed to admit of such an explanation; and that monastery, in this matter, only went along with the prevalent current. Not merely do we everywhere find daily said in the monasteries, in the second half of the 10th century, the so-called *trina oratio*, or fifteen (gradual) psalms introduced by Benedict before matins, as well as the matins, lauds, and vespers of the dead, but also a new devotional office, evidently imitated from this latter, viz. the vespers and lauds of All Saints, said in connection with vespers and lauds of the day; and the seven penitential psalms and litany introduced after prime. In fact by this date, say 950—1000, with the exception of the office of the Blessed Virgin and the "commendations," the whole groundwork of the *Prymer* (and something more, the office of All Saints) forms in the monasteries a series of supplemental daily prayers in addition to the old authorized, and still the only official service, the Divine Office of the day. The monks were not even content with this, but added after each of the hours certain psalms, two, three, or even more, for the lay benefactors and friends, *familiares*, of the monastic family, the abbey, which from their object came to bear the name *psalmi familiares;* besides a series of commemorations or suffrages of particular saints, the Holy Cross, or for peace, etc., etc. But with these further accretions, especially as the last-named have come in time to form a part of the Divine Office itself, we are not here concerned.

Still more; as if the recital of the fifteen gradual psalms before matins were not enough, in many monasteries thirty were now said during the winter half of the year with its long nights, viz. in addition to the fifteen gradual psalms those immediately following, Psalm 134 to the end of the Psalter.[2] The *Concordia regularis*, representing

---

[1] Much as "Fleury" is a name to conjure with among our modern writers who would account for the English monastic customs of the 10th century; though they would find some difficulty in giving a description from originals of the discipline of Fleury in that age apart from the English documents, the peculiarities of which the name of "Fleury" is invoked to explain.

[2] Psalms 148-150 were counted as one psalm; as indeed they are still so said at lauds.

xxii *Origin of the Prymer. Additions to it,*

the practice of English monasteries of about the middle of the 10th century, adopted another devotional expedient, viz. prefixing to the older *trina oratio*—the fifteen gradual psalms which were duly said—another, a preliminary, *trina oratio*. This was accomplished by dividing the seven penitential psalms, in imitation of the division of the gradual, into three sections, each section being followed by the Lord's Prayer and a Collect; the first three psalms being said *pro se ipso;* the next two, for the king and queen, and "familiars," and *pro se ipso;* and the last two, for the faithful departed.

Of all extant monastic consuetudinaries of the 10th and 11th centuries, the *Concordia regularis* gives the clearest view of the way in which these devotional accretions were woven into the traditional Divine Office proper. The order varied according to the time of the year, and the varying length of day and night; consequently there is a winter and a summer practice. The winter half begins universally with 1st November. The time of change from winter to summer practice varied in different localities; in the *Concordia*, that is in England in the 10th century, the change was fixed at the beginning of Lent. In the following table the devotional accretions are printed in italics, so that it is possible to distinguish at once the Church's office from these voluntary, supererogatory additions. The day hours, terce, sext, none, and the evening complin, and the *psalmi familiares* are omitted, as they do not affect the question immediately under discussion, and would only serve to complicate matters already obscure enough, and so far hard to be understood that it is "scientific" method to disburden the subject of unnecessary technicalities, and reduce it, for non-specialists, to its simplest possible expression.

TABLE OF THE MORNING AND EVENING OFFICES
ACCORDING TO THE *CONCORDIA REGULARIS*.[1]

SUMMER.	WINTER.
(from caput Quadragesimae to 1 November.)	(1 November to caput Quadragesimae.)
MORNING.	MORNING.
1. *Preliminaries (viz. the new 'trina oratio,' i. e. the seven penitential psalms divided into three sections, as explained above; and the older*	1. *Preliminaries (as in Summer).*

---

[1] SUMMER; *morning offices:* "Sic ad oratorium festinando .. cum summâ reverentiâ et cautelâ intrare ut alios orantes non impediat, ac tunc [1] flexis genibus in loco congruo et consueto, .. effundat preces magis corde quam ore ... In primâ itaque oratione decantet tres primos pœnitentiae psalmos (in

'trina oratio,' *the fifteen gradual psalms also divided into three sections*).
2. Matins of the day.
   [3. Short interval.]
4. Lauds of the day.
   [5. They go to another oratory.]
6. *Lauds of All Saints.*
7. *Lauds of the dead.*
   [8. Interval, if not yet daylight.]
9. Prime.
10. *Seven penitential psalms.*
11. *Litany.*

   EVENING.

12. *Preliminary private prayer (detail not specified).*
13. Vespers of the day.
14. *Vespers of All Saints.*
15. *Vespers of the dead.*
16. *Matins of the dead.*

2. Matins of the day.
3. *Matins of the dead.*
4. *Lauds of the dead.*
5. *Lauds of All Saints.*
   [6. Interval.]
7. *Private prayer (detail not specified).*
8. Lauds of the day.
9. Prime.
10. *Seven penitential psalms.*
11. *Litany.*

   EVENING.

12. *Preliminary private prayer (detail not specified).*
13. Vespers of the day.
14. *Vespers of All Saints.*
15. *Vespers of the dead.*

The points of difference between summer and winter in the foregoing table, and their rationale, seem to be:

(1) In the long nights, matins of the dead were thrown into the night; in the long days into the day.

(2) In summer, lauds of the dead and of All Saints, instead of

---

the second prayer, the next two; in the third prayer, the last two; then) residentibus cunctis in sedibus suis ordinatim, atque canentibus quindecim psalmos graduum singillatim, trinâ partitione; . . . atque finitis eisdem [2] incipiant nocturnum (followed by *psalmi familiares*). Post hos psalmos [3] parvissimum, uti regula praecipit et totâ aestate convenit, fiat intervallum. [4]. Post hoc, sequantur diei laudes (and *psalmi familiares* after, with commemorations or suffrages). Post quos [5] eundum est (decantando antiphonam ad venerationem sancti cui porticus ad quam itur dedicata est) [6] ad matutinales laudes de omnibus sanctis. Post quos [7] laudes pro defunctis. Quod si luce diei, ut oportet, finitum fuerit officium, incipiant primam, absque tintinnabuli signo ; [8] sin autem, expectent lucem et pulsato signo congregentur ad [9] primam. (More *psalmi familiares* after prime ; and then) more solito [10] pœnitentiae psalmos percurrant. . . . His vero finitis [11] subsequatur letania, quam universi more solito prostrati humiliter, nullo excepto, signo pulsato, compleant (with the usual appendices). Quibus finitis vacent fratres lectioni," &c. &c. (Reyner, III, pp. 80, 81).

Evening offices: "Temperius agatur vespera, cujus signa dum sonant fratres post [12] orationem in choro . . . sedeant. [13] Vesperam vero cantantes, (thereafter two *psalmi familiares* are said). Vesperis dictis (and its suffrages), there follow) [14] vesperae de omnibus sancti ; [15] et mortuorum ; [16] et vigilia usque ad Calendas Novembris " (*Ibid.*, p. 83).

WINTER ; *morning offices:* [1] as above in summer ; [2] "nocturnali peracto officio, et psalmis supradictis, [3] ac vigiliâ pro defunctis [4] cum laudibus suis, [5] atque matutinis de omnibus sancti expletis, [6] fratribus psalmodiae deditis vel lectioni . . . intervallum usquequo lucescat cum magnâ vigilantiâ custodiatur. A lucis crepusculo, dum edituus signum pulsaverit ad ecclesiam universi conveniant, [7] factâque oratione [8] laudes psallant matutinales (and the suffrages or commemorations); quas sequatur [9] prima, [10] et speciales psalmi, [11] et litania. Post haec egrediantur ecclesiam " (*Ibid.*, p. 84).

Evening offices: As Nos. [12] to [15] in summer, above.

being said before the lauds of the day, were thrown after them, and a procession was made to another oratory—a change of place reasonably enough avoided in the cold winter nights.[1]

(3) The order of these supplementary lauds was different in summer and winter; the reason for this is probably one of the mysteries of "the Pye," or rather the secret of its compiler.

Of the other printed monastic custom-books of the 10th and 11th centuries that of Udalric of Cluny, which dates more than a century later than the *Concordia*, is the only one which gives a fairly clear and connected account of the order of these services. It would not be easy to construct from the others, taken as they stand, a scheme with any certainty of being correct; the notices are merely incidental, and generally assume in the persons for whom they were written a practical knowledge of existing custom. But by the help of the table drawn from the *Concordia*, the interpretation of these consuetudinaries, in the matter in question, is easy enough; and their examination gives as a result that they all show a practically uniform observance in regard to the details under consideration.

Two points should, however, be observed:

(1) The devotional accretions whereby the Divine Office was so greatly lengthened were not said in full in Eastertide or on feast

---

[1] The practice of saying the close of lauds and vespers in another oratory is of great antiquity. It is prescribed in section 69 of the Rule of St. Caesarius for nuns as printed by the Bollandists in connection with the life of St. Caesaria, 12 Jan.; a document which in any circumstances must represent a practice of the 6th and 7th century. The foundation of Pope Gregory III. at St. Peter's (Duchesne, *Lib. pont.*, I, 422, 423, cf. 417) is another version of the same custom, though restricted to the evening office. In the *Concordia* it is reserved for the morning, and for only half the year. Cluny maintained it at both lauds and vespers, and all the year round, as may be gathered from a comparison of the various 11th century customs of that house. The "porticus" at Cluny was the chapel of the Blessed Virgin (see Udalric, lib. I, c. 3 and 41, in Migne, *P. L.*, 149, 646, 686). Bernard of Cluny once incidentally mentions the custom (in Herrgott, p. 410, "Sed sciendum," etc.). A century before these writers it was adopted from Cluny by Farfa (see the *Disciplina Farfensis* in Herrgott, pp. 50, 51, 60, 79, 80). As on the way the antiphon sung was "de sanctâ Mariâ" (p. 50), the "alius Chorus" at Farfa was doubtless the "Oratorium sanctae Mariae," described, p. 87.—The Constitutions of William of Hirschau, drawn up after he had adopted the Cluny discipline, give the most detailed description (Herrgott, pp. 545, 547, 548), and show how extremely uncomfortable this following of the practices of venerable fathers of antiquity must have been for the sick monks: their chapel was the "other oratory," and on the approach of the community in long procession, the *infirmi* were simply cleared out of it, to find refuge elsewhere as best they could (see also statute 61 of Peter the Venerable, Migne, *P. L.*, 189, 1042).

days of a high grade; or speaking technically, they were only said in full on ferial days. It is to be remembered, however, that in the 10th and 11th centuries the feast days of a high grade were comparatively of rare occurrence.

(2) These accretions were not assigned to special seasons, or portions of the year, or treated as preparations for the great feasts, but were said on ferial days throughout the year.

It is well to recall at this point the items which up to this time have come before us:

(*a*) The fifteen gradual psalms before matins (in some places increased to thirty during the winter, *i. e.* the long nights);
(*b*) The penitential psalms and litany after prime;
(*c*) The office of the dead, vespers, matins and lauds;
(*d*) The office of All Saints, vespers and lauds;
(*e*) The *psalmi familiares*, said after all the hours.

All these before the close, perhaps by the middle, of the 10th century, obtained throughout the Benedictine monasteries of England, France, Germany, and doubtless Italy.[1] Themselves an imitation of the original Divine Office, or *cursus*, as it was from long tradition called, such offices as those of the dead and of All Saints, once fairly established, were in the then temper of men's minds sure to call forth imitations. And in fact ingenious piety invented many a new *cursus;* those of the Blessed Virgin and of the Holy Cross[2] are the first to appear; to which by and by were added those of the Incarnation, of the Holy Trinity, of the Holy Ghost. Each represented a special devotional attraction of some individual, and each was said in the same way which the customary recitation of the office of the dead and of All Saints had made familiar, viz. as a private daily devotional addition to the Divine Office itself, in strict

---

[1] Even where only a portion of these accretions is mentioned in any particular document in the 10th century, it is not safe to conclude from silence that the items not mentioned were not also said. Thus the life of St. John of Gorz (*M. G. SS.*, iv. 359) mentions only the "ternae orationes" of fifteen (in winter thirty) psalms; and the seven penitential psalms and the litany after prime. The Verdun St. Vannes customs say nothing of these, but give details as to the daily offices of the dead and All Saints (Martene, *de ant. Mon. rit.*, p. 300 b). Yet there can be no doubt they both represent, in these details, the same stage and practice of the same monastic movement in two of the episcopal cities of Lorraine. The compiler of the Verdun customs, an interesting man, a physician, and an authority on diet, not to say on cookery, evidently looks back with pleasure, if not with regret, on the good old days before the "movement" began.

[2] See note 1, p. xxvi.

imitation of it, and, like the Office, as a *daily* exercise throughout the year.[1]

Of these numerous later products of an exuberant piety only one—the office of the Blessed Virgin—was destined to take its place, as an additional *cursus* to the Divine Office, alongside of the office of the dead, and like it secure public recitation in the church, eventually ousting even in the monasteries the long-established older *cursus* of All Saints. It will be proper therefore to bring together here the scanty early notices of the office of the Blessed Virgin.

(1) The contemporary biographer of St. Udalric, bishop of Augsburg, who was provost of the cathedral, and knew the saint well in his later days, writes that, finding himself able by the Emperor's permission to throw off on his nephew the burden of the secular duties attaching to his high station, Udalric threw himself almost unreservedly into prayer and acts of devotion; unless interrupted by necessary duties, it was his custom to say the Divine Office daily along with the chapter in the choir of his cathedral; he also added thereto, as an act of personal and private devotion, "one *cursus* in honour of St. Mary, Mother of God; another in honour of the Holy Cross; and a third in honour of All Saints, besides the whole psalter daily."[2] This notice occurs almost at the beginning of the "Life"; but the work is written without regard to chronology, and from later notices as to the appointment of the nephew,[3] it is clear that the passage just quoted must relate to quite the last years of Udalric's life, say about 970 or 971.

(2) In the chronicle of Hugh of Flavigny a story is told how it was the habit of Berengerius, bishop of Verdun (940—962), to go to the church to make long prayers before matins began, and how on

---

[1] So Franco, abbat of Lobbes, about the middle of the 12th century, "nec enim communi horarum regularium vel cursuum debito contentus, Trinitatis insuper Incarnationisque . . . cotidianum devotum cursum frequentabat" (*Gesta abb. Lob.* in *M. G. SS.*, xxi. 330). And at an earlier date St. Stephen of Grandmont, "exceptis enim ecclesiastico officii regularibus debitis . . . a prima die qua venit in eremum (in 1076) usque ad ultimum diem vitae suae, ordinem de sancta Trinitate cum novem lectionibus et horis canonicis singulis diebus ac noctibus devotissime celebravit" (*Vita*, § 20, Migne, *P. L.*, 200, 1017-1018).

[2] "Ille vero quantum secularibus curis se absolutiorem esse persensit, tantum se ipsum in Dei voluntate facere nitebatur obligatiorem. Cursus scilicet cottidianus cum matriculariis in choro ejusdem matriculae ab eo caute observabatur, quandocumque ei domi manendum aliae occupationes consenserunt. Insuper autem unum cursum in honore sanctae Mariae genitricis Dei, et alterum de sancta Cruce, tertium de omnibus sanctis, et alios psalmos plurimos, totumque psalterium, omni die explere solitus erat, nisi si eum impediret aliqua inevitabilis necessitas" (Gerhardi Vita S. Oudalrici Ep., *M. G. SS.*, iv. 389).

[3] See the narrative, *ibid.*, p. 407, *seqq.*

one occasion in the darkness of the building, when entering the choir he stumbled over Bernerius, the provost of the cathedral, who was lying prostrate on the ground reciting the matin office (*matutinarium cursum*) of the Blessed Virgin.[1] The same story is told much more briefly by the somewhat earlier author of the *Gesta episcoporum Virdunensium*, who uses the expression that Bernerius was saying the "memory" of the Blessed Virgin (*Beatae Mariae memoriam celebrantem*).[2] But apart from the question that there can be hardly a doubt the same *thing* is meant, Hugh of Flavigny has more detailed and authentic sources of information (evidently the necrology of the monastery of St. Peter, called later St. Vannes, at Verdun, in which Bernerius became a monk).

(3) The Einsiedeln Customs, drawn up not long after the year 970, as it would seem, and certainly before 990 or 995, not only confirm the existence and the spread of such a *cursus* of the Blessed Virgin in Germany at this time, but they also show that the transition from the stage of a mere private devotion to an actual place in the public office in the church was already accomplished. They assign, for the period from the octave of Easter to Advent (provided the days were not occupied by a feast), a votive office (with three lessons) of the Holy Cross to Fridays, and one of the Blessed Virgin (also with three lessons) to Saturdays, apparently along with, and not in substitution of, the ordinary ferial office of those days.[3] Of course this is different from the daily recital, after the Divine Office, which obtained somewhat later; but a step forward at the least is taken.

Soon after the middle of the 11th century, St. Peter Damian gives ample evidence that a devotional and private daily recitation of the office of the B. V. must have been commonly practised amongst even the secular clergy in Italy. He moreover specially mentions a case where, in a monastery, the custom was about the

---

[1] *M. G. SS.*, viii. 365.   [2] *M. G. SS.*, iv. 46.
[3] "Per totam quinquagesimam paschalem (*i. e.* to the octave of Pentecost inclusive) infra ebdomadam fiant tres lectiones similiter; sexta quoque feria et septima, si sanctorum natalitia non affuerunt, de sancta Cruce et de sancta Maria tres eodem modo compleantur. Hoc quoque de sancta Cruce et de sancta Maria non dimittatur usque in Adventum Domini" (O. Ringholz, *Des Benediktinerstiftes Einsiedeln Thätigkeit für die Reform deutscher Klöster*, p. 41).—The *Concordia regularis* (p. 82), and Aelfric's Eynsham Customs (in Kitchin's *Winchester Obedientiaries' Rolls*, p. 177), say nothing of an office, but prescribe for these days that the principal mass shall be of the Holy Cross, and the Blessed Virgin, deriving the practice doubtless from Alcuin, whose own prescription, it can hardly be doubted, was based on the devotion of the Anglo-Saxon Church before his days.

xxviii *Origin of the Prymer. Office of the Blessed Virgin.*

year 1053 introduced of saying the hours of this office in choir along with the regular office of the day.[1] From the terms which he uses (*novae adinventionis pondus*) it is clear that in Northern Italy, at least, this must have been at the time a hitherto unheard-of novelty. But it does not seem open to doubt that about this time at the latest, the practice must have been in vogue at Monte Cassino; for Peter the Deacon, the chronicler of that house, writing in the early years of the 12th century a commentary on the Rule of St. Benedict, narrates that Pope Zacharias (who died 752) imposed on the community of Monte Cassino a strict obligation always, as well in summer as in winter, to say before the night and day office, as soon as the brethren assembled in choir, the office of St. Benedict; and after the regular office, the office of the Blessed Virgin Mary. And, as if to preclude all doubt as to the nature of these offices of St. Benedict, and the B. V., he describes them as being "offices of the seven hours" (*septem horarum officia*).[2] Whatever be thought of the account Peter gives of the origin of the "custom," it is certain that that custom must, when he wrote, have been already of long standing at Monte Cassino; during a couple of generations at least. And if the stringent terms which he uses in regard to the obligation raise some suspicion that there were grumblers who did not eye the custom favourably, yet it must have existed long enough for all knowledge of the precise circumstances attending its introduction to die out; otherwise his fellow-monks would have at once detected the error.

The schemes printed in the present volume[3] are sufficient evidence that the office of the Blessed Virgin must have been used in

---

[1] See Batiffol, *Hist. du Brév. Romain*, pp. 185-186.
[2] See Martene, *de ant. Mon. rit.*, lib. I, c. 2, § 17. There can be no doubt as to the origin and authenticity of the passage. Ang. de Nuce (*Chron. Cassinens.*, 1668, app. p. 19) draws it from *Cod. Cassinens.*, 257, as to which see *Bibliotheca Cassinensis*, IV, *Florileg.*, p. 5, "Sub districto praecepto (writes Peter) Cassinensi congregationi Zacharias papa observare praecepit, constituens ut omni tempore tam aestatis quam hiemis ante nocturnale vel diurnale officium mox ut fratres in choro convenerint incipiant officium de sancto Benedicto; et eo expleto inchoent officium quod regula praecipit; adjuncto etiam sanctae Dei genitricis et virginis Mariae officio." Above he describes them as "canonica septem horarum officia in commemoratione B. P. Benedicti salvo eo quod in honore S. Dei Genitricis persolvi consuetudo est."—The author of the life of St. Stephen of Grandmont, recounting how the Saint said daily the office of the Blessed Virgin from the year 1076 onwards, counts it with the office of the dead as already in that neighbourhood an integral part of the Divine Office: "Ecclesiastici officii *regularibus debitis*, agenda videlicet diei et beatae Mariae et fidelium defunctorum" (Migne, *P. L.*, 200, 1017).
[3] See p. lxxv.

England at even an earlier date, whether in the form of a daily addition to the Divine Office, or as a votive office on Saturday does not appear. Apart from the probable evidence of date afforded by the volumes in which they are found (always uncertain and unsatisfactory, however, as such evidence must be, where mere undated handwriting has to be depended on), the statutes of Lanfranc are clear proof that such an office was not introduced into English monasteries by Norman monks;[1] nay more, they are proof too that, if it had been in use in England previously, it was abolished by the new-comers, the men of model observance, as mere Englishry. There can be little doubt that the offices of which the schemes are here printed are to be brought into connection with that spread of devotion to the Blessed Virgin which was so marked a feature of the English Church from the close of the 10th century to the Conquest; of which to this day the Feast of the Conception is speaking evidence, originating as it did (so far as the Western Church is concerned) in England, and spreading from thence over the rest of Europe; a devotion which was thrown into the background by the Norman Conquerors, but which, with the gradual recovery of Englishry, asserted itself again in the later Anglo-Norman days, and finally found its natural theological expression in the controversy between Nicholas, the monk of St. Albans, and the great St. Bernard.[2]

Cluny was somewhat late in admitting this office of the Blessed Virgin; and even when adopted, it did not enter into the round of daily devotion of the community. The fact is, Cluny had already overburdened itself with these accretions; worthy Udalric asseverates and vows that the monks bore it all with freshness, alacrity, and joy. That may be; but the reader who will have the patience to read him (and especially the 39th chapter of his first book) will be apt to think that he is himself very good evidence that the monks of Cluny monastery must have been pretty well breathless before they got to the end of the day.[3] The office of the B. V. was first intro-

---

[1] The office of the Blessed Virgin is nowhere mentioned in Lanfranc's Statutes for Benedictines, which in more than one particular prescribe the contrary of older English customs in a way so express as to show that his directions are aimed at them in a prohibitory sense.

[2] See an article on the "Origins of the Feast of the Conception of the Blessed Virgin" in the *Downside Review*, v. (1886), p. 107 *seqq*. M. Vaucandard, the most recent historian of St. Bernard, has finally elucidated the theological question at issue between the English monk and the French saint.

[3] Migne, *P. L.*, 149, 668, and cap. 41, 687-688; cf. stat. 31 of Peter the Venerable in Migne, 189, 1084.

duced by abbat Hugh (1049—1109), but he prudently restricted its recitation to the monks who were in the infirmary, and to the chapel of sick monks only. Cluny in its then mind could hardly subtract itself from the practice of a devotion which, to use a plain term, had become fashionable; and the infirmary chapel, dedicated to the Blessed Virgin, naturally recommended itself as a ground where, on the one hand, the need felt to be on a level with the times, and on the other the sheer impossibility of undertaking new devotional duties, could both be conveniently reckoned with. In the days of abbat Peter, some time before 1146 or 1147, the complin of the Blessed Virgin, which had not been hitherto said at Cluny, was added to the infirmary *cursus*.[1]

With the 12th century, and the institution of the White Monks of the order of Citeaux, and the White Canons of the order of Prémontré, and the Black Canons of St. Augustine, a new period opens in the history of these accretions to the Divine Office. The White Monks and White Canons, who were the expression of the most ardent piety of the time, resolutely struck out a new line for themselves. They began by simply sweeping aside all these novelties, in each case with one exception. They cleared them out of the way, and reduced the Office to the early simplicity and straightforwardness[2] which from the time of St. Benedict of Aniane it had gradually lost through the heaping upon it of productions of devotion, privately commendable doubtless, but not always publicly prudent.

In their somewhat ruthless reform Citeaux preserved the daily recital of the office of the dead;[3] Prémontré, of the office of the Blessed Virgin.[4] But as it has happened before and since, new and powerful religious orders, which seem at first glance to carry all before them with a rush, are found in fact, when the whole length and breadth of the situation is patiently considered, to have exercised a less absorbing influence than the trumpet of common fame gives out. Citeaux and Prémontré were powerful no doubt, but the

---

[1] "Quidquid dicit conventus dicunt (infirmi); et, ex praecepto domni abbatis Hugonis, insuper omnes horas de sanctâ Mariâ (Bern. Clun., lib. I, cap. 23, in Herrgott, p. 189); see also the 60th Statute of Peter the Venerable, Migne, 189, 1041.

[2] This is clear enough on a comparison of chapters 68 and 74 of the original Customs of Citeaux (Ph. Guignard, *Monuments primitifs de la Règle Cistercienne*, p. 161, 176) with the *Primaria instituta Canonicorum Praemonstratensium*, dist. I, c. 1, 2, in Martene, *de ant. Eccl. rit.* (Antv. 1764), III, p. 325.

[3] *Consuetudines*, c. 50, in Guignard, p. 137.

[4] "Post missam dicitur prima de Sancta Maria" (*Primaria instituta*, dist. I, cap. 2).

current was still set in the channel we have been following, and with a force they could not stem; with all their popularity and power, the direction of the future in this matter was not with them.

The Black Canons, as in their organization, so in their practice, adopted a directly contrary policy. The Cistercians and Praemonstratensians, imitating Cluny, though with modifications, were a highly centralized organization, having a personal head, the abbat of Citeaux or Prémontré, and a common centre, those abbeys themselves, wherewith the whole order was brought into continual and direct communication by means of frequent general chapters held in these mother-houses. The Black Canons adopted the older Benedictine system, with no necessary dependence on a central point, and no common head. Their houses assumed, therefore, more the character of diocesan institutions. And whilst Citeaux and Prémontré each drew up a complete set of office books to be copied down to every jot and tittle, and followed with minute exactitude in every house of their respective orders,[1] the devotion and piety of the Black Canons in their early fervour imitated as far as possible the practices to be found in the monasteries and churches of best-established repute in their own neighbourhood. Thus in the constitutions for these canons regular drawn up by Peter de Honestis, of the monastery of St. Mary de Portu near Ravenna, confirmed by Pope Paschal II. in 1117, which were very soon widely observed in Italy and Germany, it is prescribed, in regard to diversity of hours and offices, on ferial days, and Sundays, and feasts, etc., that as diversity of practice exists in different places, the local order and use of the more observant churches of the district should be followed.[2] He lays down the same practical rule, especially in regard to the various accretions to the Divine Office. "As regards the three prayers[3] before matins, in

---

[1] For the condition of Cistercian office books in early days see *Vita S. Stephani Obazin.* in Baluze, *Miscellanea*, iv. 120 (original edition). Citeaux was more successful than Prémontré in securing uniformity; see the description of the "manuscrit-type" in Guignard, préf. p. v, *seqq.* For Prémontré efforts, *M. G. SS.*, xxiii. 526, 585; xxiv. 655, 672.

[2] "Horarum autem et officiorum diversitas fit pro die, festo, hora et tempore. Aliter enim fiunt diebus ferialibus, aliter diebus dominicis," &c. &c. "Verum in aliquibus horum, plurima quorumdam officiorum pro temporibus diversis et locis invenitur varietas, quam in singulis partibus majorum ecclesiarum et rectiorum usus edoceat" (*Regula Portuensis*, lib. III, c. 8; in Amort, *Vetus disciplina Canonicorum*, Venet., 1747, p. 369).

[3] That is, three preliminary short prayers often said before the 15 psalms, corresponding to the 7 penitential psalms with collects before matins in the *Concordia*. See such prayers in Hergott, pp. 593-4, from a Monte Cassino Breviary of the 11th century.

the morning before prime, and at night after complin; the gradual psalms; the lauds and vespers of All Saints; the hours of the Blessed Virgin, if the devotion of the brethren observes them (*si fraterna devotio habeat*); matins, lauds, mass, and vespers for the dead; the penitential psalms in the morning; and the *psalmi familiares* after the hours, and whatever other things are necessary, let the use, order, and custom of those who have gone before us inculcate what is to be done."[1]

Other Constitutions were drawn up for the Black Canons about the same time by Manegold of Lauterbach, a man influential and revered, who had been deeply concerned in the ecclesiastical politics of the day, and so formed a contrast to "Peter the sinner, clerk, with his brethren," who were the authors of the Ravennese code. Manegold's compilation was primarily designed for the monastery of Marbach in Alsace, which he had founded, but it soon obtained wide acceptance elsewhere. He mentions as of daily observance the *trina oratio*, to be followed by the fifteen gradual psalms, before matins; the office of the dead; the office of the Blessed Virgin, the hours of which were to be said after the relative hours of the ordinary office; the seven penitential psalms and litany after prime.[2] In these German Constitutions, the vespers and lauds of All Saints, mentioned in those of S. Mary de Portu, have fallen out, and the office of the Blessed Virgin is assumed to be generally said; whereas the Italian Peter de Honestis has, with regard to this latter, a limitation (*si fraterna* &c.) showing that in many monasteries at the least it was not said in his neighbourhood.

So far the discussion has been concerned with the religious orders. It remains to consider briefly the adoption of these devotional accretions in their public service in the Church by the secular clergy, viz. those who may specifically and absolutely be called

---

[1] *Reg. Portuens.*, lib. III, c. 17, in Amort, p. 373.
[2] In Amort, pp. 386-387; see also §§ 12, 18, 24, 35, 37, 50, 52; less correctly from another manuscript in Martene, *de ant. Eccl. rit.*, III, 306 *seqq.*—S. Stephen of Obazine and his companions used all these accretions (including both the hours of the Blessed Virgin and of All Saints) whilst they were still seculars, and before they had made up their minds to join themselves to a religious order (*Vita* in Baluze, *Miscell.*, IV, 80-81; the passage does not occur in the abridged Life in the Bollandists). The compiler of the *Ordo divini officii* in Amort, p. 932 *seqq.* is a strong orthodox Romanizer, as appears from his frequent quotations from the Micrologus (*i. e.* Bernold of Constance), and he consequently has but small liking for these novel accretions; he mentions, however (lib. VIII, c. 5, p. 1046), the 15 gradual psalms, and (lib. VII, c. 22, p. 1042-3) the daily office of the dead.

"*the clergy*" proper, *i. e.* all clerics who do not belong to a religious order.

It has been already pointed out, that the spread of "devotional" practices is, as a general, if not universal, rule, from the religious orders to the clergy. Just as in earlier centuries, six and seven hundred years or more before, the clergy adopted matins from monks first as a matter of devotional imitation, and found them at length imposed as a duty and obligation, it was inevitable that the accretions to the Divine Office, which began from the time of Benedict of Aniane, should be taken up by the secular clergy and become at length a part of the daily *pensum*. In view of the unvarying tenor of the story, whether in ancient days or modern times, the wonder is that the clergy did not adopt these at an earlier date than that when they were actually received in non-monastic churches. The office of the dead seems to have been the first item of these offices of supererogation to make its way into the office as publicly said by the clergy.[1] It is, of course, to be understood that this item, as well as the rest later, was not imposed by some general order, but was adopted or not in particular churches according to the discretion or the zeal of individual bishop and individual chapter. When once, however, the current set in that direction, it was only a question of time that the whole of these additions would be publicly said, and become of obligation by and by from mere custom in the churches of the secular clergy no less than in those of monks and regular canons. The Black Canons, without design, but in practice, were just the means whereby these monastic observances might be expected to be the more quickly communicated to the cathedral and collegiate churches, and the secular clergy at large. For whilst now forming a religious order in the strict sense of the word, and adopting the devotional practices usual among the monks, they still remained themselves clerics, and professedly a part of the clerical, not the monastic body, and were designed by their very

---

[1] Batiffol, *Hist. du brév. Rom.*, p. 190, quoting John of Avranches, who wrote between 1061-67, and gives the custom at least in Normandy. In Germany the practice must have found its way into some cathedral churches a century earlier, *e. g.* Augsburg: "aliis orationibus firmiter insistebat (sc. Udalr. episc. Augustens.) usque dum signum ad vigilias defunctorum sonaret; quo audito statim surrexit et cum fratribus vigiliam celebravit et primam. Prima vero expleta, fratribus solito more crucem portantibus, ipse remanens in aecclesia," etc. (*Vit. S. Oudalrici Augustens.* in *M. G. SS.*, iv. 391). The whole context shows that the *fratres* in question were the cathedral chapter, and the *ecclesia* the cathedral church.

institute to take a share in the pastoral and other ministerial duties incumbent on the secular clergy. And, as an accident, the simple and unassuming character of their piety contributed to recommend their practices to the favourable notice of their clerical brethren.[1]

How, and by what steps, and when, in different localities they were in fact received, it would be possible to state only after an examination, impracticable at present for any individual, of the extant early cathedral statutes and ordinalia. But it was certainly in the course of the 12th and 13th centuries, for the most part perhaps even in the 12th, that the change took place.[2] And it was thus coincident with the general settlement of cathedral chapters on the new model, and with the erection of new and more magnificent cathedral churches, an occasion which would be taken advantage of, there is every likelihood for expecting, to revise the Church books and ceremonies. By the end of the 13th century, at the very latest, the process must have been complete.

Unfortunately no formal directory or ordinal of so early a date exists for any English cathedral. But there are in various documents scattered indications, each one slight enough in itself, but in fact sufficient to make it reasonably sure that the accretions, even as a whole, may have formed part of the public office as said in our English cathedral churches as early as the first half of the 13th century. Thus an incidental notice in the Sarum tractate *de officiis*, dating at the latest about 1230, shows that the offices of the dead

---

[1] The writer of the history of the foundation of Llanthony might be considered a partial witness. But the highly critical "Burnellus," who saw through the weaknesses of every order, and especially of the "canons secular," cannot be gainsaid (see *Nigelli Speculum Stultorum* in Wright's *Satirical Poets of the Twelfth Century*, i. 93; the author, Nigel "Wireker," the Canterbury monk, was own brother to no less a personage than the powerful Chancellor, William Longchamp, Bishop of Ely).

[2] A Rheims Ordinale at the British Museum (MS. Reg. 11, B. xiii), of early 13th century, shows the devotional offices of the dead, of All Saints, and of the Blessed Virgin, as already established in that church. A Treves Ordinale of about the latter half of the same century (Harl. MS. 2958) mentions none of these; only the fifteen gradual psalms after prime (apparently in Lent only). Also in Lent, besides many psalms and preces of no account here, the seven penitential psalms at prime; and during the whole year (including Lent) on ferias, one of the seven penitential psalms after each of the hours. Possibly also, in Lent, before prime, the matins of the dead: "ante primam cantande sunt vigilie cum novem lectionibus per totam quadragesimam" (f. 22, b.). These two Ordinalia show very well the different ways in which different secular churches approached the adoption of these devotional accretions as a whole.

It is to be observed that the vespers and lauds of All Saints never gained any general acceptance in secular churches, and indeed from this time forward gradually fell into disuse in the monasteries themselves. So that at the time of the formation of the *Prymer*, this office was not a commonly current devotion.

and of the Blessed Virgin were then daily said in the church of Salisbury.[1] The custumals of Lincoln cathedral, dating from the third quarter of the 13th century, show that the daily recital of the office of the Blessed Virgin was the settled practice of that church.[2] Of devotional accretions to the office, the statutes of St. Paul's, drawn up before the year 1305, mention the office of the dead, the fifteen psalms, and the commendations.[3] It is to be observed that these are mere chance notices, and seeing that the whole body of accretions are found at a later date in the Sarum books, there is little reason to doubt that all the items had here, as elsewhere, found admission by the beginning of the 14th century, although only some of them are specifically mentioned in the fragmentary records of that age which have survived to the present day.[4]

It does not, of course, follow that each item was assigned exactly to the same place as that in which it is found in the table from the 10th century *Concordia*, given above. With a general liturgical uniformity in the West during the middle ages, there existed an infinite variety in point of minute and indifferent detail. Thus a competent and well-informed liturgist of the second half of the 14th century was able to say that the daily recital of the offices of the Blessed Virgin and of the dead was now obligatory on all, and that by virtue of the general custom of all nations. By the laudable practice of many, other particular offices are also observed, as the penitential and gradual psalms, and so forth. The vespers and matins of the dead are (he says) generally said in the evening, and lauds next morning, after lauds of the day. The office of the Blessed Virgin was usually said before each hour of the regular office, except complin; but the Franciscans say matins, lauds and vespers before matins and vespers of the day, and the other hours after the relative hour of the day. Some religious and seculars said the fifteen psalms, according to the original institution, before matins;

---

[1] Section 52 (in Rock's *Church of our Fathers*, IV, 2, p. 36; *Registrum S. Osmundi*, ed. Jones, I, p. 90).

[2] H. Bradshaw and Chr. Wordsworth, *Statutes of Lincoln Cathedral*, I, 289, 290, 385. Office of B. V. at Wells in 1207 (*C. M. Church Early History*, p. 78).

[3] Sparrow Simpson, *Registrum Statutorum eccl. cathedr. S. Pauli Londinens.*, pp. 47, 54—56.

[4] A reference to the so-called "Antiphonar" of Hereford in the Cathedral library would be here desirable, as it seems to be of the 13th century. It is unnecessary to cite later books, *e. g.* at Exeter, Hereford: the detail can be easily filled up. For York the sources seem curiously defective, on account especially of the paucity of interesting rubric in the York Breviary; but see vol. i. p. 213. It will be enough for the present purpose to follow up Sarum.

xxxvi *Origin of the Prymer. Definition and Contents of it.*

others divided them into five groups of three, and said them after the five lesser hours of the office of the Blessed Virgin; some said the penitential psalms after prime; others omitted them; others said them after prime, but only in Lent, a restriction first introduced into the Papal Chapel by Innocent III., and adopted by the Franciscans, although this practice is designated as exceptional.[1]

The following table will show the Salisbury custom and accommodation of these devotional additions to the regular and traditional Divine Office proper.[2] The gradual and penitential psalms were said on ferias in Lent only; the fifteen gradual psalms, followed by the Litany, after terce; the penitential psalms were divided over the hours of the day, and one each was said after lauds, prime, terce, sext, none, vespers, complin.

FERIAS OUT OF LENT.

EVENING.	MORNING.
1. Vespers of the day.	4. Matins and lauds of the day.
2. *Vespers of B. V.*	5. *Matins and lauds of B. V.*
3. *Vespers and matins of dead.*	6. *Lauds of the dead.*

FERIAS IN LENT.

1. Matins and lauds of the day.	said before mass of the day. After mass of the day—
2. *Matins and lauds of B. V.*	
3. *Lauds of the dead.*	10. *Vespers of the dead.*
4. Prime.	11. Vespers of the day.
5. *First penitential psalm.*	12. *Vespers of the B. V.*
6. Terce.	
7. *Fifteen gradual psalms.*	IN THE EVENING.
8. *Litany.*	
9. *Second penitential psalm.* The rest of the penitential psalms distributed as explained above. Sext and None	13. *Matins of dead.*
	14. Collation.
	15. Complin of day.

---

[1] See Radulphus de Rivo, *de Canonum observantia liber*, in Hittorp (ed. 1610), col. 1145; 1146 (office of dead); 1146-7 (office of B. V.); 1148, 1133 (the 15 and 7 ps., litany, etc.); 1137 (lenten additions).

[2] It is drawn up on the prints of Procter and Wordsworth (P.), and Seager (S.); the rubrics of the latter's "MS. L." are useful for clearing up some obscurities of the printed breviaries.

For the office of the dead, see P., vol. II. p. xliv, xlv, xlvii, xlix, dxcii, dxciii, dxciv; S. fasc., I, p. lv.

For the office of the Blessed Virgin, see S., fasc. 2, § 115 (p. 174), 125 (p. 178); p. xlv, xlvi, xlvii, xcvii, and p. xii of the third pagination. I do not understand the explanation given in the Index of vol. II. of P.: "Mattins and Vespers of S. Mary were said in choir before those of the day; the other hours of the Virgin after the day hours" (p. mdxxi). According to Radulphus de Rivo, this was the use of the Franciscans, but it does not appear to be the practice described in the Sarum rubrics.

For the gradual psalms and litany: P., vol. II. dlxxxix, dxc, dxci; vol. I. p. 249.

For the penitential psalms: P., vol. II. dlvii, dlxxxviii.

For the commendations: P., vol. II. xlviii, xlix, dlxxxix.

The *other hours of the Blessed Virgin* were recited out of choir; prime, terce, sext, and none in the chapel of B. V. before the Lady Mass; complin was said by each one privately after complin of the day.

Having followed up the story of the particular items of which the *Prymer* in its groundwork is made up, we are now in a position to answer the question—What was the relation of this favourite lay-folks' prayer-book to the authorized and official service books of the Church? The answer is that the *Prymer* consisted of those devotional accretions to the Divine Office itself, invented first by the piety of individuals for the use of monks in their monasteries, which accretions were gradually and voluntarily adopted in the course of two or three centuries by the secular clergy so generally, that by the 14th century they had, by virtue of custom, come to be regarded as obligatory, and practically a part of the public daily (or only Lenten) office itself. These accretions, besides the Litany, fall into two classes: (1) mere special psalms, gradual, penitential, the commendations; (2) offices (of dead, of B. V.) framed on, and following, the model of the hours of the Divine Office.

"If a man took the *Prymer* to church, would he hear the same service, or set of services, in Latin?" The foregoing table from the Sarum books gives a sufficient reply. So far as the items printed in italics are concerned, he would find them in the *Prymer;* but it is to be added, that he would hear them said with much less solemnity than those portions not in italics, which constitute the old office proper.

It may be further asked—How came precisely the accretions to be taken for the basis of the *Prymer*, and these only? Quite apart from a fact which experience shows to be true, viz. that the popular instinct always seizes on the devotional, and if possible the latest devotional, accessory, it seems easy to explain the original constitution of the *Prymer* on other grounds. There is a constant desire in a certain set of lay folk to imitate the clergy as far as they can; and this tendency is not restricted to any particular class or period. An observant foreigner travelling in England nearly four centuries ago, noted it among our own people. The instance he records aptly illustrates the very subject under discussion. "Although Englishmen (he writes) all attend mass every day, and say many Paternosters in public, the women carrying long rosaries in their hands, and those who can read carry with them the office of Our Lady, and say it in church in a low voice with some companion, verse and verse after the manner of churchmen, they always hear mass on Sundays in their parish church," etc.[1]

The perplexing intricacies of the Breviary, with its continually varying texts, apart from its size, put an adaptation of the old daily office for common use out of the question. But the accretions, now by this time popularly looked on as an integral part of the office, afforded just the material that was wanted. They were, with the exception of the office of the Blessed Virgin, invariable. This latter, in the Sarum (and other) books, does indeed vary with the season of the year; so that on referring to a Breviary, the enquirer must not expect to find the office exactly the same as that found in a *Prymer*. But the variants of the seasons are not so considerable as to have made it otherwise than easy for the compiler of the *Prymer* to frame, what was convenient for his purpose, an invariable office. Looking at the book as a whole, we cannot but be struck with its appropriateness for the end in view. What could appeal more directly to the devout and pious mind than these psalms of degrees, these psalms of penitence, or that wonderful 118th psalm, which constituted not merely the Sarum "commendations," but also the day hours, prime and terce, and sext and none, said in every secular church, said by every secular priest, day by day and all the year round throughout England? Or again, what more readily appealed to men in those days than the offices which were the expression of devout reverence to the Spotless Mother of our Divine Lord, of piety and duty towards those who have gone before, to rest, we would fain trust, in the sleep of peace?

And this recalls me to the quotation with which I began. After what has been said it seems to me that there is no need to criticize it in detail, and indeed it seems to me to be wrongly conceived in nearly every point of detail throughout, especially as Mr. Bradshaw himself seems to have regarded his theory rather as a *ballon d'essai*. Should, however, any one else take up the same thesis, I will endeavour to give satisfaction on each point. There can be no need to add words of explanation why the *Prymer* in English makes its appearance in the 14th century,—possibly in the second half rather than in the first.

EDMUND BISHOP.

[1] *Italian Relation of England* (Camden Society), p. 23.

II.

Some Historical Notes.

FROM the fact that almost all mediæval prayer-books in MS. or in print agree in containing a definite series of devotions with or without certain varying additions, we may feel sure that but one prayer-book was in common use in the Middle Ages. We may believe this book to have been known as the *Prymer*, for the early printed copies bear that title, and the prayer-book is almost invariably alluded to in mediæval documents as the *Prymer*, or its Latin equivalent, *primarium*. The book is met with in Latin, in English, and in both languages. The MS. copies (I do not propose to go into the matter of the printed versions) contain almost invariably, often with additional matter—

1. The Hours of the Blessed Virgin Mary.
2. The 7 Penitential Psalms.
3. The 15 Gradual Psalms.
4. The Litany.
5. The Office for the Dead.
6. The Commendations.

Distinction between the Prymer and its additions.—The following extract points to the distinction between the contents of the *Prymer* proper and the additions which it at times contained:

"my prymere with the sawter and opere praiers."
Somerset House Wills, Wattys, leaf 219, A.D. 1479.

The Uses and Classes of Prymers.—The word Use is a liturgical term, meaning the customary use or arrangement of the public services of a diocese. And this arrangement, carefully laid down in the service books of any particular diocese, yet remains, with a few exceptions, to be really investigated. We may speak therefore of a York, or Sarum, or Hereford book, but it does not follow that the Use is co-terminous with the limits of a diocese, or that its use is inevitable throughout the diocese. The Use of Sarum is generally considered to have extended far, and this is strongly supported by remaining Prymers—most of them follow the Sarum arrangement.

As time goes on, and a more thorough knowledge of Prymers and service books generally is obtained, a better classification of all will be laid down; but, in the meantime, the following attempt will be found useful:

   I. Latin versions, some having the Hours noted as according to Sarum Use. These books may be taken to form by far the main body of mediæval Prymers remaining.

  II. Latin versions, with the Hours noted as secundum usum or consuetudinem Anglie. These books, in every respect, follow the text of No. I.

 III. English versions, following very closely indeed to Nos. I and II, but with some slight variations.

 IV. English versions, following in the main Nos. I and II, but with fewer Memorials in the Lauds of the Hours, a distinctly shorter Litany, and some other slight variations. To this class our text belongs.

  V. Latin versions, according to the Use of York. At present only three MS. Prymers of this Use are known, one in the British Museum, one in the Library of York Minster, and one in the possession of Mrs. Willett, Cudwells, Lindfield, Hayward's Heath. In none of these books is the order of contents quite that commonly met with.[1]

---

[1] York Prymers.

British Museum, Harleian MS. 1663, alluded to as **H.**

Size, A little thick book.
Binding, Modern.
Illumination, None.
Date, Less early in the century than M (on Mr. Warner's authority).
Condition, Good, but much used.

CONTENTS.

1. The Calendar	lf. 1.
2. The Hours of the Blessed Virgin Mary	lf. 7.
3. The 7 Psalms	lf. 47.
4. The Litany	lf. 58, bk.
5. The Office for the Dead	lf. 70.
6. The Commendations	lf. 123.
7. The Psalms of the Passion	leaves 141-148.

Some Historical Notes.   xli

VI. Latin versions with rubrics.

To the above we may add

The Use of Hereford. Though at present, so far as I am aware, no copy of this Use, MS. or printed, is known, we

---

Mrs. Willett's, alluded to as **W.**

Size, A little book.
Binding, Modern.
Illumination, None.
Date, Less early in the century than M (on Mr. Warner's authority).
Condition, Good, but much used. The soiling of the lower corners of the leaves, due to continued holding of the volume in use, forms an interesting feature.

CONTENTS.

1. The Hours of the Blessed Virgin Mary ... ... lf. 1.
2. The 7 Psalms ... ... lf. 30.
3. The Litany ... ... lf. 39.
4. The Office for the Dead ... ... lf. 48, bk.
5. The Commendations ... ... lf. 80, bk.
6. The Psalms of the Passion followed by a V7 and R7... ... lf. 91, bk.
7. A Prayer, *Domine ihesu criste fili dei uiui*, qui etc. ... lf. 97.
8. The 15 Psalms ... ... lf. 98.
9. Two prayers, Aue ihesu *criste*, uerbum etc., and Aue lux mundi, etc.; A memorial of Archbp. "scrupe"; Part of St. John's gospel; Two prayers, Deus qui manus, etc., and O intemerata, etc.; A memorial of St. Anne; The 15 O'es; A prayer, Gracias tibi, etc.; Memorials of St. Blase, the Name of Jesus, St. Stephen, St. William, St. Peter, St. Thomas of Canterbury, St. Ninian, St. Laurence, and St. John of Beverley ... ... leaves 101-125.

The York Minster MS. 16 G 5, *alluded to as* **M.**

Size, Quarto.
Binding, Modern.
Illuminations, Several, but of little merit; others from other books have been pasted in.
Date, Early 15th century (on Mr. Warner's authority).
Condition, Good, but much used.

CONTENTS.

1. On fly-leaf, post-Reformation insertions.
2. Calendar.
3. "York Hours of the Cross" (See *Lay-Folks' Mass Book,* E. E. T. S.) ... ... lf. 1.
4. Hours of the Blessed Virgin Mary ... ... lf. 2, bk.
5. Various devotions ... ... lf. 25, bk.
6. The 7 Psalms ... ... lf. 31.
7. The Litany ... ... lf. 37.
8. The 15 Psalms and the 117th psalm ... ... lf. 43.
9. The Psalms of the Passion ... ... lf. 45.
10. Two Memorials ... ... lf. 52.
11. The Office for the Dead ... ... lf. 52, bk.
12. The Commendations ... ... lf. 66, bk.
13. Numerous devotions ... ... leaves 75-112.

Printed York Prymers will be found at Ushaw College, near Durham; Lincoln Cathedral; York Minster; St. John's College, Cambridge; and Emmanuel College, Cambridge.

may feel sure that a Hereford Prymer would differ from the common text in, at any rate, the Office for the Dead, because the Hereford Office, as given in the Appendix to the Surtees Society's York Manual, reads in the first Versicle and Response of the third Nocturn of Mattins—

"Versus. Animæ eorum in bonis demorentur.
Responsorium. Et semen eorum hæreditet terram."

This may form some test for the discovery of the Hereford Prymer.

A *Durham Prymer.* The British Museum MS., Harl. 1804, may be a Prymer following a Durham Use. It has internal evidence in the "Obits" of a very close connection with Durham.[1]

The Name well known.—The following affords some evidence of the lay-folks' familiarity with the *Prymer* in 1493:

"To my cousin Joane ffitzlowes
my litill englissh booke like
a prymer."—*Somerset House Wills*, Vox, 19, 1.

The frequent legacy of a Prymer points also to a very common knowledge of the book,

"To my sone Thomas . . . a Prymar."
Testamenta Eboracensia, Vol. IV, A.D. 1497.

We shall, I think, do well to bear clearly in mind the important fact that in testamentary dispositions of the *Prymer* no explanation of the book is afforded, but it is almost invariably alluded to as *a* Prymer—*my* Prymer—my *great* or my *little* Prymer, or my Prymer bound in this or that particularly mentioned cover. Against

---

[1] **The Durham Prymer.**

Size, A little book.
Binding, Modern.
Illumination, None.
Date, About 1500 (on Mr. Warner's authority).
Condition, Good.

CONTENTS.

The Calendar	lf. 1.
"Obits"	lf. 13.
Three Prayers	lf. 16.
The Hours of the Blessed Virgin Mary	lf. 18.
Memorials "Ad *matutinas* suffragia"	lf. 65.
The 15 Psalms with intervening devotions	lf. 71, bk.
Memorials	lf. 76, bk.
The 7 Psalms	lf. 82, bk.
The Litany	lf. 90, bk.
The Office for the Dead	lf. 100, bk.
Various devotions	leaves 130-138, bk.

this we may in a measure set the following extract, which is however an extremely rare instance. Indeed, amongst many hundreds of bequests of Prymers I can recall no other of a similar character.

> "Item lego Isabellæ Roos unum Primarium de Sancto Spiritu."—*Test. Ebor.*, Pt. 11, p. 65.

The following is a curious reference to the *Prymer*. After some inquiry I am still unable to explain it; the reading may, I believe, be relied upon:

> "a Prymor whiche is called my Bretar' (*sic*) boke."
> *Test. Ebor.*, v. 4, p. 274 (A.D. 1507).

On the question of the pronunciation of the name Dr. Furnivall writes: "The old spelling *primmer* that occasionally turns up, shows how the word was pronounced. I never heard prīmer till a few years ago, when the shilling primmers were started; and then folk thought they were for cramming or priming boys for examination."

It is unfortunate that MS. Prymers should, in Libraries, be classed as Books of Hours, or Horæ. The MSS. so called, whether they contain the common contents of the *Prymer*, or whether they contain any kind of Hour Office, are as a rule all classed together under that heading, though in most cases they prove to be Prymers. Many hundreds, perhaps thousands, of instances occur of mediæval allusions to the *Prymer*, *Primer* or *Primarium*; but there are, I think, very few contemporary allusions to Books of Hours or Horæ.

Earliest mention of the Prymer.—The earliest mention of the book, yet available, is perhaps the following, where a lady leaves a

> "Primer which was my sister Margaret's."
> *Gibbons's Early Lincoln Wills*, under date 1323.

Foreign Prayer Books.—A similar book was in use in the middle ages on the Continent, and the list of its contents will, I think, be found the same, if we except the Gradual Psalms.

A Prymer now in a Parish Church.—In the library of the parish church at Tiverton is preserved a Latin version of the *Prymer*. Through the kind help of Canons Edmonds and Hingeston-Randolph, we may feel sure that its connection with the church dates only from post-Reformation times.

Manner of using the Prymer.—Dr. Furnivall writes:—"The point I want to know is—If a man took the *Prymer* to church, would he hear the same service or set of services in Latin? Is the

Prymer a translation of a public service-book, or one of private devotion, or partly of both?"

To this we may reply, that the book is a translation, or, in the case of the Latin versions, a copy of different parts of the Breviary and Manual, the order of devotions in the Hours of the Blessed Virgin slightly differing from those in the Breviary; the Manual does not contain them. Indeed the Breviary was perhaps used sometimes in place of the *Prymer*,

"a litel Portose, the whiche the saide Sir Thomas toke wt hym alway when he rode."—*Test. Ebor.*, Pt. 11, p. 227.

Sir Thomas was a layman. From Cavendish's *Life of Wolsey*, we know the book to have been used at home in at any rate one instance. From the fact of mediæval pews still retaining their book-rests, as well as for other reasons, we know the book to have been used in church. In an article on the church of East Budleigh, Devonshire, dated pews are thus spoken of :—

"The book boards are 5 inches, and the seats 13 inches wide, both fixed perfectly horizontal . . . . . that year [1537] being recorded on one of the pew ends."—Vol. XXIV of *Transactions of the Devonshire Association for the Advancement of Science and Art.*

Though not of pre-Reformation date, the following throws some light on the use of the book in church, and is in addition of peculiar interest.

"*Brawling or Misconduct in the Church of Wolsingham.*

The personal answer of Arthur Chapman of Wolsingham, blacksmith, aged 30 years, 3 Feb. 1570.

He saith that upon St Mathewe day last, he, this examinate, was in the church of Wolsingham the tyme of the morning praier; at what tyme this deponent was redinge of an ynglish boke, or prymer, while as the preist was saynge of his servic no nyndynge what the preist redd, but tendynge his own boke and praier. Mary, he redd not allowde to the hynderenc of the priest, to his knowledg, but the priest after the first lesson willyd him, this examinate to reid mor softly, to whom this examinate answered that he wold mak amends for that fault, and further this examinate said nott. Arthur Chapman.

. . . .

The personal answer of Arthur Chapman ad positionem additionalem.

The said Arthur saith that he had a primer in english, which he haith had a twelvemonth and more; which

primer is in this Juge's hands, and which he, the said
Arthure, haith used to prai on, and at such tymes as he
now is blamed for."—*Depositions and other Ecclesiastical
Proceedings from the Court of Durham*, Surtees Society,
pp. 231-2.

Though not expressed, we may believe the following extract to
represent a very general fact—

"Johanni Swan juniori meum Primerium quo cotidie utor."
Test. Ebor., Vol. II, A.D. 1459.

Perhaps not the least noteworthy and interesting fact in connection with the story of the old prayer-book may be found in the traces of thumb-marks so often found on the lower corners of the leaves. The Prymer Brit. Mus. MS. Sloane 2474 in this respect tells a tale most vividly of long and continued holding, which can have only been for devotional purposes.

The Prymer represented in its illuminations. In the Museum MSS. Sloane 2474 and Harl. 1251 the Placebo pictures represent mourners with books which we may very reasonably believe to be Prymers. In the Museum MS. 25,698, described in the Museum Catalogue as ". . . Miniatures cut from a book of Hours (?) Flemish, late xv," is a representation of a mediæval deathbed, in which one of the figures is depicted as reading a book which may very well be a foreign Prymer. In the same volume is represented the interior of a church during service time, and here again two of the lay-folks are seen reading from prayer-books. In the Museum MS. 34,294 is represented a book depending in a leather casing from the girdle. Prymers similarly bound still exist. In the Museum MS. 28,962, the prayer-book is seen in use on leaves 281 *b* and 312.

A King's Prymer.—From the Museum authorities we learn that the Prymer MS., Kings 9, belonged to Henry the VIIIth. The volume contains his handwriting.

The Prymer of a lady of the court of Henry VII. In the description of MS. 17,012 in the Museum Catalogue we read as follows:—

". . . It appears to have belonged to a lady of the court of King Henry VII, and, afterwards, of Henry VIII, for it contains the autograph inscriptions and signatures of Henry VII. himself and his Queen Elizabeth of York, Henry VIII and his Queen Catharine of Arragon, and the Princess Margaret, afterwards Queen of Scotland, all addressed to a lady towards whom Henry VII uses the term 'your lovynge maistre,' ff. 20 b, 21. It contains also autographs of the following persons . . . . . Princess, subsequently Queen, Mary, f. 192 b, and Yolande L 'de Savoye,' daughter of Philibert, I Duke of Savoy, f. 196 b . . ."

Mus. Catalogue, MS. 17,012.

Above the signature of the pious Catherine of Arragon, and all in the same hand, is written

"I thinke the prayrs of a frend be most acceptable vnto god and be cause I take you for one of myn assured I pray you to remembre me in yours

Katherine [y]e [Qu]e[ne]."

At leaf 180 we find :—

madam wan you ar dysposyd to pray
remember your assured saruant alw[ay]

madame when ye most deuoutyst be
haue yn remembrance f and p

A Queen's Prymer (?).—The Museum Catalogue describes MS. Sloane 2565 as having the "Arms of Q. Mary on covers."

An Abbot's Prymer (?).—The Museum MS., Harl. 928, contains at the beginning an insertion to the effect that "the first owner of this booke was Ambrose de la reene, Abbot of Glastonburie," and on the same page the book is described as having been written "in the yeare of grace 1428, the 16 of Septem, in that famous Abbie of Glastonburie," but this entry is not in a contemporary hand, though the volume itself is clearly of the period assigned. The many hundreds, probably thousands, of Prymers which belonged to the more humble classes we can, unfortunately, no longer identify, though numberless testamentary bequests remain to tell their tale.

An Oath administered on a Prymer.—

"ii. The confession of Henry Leverett, of Wisbech, in the I. of Ely, shoemaker, ... (1) That he joined in an assembly of 22 shoemakers, 21 July, at the mill hill called the milfeld, in Wisbech, for the purpose of raising their wages, and that none should work unless their masters gave them 18d. for sewing every dozen pair of shoes, instead of 15d. as before; that he took a primer out of his bosom, and one Edward, servant to Robert Smythe, administered to him an oath to that effect."

Letters and Papers of the Reign of Henry VIII,
No. 1454 (Rolls Series, Vol. XIII, Pt. 1).

Certain Children accustomed to say the Hours daily.—

"Item, y wol and ordeyne þat vij pore children þat wol go to scole to Oxonford or Cambrigge, and namely such as be kynne or god children to me, haue euery of hem vij nobyll by yere to þaire scole duryng the terme of vij yere, and say euery day our lady matyns and houres."—Archbp. Stafford's *Register* at Lambeth, lf. 170, bk.

The Contents of the Prymer highly esteemed.—We often find mention in mediæval Wills of those devotions which form the *Prymer*. Priests were directed

"to say every Sonday, Tuysday, and Thursday the antem Ne reminiscaris, the vij Psalmes of Penaunce, ye Lateny, ye Colettes Inclina, Miserere, Fidelium; and, every Monday in the weke, Wednnsday, Friday, aud Setterday Commendacion, Placebo with Dirige."—*Test. Ebor.*, vol. iv., p. 180, etc., etc.

Illuminated Prymers.—Most *Prymers* contain very interesting little pictures. Of the six divisions of the book, the first (the Hours) will often have at its commencement a representation of the Annunciation; the fifth division (Office for the Dead) will often have at its commencement a picture representing the interior of a church during the singing of the Office for the Dead; and the sixth division (Commendations) will often have before it a representation of a graveyard, the graves lying open, and the souls (small naked figures, three in number) being carried up in a large white cloth to the Almighty, who is depicted above.

Amongst the more interesting of the representations in the *Prymers* in the British Museum we may (not confining ourselves to English examples alone) specially note MS. No. 18,192, leaf 196, containing a representation of Communion. MS. 16,997, leaf 119, a representation of a choir with the suspended pyx (a rare example?). MS. Kings 9, St. Michael and the Devil beside the soul of the dead man, the Devil with a scroll of the dead man's sins. MS. Harl. 2934, a corpse lying outside a coffin. MS. Eg. 1070, leaf 53, Death; leaf 72, Exorcism; leaf 100, Sacramental wafer. MS. 19,962, Creation. MS. Eg. 937, leaf 7, back, a man in his nightdress praying in his bedroom. MS. 25,698, a mediæval death-bed. MS. 17,280, Benediction; a nude figure on an altar tomb; many illustrations of Bible history. MSS. 24,098 and 34,294, Superb illuminations. MS. 27,913, leaf 48, a bier. MS. 31,240, a Bleeding

Host in a monstrance; a schoolmaster with birch and boys with books; Last Sacrament; the Host in the chalice. MS. Eg. 1147, a corpse being borne to the grave. MS. 18,850, leaf 272, Parish coffin. MS. 17,026, leaf 38, Communion without houselling towel. Sloane 2471 Placebo picture shows a layman with a book, seated in the chancel near the officiating priest.

Owners' writings in Prymers.—At the end of the very small Museum *Prymer*, Harl. 1251, is written

> "Thys boke ys myne, eleanour worcestar.
> and I yt loos and yow yt fynd,
> I pray yow hartely to be so kynd,
> that yow wel take a letel payne,
> to se my boke brothe home agayne.[1]
> E. Worcester."

At the commencement of the Museum MS., No. 18,629, which is however deficient in the 15 Psalms and Commendations, is written:—

"In the yere of our lord mcccciiij & vij, The first daye of the Moneth of Janyu*er*, the Banys where solempnished & published betwixt Annes Skerne, late Wedow of the p*ar*ishe of kyngeston�, of the to on p*ar*ty, And Peres Courteys, the kyng*es* warderober of london̄, of the p*ar*ishe of Saynt Andrews, in Barnardcastel in̄ london̄, to the oñ othr p*ar*ty. Itm̄, the second Bayn̄ was maad, don̄ & published wi*thi*n̄ the seid Chirche, the vj daye ensuyng. Itm̄, the third Bayn was publisshed within the seid Chirch the xiij daye of the seid moneth of Janyu*er*.

Me*m*orandu*m*, that the Banys were asked & publisshed the xiij daye of Janyu*er*, betwixt Maist*er* Peres Courteys of the p*ar*ishe of Saynt Andrews, in Barnardcastel, of the to on p*ar*ty, And Annes S[k]erne, wedow, of the p*ar*ishe of kyngeston̄, of the to othr p*ar*ty. Itm̄, the second Bayn it was asked the xx daye of Janyu*er*. Itm̄, the thyrd Bayn̄ it was asked vpon the xxv daye of Janyu*er*.

And so aft*er* the Banys doon̄ & fynyshed, according to the Chirch lawes, The seid Maist*er* Peres Courteys and the seid Annes were wedded, a fayve of þe clok, solempny wi*thi*n̄ the Chirch of Saynt Andrews in̄ Barnardcastel, the xxix daye of Janyu*er*, on the presence of Maistresse Stokton; Maistre helys, gentylman; Sir Dyd[i]er Burges, p*ar*sone of Saynt Andrewe of Canterbury; Thomas Stokton̄); Thomas Stokton̄); Richard Butler, Clerk of the seid

---

[1] These last four lines are by no means uncommon in 15th-century books

Chirch of Saynt Andrews; Thomas H.....; Thomas Leuell; Robert Durant; Iamys John Boylet, and Margery Grent . . . ." Brit. Mus., MS. 18,629, lf. 1.

In the Museum *Prymer*, MS. 2 A XVIII, we find in the Calendar many entries of events of national interest, as for instance:—

"January." The xxviijth daie of January deceassed the noble prynce Henry the eight, the yere of our lorde 1546.

Under September the 5th, in the same volume, we find the unusual entry:—

"here endythe the canycular dayes."

Under November the 28th:—

"this saturday was bore at westminstre at nyght, after the ix^t houre a quarter, my ladi margaret, the ij^d child to the king harri the vij^t, *Anno domini* 1489."

Not a few Prymers contain, scribbled on the fly-leaves, various prescriptions for common ailments: the last-mentioned MS. will supply one:—

"Kolla quyntyta ys for a purgacyon; ye must have yt of the pottycary; hyt wyll cost iij^d the ovnce.

take a penyworthe of hyt, and quarter hyt in fowre, & then take on of the pecys & ley it in stepe in half a peynt of ale, ye space of an owre; & then strayn the ayle, & wryng it hard owt of ye ayle, then put ij spon fulle off suger into ye sayd ayle, & drynk it luk warm, fasting."

At the end of the Museum *Prymer*, Harl. 3835, is written:—

"If thow art young then mary not ekit:
if thou art old thou hast more wite.
for young mens wifes [may n]ot be taught,
and olde mens wifes be good for naught."

In the Museum *Prymer*, 2 A XVII, at the foot of the Calendar for March, is written:—

"In marche, after the fyerst c,
tacke the prime wher euer he be,
the thyerde sondaye without mys
estur daye yt is.

yf the prime on the sondaye be
tacke hym for on of the three."

In the *Prymer* at Tiverton parish church occurs the following, kindly communicated by Canon Edmonds:—

"Thys boke is won and Crysts cursse ys a nothyr.
he that stelyth the toyn shall have the tothyr."[1]

In the Museum *Prymer* Harl. 2367, under the 28th of May, is scribbled

"my mother decessed upon thys daye."

In the Museum *Prymer* MS. 27,948, leaf 63 b, we find scribbled:—

"Ihesu my lord, ihesu my god, ihesu my creature, ihesu my sauiour, ihesu my blis, ihesu my socour, ihesu my helpe, ihesu my comfort, ihesu my myrthe, ihesu my solas, ihesu my leder, ihesu my techer, ihesu my wischer, ihesu my counseler, ihesu my maker, ihesu my founder, ihesu my mercy, ihesu haue mercy, ihesu lord mercy, ihesu, ihesu, grammercy, father and sone and holy gost, iij persons and oo god, grammercy, amen. quod lednam."

Prymers containing Owners' Portraits.—According to the Museum Catalogue, the MS. *Prymer*, 2 A XVIII, contains on lf. 24 b. the portraits of the owners of the volume. Both are represented as kneeling in an attitude of prayer, and before each lies an open volume, which we may take to represent the *Prymer*.

The same Catalogue also assigns a figure on lf. 65 b., of MS. 18,629, as that of the owner of the volume.

Prymers containing Owners' Names.—These are numerous; see, for instance, the Museum MS., Burn. 334, belonging once to "John burlay of Roydoun"; and Arundel 203, with name of "Thomas Parker of Wyllyngton, Sussex."

The facsimiles of this volume.—Plate II is a reproduction from the Museum *Prymer*, MS. 17,012, described above as that of a lady of the court of Henry VII. Plate III is from a volume described, of which the following is the description in the Museum Service-book Catalogue:—

"Horæ et Officia, ordine sequenti:—Kalendarium;—Lectiones ex evangeliis Horæ B Mariæ Virginis;—Septem psalmi pœnitentiales;—Litania;—Officium Mortuorum;—

---

[1] The Harleian MS. 1251 also contains this inscription. On a blank space, in the middle of a little Prayer-book, we find in red ink:—

"Of youre charite pray for the sowlys of John Edwarde, and Margaret hys wyffe, And for Elizabethe ther doughter, professed yn syon, for whos vse thy[s] boke was made" (Brit. Mus., MS. Cott., Appx. 14, lf. 56 b.).

In this book the Hours of the Holy Spirit are substituted for those of the B. Virgin, or we might designate the book a Nun's *Prymer*.

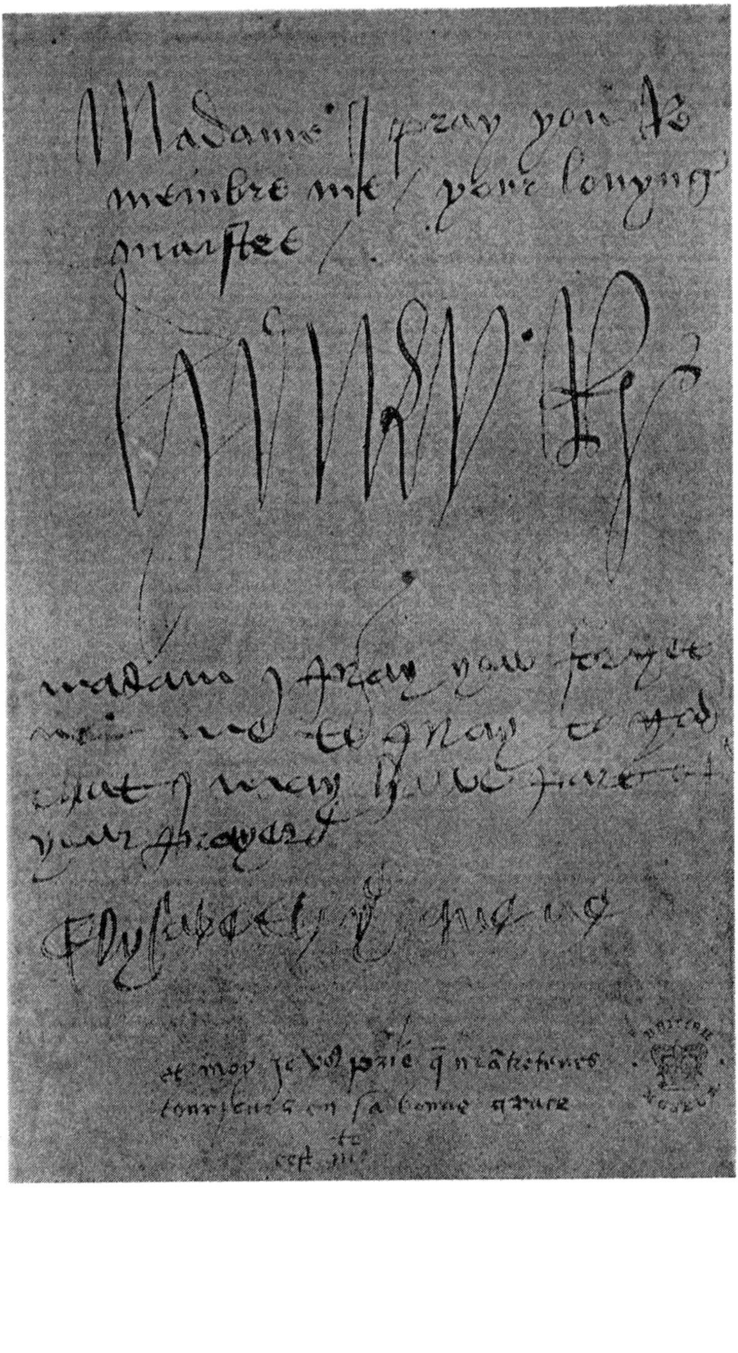

PLATE II

Madame I pray you to
meimbre me your louyng
maistre

HENRY R

madame I pray you forget
not me to pray to god
that I may have parfet
your hiewase

Elysabeth

et moy je vo9 prie q[ue] a kehenrs
tourjours en sa bonne grace
cest ...

PLATE III

Horæ abbreviatæ pro unoquoque die septimanæ;—Commemorationes Sanctorum et dierum festorum;—Oratio ad Virginem, et Officia varia abbreviata;—Lectiones evangelicæ de Passione Christi;—Historia Biblica, versibus expressa incip "Verbum a principio procedens eterno." On vellum, finely written and illuminated, for the use of René of Anjou, titular king of Naples, who died in 1480. At the commencement is a large shield of his arms emblazoned; and his badge of a sail inflated by the wind, with the motto *En Dieu en soit*, is often repeated. At fol. 43 *b* are some prayers added, in which he is prayed for by name; and at fol. 53 is a miniature representing him as a crowned skeleton, with a banner of his arms beneath; a subject which is found also in a MS. written by René, preserved in the Bibl du Roi, No. 58, Fonds Gaignières. It is possible that this, and two or three other miniatures in the volume, were painted by René himself. From a memorandum at the end of the volume, it appears that this volume was subsequently presented to King Henry VII. of England by his chaplain, George Strangways, Archdeacon of Coventry. Small Quarto. [Bibl. Eg. 1070] middle xv France.

III.

The Distribution of the Psalms of the Prymer.

The following Table will show the distribution of the 52 Psalms in the common versions of the *Prymer*. Sarum follows the Table; York adds 3, Psalms 1, 2, and 5 (see Prime of the Hours); and the Versions in English repeat the De Profundis as part of the concluding devotions of the Hours.

	Matins	Lauds	Prime	Tierce	Sext	None	Evensong	Compline	7 Psalms	15 Psalms	Placebo	Dirige	Commendations
Ps. 120. Ad dominum cum				+						+	+		
Ps. 25. Ad te domine leuaui												+	
Ps. 123. Ad te leuaui oculos meos					+		+			+			
Ps. 119. Beati immaculati													+
Ps. 128. Beati omnes						+				+			
Ps. 32. Beati quorum									+				
Ps. 41. Beatus qui intelligit												+	
Ps. 149. Cantate domino		+										+	
Ps. 19. Celi enarrant	+												
Ps. 138. Confitebor tibi												+	
Ps. 118. Confitemini domino				+									
Ps. 63. Deus deus meus		+										+	
Ps. 54. Deus in nomine tuo				+									
Ps. 67. Deus misereatur		+											
Ps. 130. De profundis									+	+	+		
Ps. 116. Dilexi quoniam											+		
Ps. 7. Domine deus meus												+	
Ps. 8. Domine dominus noster	+												
Ps. 102. Domine exaudi								+					
Ps. 143. Domine exaudi								+					
Ps. 24. Domini est terra	+												
Ps. 6. Domine ne in furore									+			+	
Ps. 38. Domine ne in furore									+				
Ps. 131. Domine non est							+		+				
Ps. 139. Domine probasti me													+
Ps. 27. Dominus illuminacio												+	
Ps. 23. Dominus regit me												+	
Ps. 93. Dominus regnauit		+											
Ps. 134. Ecce nunc										+			
Ps. 133. Ecce quam bonum												+	
Ps. 30. Exaltabo te domine												+	
Ps. 40. Expectans expectaui													+
Ps. 126. In conuertendo					+	+				+			
Ps. 100. Iubilate deo		+											
Ps. 43. Iudica me deus													+
Ps. 122. Lætatus sum					+		+			+		+	
Ps. 146. Lauda anima mea			+										
Ps. 117. Laudate dominum												+	
Ps. 148. Laudate dominum de		+										+	
Ps. 150. Laudate dominum in		+											
Ps. 121. Leuaui oculos						+				+	+		
Ps. 132. Memento domine										+			
Ps. 51. Miserere mei deus									+			+	
Ps. 127. Nisi dominus edificauerit						+				+			
Ps. 124. Nisi quia dominus					+	+				+		+	
Ps. 42. Quemadmodum						+	+						
Ps. 125. Qui confidunt										+		+	
Ps. 129. Sæpe expugnauerunt								+		+			
Ps. 65. Te decet ymnus							+						
Ps. 13. Usquequo													
Ps. 95. Venite	+											+	
Ps. 5. Verba mea auribus													

For some authority for the following attempt, see:

Sarum MSS.

British Museum MS. Sloane 2471
,, ,, ,, ,, 2565
,, ,, ,, ,, 2633
,, ,, ,, Royal 2 A VIII
,, ,, ,, Harl. 2976
,, ,, ,, ,, 2985

See p. xci for Sarum readings. See also Breviaries and Manuals of Sarum Use, and many other Prymers with the Hours noted as according to Sarum.

York MSS.

British Museum MS. Harl. 1663 (MS. **H**).
Mrs. Willett's, Hayward's Heath (MS. **W**).
York Minster MS. 16 G 5 (MS. **M**).

See footnotes for York readings. See also Breviaries and Manuals of York Use.

IV.

An Attempt to define the Structure of the Prymer according to the Uses of Sarum and York.

THE HOURS OF THE BLESSED VIRGIN MARY.

Matins.

Commences, Domine, labia mea aperies.
    Et os meum annuntiabit laudem tuam.
The opening, Deus, in adiutorium meum, intende.
    Domine, ad adiuuandum me, festina.
    Gloria patri, etc.
    Sicut, etc.
    Alleluia.
The Invitatory, Aue maria, etc.
The Venite, with the Invitatory interwoven.
The Hymn, Quem terra.
The 3 Psalms, Domine dominus noster, Celi enarrant, and Domini est terra.
The Anthem, Benedicta tu.
The V⁊ and R⁊, Sancta dei, etc.; Intercede, etc.; the Pater noster[1]; the V⁊ and R⁊, Et ne nos, etc.; Sed libera, etc.; the V⁊ and R⁊, Jube, domine, etc.; Alma virgo, etc.; 3 Lessons, with their V⁊s and R⁊s (see Text, p. 5); the V⁊s and R⁊s of the first and second Lessons in **Sarum** (and in Pt. 1) being transposed in **York**, excepting the last R⁊ of the first and second Lessons.
The Te Deum.
A V⁊ and R⁊, differing from our text in Pt. 1, and reading in both Uses.
    Ora pro nobis, sancta dei genitrix,
    Ut digni efficiamur promissionibus Christi.

---

[1] The Ave Maria in Pt. 1 is not usual.

lvi *The Structure of York and Sarum Prymers.* (*The Hours.*)

Lauds.

The opening, Deus in adiutorium, etc., to Alleluya inclusive (see Matins); 8 'Psalms,' Dominus regnauit, Jubilate, Deus deus meus, Deus misereatur, Benedicite, Laudate dominum de celis, Cantate domino, Laudate dominum in sanctis eius.

The Anthem, O admirabile.

The Chapter, in **Sarum**, Maria virgo; in **York**, In omnibus requiem, etc.

The Hymn, O gloriosa domina.

The V7 and R7, Elegit eam deus & preelegit eam. Et habitare facit eam in tabernaculo suo.

The Benedictus.

The Anthem, O gloriosa dei genitrix.

A V7 and R7, in **Sarum** perhaps generally Ostende nobis, domine, misericordiam tuam. Et salutare tuum da nobis; in **York**, Domine, exaudi orationem meam. Et clamor meus ad te veniat.

The prayer, Concede nos.

In **Sarum** now follow 16 anthems, each followed by a V7, R7, and prayer.[1]

Lauds concludes (in both Uses) with the Hour of the Cross, with its V7 and R7 always the same, Adoramus te, etc., Quia per, etc., and the prayer, Domine Jesu Christe.

Prime.[2]

The opening, Deus in adiutorium, to Alleluya, inclusive.

The Hymn, Veni creator.

In **Sarum**, 3 Psalms, Deus in nomine, Laudate dominum, and Confitemini domino; in **York**, 4 Psalms, Beatus vir, Quare fremuerunt, Verba mea auribus, and Laudate dominum, only the last being common to both Uses at this point.

The Anthem, in **Sarum**, O admirabile; in **York**, Quando natus.

The Chapter, In omnibus requiem, 8 V7s and R7s (see Text), and the prayer Concede nos.

The Hour of the Cross, with its V7 and R7; and the concluding prayer, Domine Jesu Christe.

---

[1] Each Anthem, with its V7, R7, and Prayer, is known as a *Memorial.* (See Table of Six Sarum Prymers.)

[2] The structure of the Hours of Prime, Tierce, Sext, and None is exactly alike, excepting that in York Prime has 4 Psalms.

The Structure of York and Sarum Prymers. (*The Hours.*) lvii

Tierce.

The opening, Deus, etc.
The Hymn, Veni creator.
3 Psalms, Ad dominum cum tribularer, Leuaui oculos, Letatus sum.
The Anthem, in **Sarum**, Quando natus, etc.; in **York**, Rubum quem viderat.
The Chapter, Ab initio, 8 V/s and R/s, and the prayer Concede nos.
The Hour of the Cross, with its V/ and R/, and the prayer Domine Jesu Christe.

Sext.

The opening, Deus, etc.
The Hymn, Veni creator.
3 Psalms, Ad te leuaui oculos meos, Nisi quia dominus, and Qui confidunt.
The Anthem, in **Sarum**, Rubum quem; in **York**, Germinavit radix.
The Chapter, Et sic in syon, 8 V/s and R/s, and the prayer Concede nos.
The Hour of the Cross, with its V/ and R/, and the prayer Domine Jesu Christe.

None.

The opening, Deus, etc.
The Hymn, Veni creator.
3 Psalms, In conuertendo, Nisi dominus, and Beati omnes.
The Anthem, in **Sarum**, Germinavit radix; in **York**, Ecce maria.[1]
The Chapter, Et radicaui, 8 V/s and R/s, the two last of which in **York** read, Elegit eam deus & preelegit eam. Habitare facit eam in tabernaculo suo, and the Prayer, Concede nos.
The Hour of the Cross, with its V/ and R/, and the prayer Domine Jesu Christe.

Vespers.

The opening, Deus, etc.
5 Psalms, Letatus sum, Ad te leuaui, Nisi quia, Qui confidunt, and In conuertendo.
The Anthem, Post partum.
The Chapter, Beata es virgo.
The Hymn, Aue maris stella.

---

[1] Ecce maria genuit nobis saluatorem; quem iohannes uidens exclamauit dicens, ecce agnus dei, ecce qui tollit peccata mundi. Alleluia.

lviii *The Structure of York and Sarum Prymers.* (*The Hours.*)

A V⁊ and R⁊, differing in **York** from our text, and reading, Sancta dei genitrix. Intercede pro nobis.
The Magnificat.
The Anthem, Sancta maria succurre.
A V⁊ and R⁊, differing from our text, and reading in both Uses, Domine exaudi orationem meam. Et clamor meus ad te veniat.
The prayer, Concede nos; the Hour of the Cross, with its V⁊ and R⁊; and the prayer, Domine Jesu Christe.

Compline.

The V⁊ and R⁊, Conuerte nos, deus, salutaris noster. Et averte iram tuam a nobis.
The opening, Deus, etc.
4 Psalms, Usquequo, domine, Judica me, Sæpe expugnauerunt, Domine non est.
The Anthem, Cum iocunditate.
The Chapter, Sicut cynamomum.
The Hymn, Virgo singularis.[1]
A V⁊ and R⁊, differing from our text, and reading in both Uses, Ecce ancilla domini. Fiat michi secundum verbum tuum.
The Nunc Dimittis.
The Anthem, in **Sarum** Glorificamus te; in **York**, Ecce completa sunt.[2]
A V⁊ and R⁊, differing from our text, and reading in both Uses, Domine, exaudi orationem meam. Et clamor meus ad te veniat.
The Prayer, Gratiam tuam; the Hour of the Cross,[3] with its V⁊ and R⁊;[4] and the prayer, Domine Jesu Christe.[5]

Concluding Devotions of the Hours.

The Salve Regina, to post hoc exilium ostende.
Sarum then adds, O clemens, O pia, O dulcis uirgo maria.
Both Uses then read :—

---

[1] Really the second part of the hymn, Aue maris stella.
[2] Ecce completa sunt omnia que dicta sunt per angelum de virgine maria.
[3] Immediately followed by the Recommendation in York:
　　　　Has horas canonicas cum deuocione,
　　　　Christe tibi recolo pia racione,
　　　　tu qui pro me passus es amoris ardore,
　　　　sis michi solacium mortis in terrore.
The reading of the Recommendation varies slightly in some MSS.
[4] The Hours end here in **W** (Mrs. Willett's MS.).
[5] Followed by the Recommendation in Sarum.

Uirgo mater ecclesie,
  eterna porta glorie,
  esto nobis refugium
  apud patrem & filium.
O clemens.
Uirgo clemens, uirgo pia,
  uirgo dulcis, O maria,
  exaudi preces omnium
  ad te pie clamantium.
O pia.
Funde preces tuo nato
  crucifixo, uulnerato,
  & pro nobis flagellato,
  spinis puncto, felle potato.
†O dulcis.
Gloriosa dei mater,
  cuius natus extat pater,
  ora pro nobis omnibus
  qui tuam memoriam agimus.

Sarum.

O maria.
Dele culpas miserorum,
  terge sordes peccatorum,
  dona nobis beatorum
  vitam tuis precibus.
O mitis.
Ut nos solvat a peccatis
  pro amore sue matris,
  & ad regnum claritatis
  perducat nos rex pietatis
O clemens, O pia, O dulcis, o
  mitis maria.

York.

O mitis.
Vt nos soluat a peccatis
  pro amore sue matris,
  et ad regnum claritatis
  perducat nos rex pietatis.
O casta.
Dele culpas miserorum,
  terge sordes peccatorum,
  dona nobis beatorum
  uitam tuis precibus
O maria deo digna
  uirgo mater & benigna,
  nobis succurre miseris,
  ne dampnemur cum impiis.
†O dulcis maria, salue.

The Hail Mary.[1]

---

† All between this dagger and that below is omitted by **M** (York Minster MS.).
[1] **H** (British Museum MS.) and **W** omit this Hail Mary.

lx *Structure of York and Sarum Prymers.* (*Psalms and Litany.*)

All then concludes with the prayer Omnipotens sempiterne (see Pt. 1, p. 34).

THE 7 PENITENTIAL PSALMS.

In both Uses the 7 Psalms conclude with the Antiphon, Ne reminiscaris, domine, delicta nostra, vel parentum nostrorum, neque vindictam sumas de peccatis nostris.

THE 15 GRADUAL PSALMS.

Sarum.	York.
The 15 Psalms conclude with the Anthem, Parce domine, parce populo tuo quem redemisti precioso sanguine tuo, ne in eternum irascaris nobis.	Apparently the **York** Prymer did not contain the 15 Psalms as part of the Prymer proper.

THE LITANY.[1]

York.	Sarum.

Kyrieleison.
*Chr*iste*leison.*
[Kyrieleison.]
*Chr*ist*e*, audi nos.
Pater de celis, deus, miserere nobis.

---

[1] Where possible, the text is from MS. Harl. 1663. The Sarum, the saints' names in which vary slightly in the MSS., is from MS. Sloane 2565.

The Sarum MS. incorrectly gives apostles and evangelists instead of angels and archangels.

The Sarum MS. does not follow exactly the order of the names, and gives Thaddeus in place of SS. Jude, Marcial, and Timothy.

The Structure of York and Sarum Prymers. (The Litany.)

York.   **Sarum.**

Fili, redemptor mundi, deus, miserere nobis.
Spiritus sancte, deus, miserere nobis.
Sancta trinitas, vnus [deus], miserere nobis.
Sancta maria, ora *pro nobis*.
   ,,   dei genitrix, ora *pro nobis*.
   ,,   uirgo uirginum, ora *pro nobis*.
Sancte michael, ora *pro nobis*.
   ,,   Gabriel, ora *pro nobis*.
   ,,   Raphael, ora *pro nobis*.
Omnes sancti angeli & archangeli, [orate pro nobis].
Omnes sancti beatorum spirituum ordines, [orate pro nobis].
Sancte Iohannes baptista, ora *pro nobis*.
Omnes sancti patriarche et prophete, orate *pro nobis*.
Sancte Petre, ora pro nobis.
   ,,   Paule, ora pro nobis.
   ,,   Andrea, ora pro nobis.
   ,,   Iacobe, ora pro nobis.
   ,,   Iohannes, ora pro nobis.
   ,,   thoma, ora pro nobis.
   ,,   Iacobe, ora pro nobis.
   ,,   Philippe, ora pro nobis.
   ,,   Bartholomee, ora pro nobis.
   ,,   Mathee, ora pro nobis.
   ,,   Symon, ora pro nobis.
   ,,   Iuda, ora pro nobis.
   ,,   Mathia, ora pro nobis.
   ,,   Barnaba, ora pro nobis.
   ,,   Marce, ora pro nobis.
   ,,   Luca, ora pro nobis.
   ,,   Marciales, ora pro nobis.
   ,,   Thimothee, ora pro nobis.
Omnes sancti apostoli & euangeliste, [orate pro nobis]
Omnes sancti discipuli domini, orate pro nobis.
Omnes sancti Innocentes, [orate pro nobis].
Sancte Stephane, ora pro nobis.
   ,,   Line, ora pro nobis.
   ,,   Clete, ora pro nobis.
   ,,   Clemens, ora pro nobis.

The Structure of York and Sarum Prymers. (The Litany.)

York.		Sarum.	
Sancte Corneli,	ora pro nobis.	Sancte fabiane,	ora pro nobis.
,, Cipriane,	,,	,, sebastiane,	,,
,, Sixte,	,,	,, cosme,	,,
,, thoma,	,,	,, damiane,	,,
,, Laurenti,	,,	,, prime,	,,
,, Vincenti,	,,	,, feliciane,	,,
,, Grisogone,	,,	,, georgi,	,,
,, ffabiane,	,,	,, *chris*tofore,	,,
,, Sebastiane,	,,	,, Victor, cum sociis tuis, orate pro nobis.	
,, *Chris*tofore,	,,	,, Dyonisi, cum sociis tuis, orate pro nobis.	
,, Georgi,	,,	Omnes sancti martires, orate *pro nobis*.	
,, dyonisi, cum *sociis tuis*,	,,	Sancte siluester,	,,
,, maurici, cum *sociis tuis*,	,,	,, leo,	,,
,, Eustachi, cum sociis tuis,	,,	,, iheronime,	,,
,, Blasi,	ora pro nobis.	,, augustine,	,,
,, Joha*nn*es & paule,	,,	,, ysidore,	,,
,, cosma & damiane,	[,,]	,, iuliane,	,,
,, Marcelline & petre,	[,,]	,, gildarde,	,,
,, Albane,	,,	,, medarde,	,,
,, Osuualde,	,,	,, albine,	,,
,, Edmunde,	,,	,, eusebi,	,,
,, Omnes sancti martires, orate *p. n.*		,, suuichine,	,,
,, Siluester,	ora pro nobis.	,, vrine,	,,
,, Leo,	,,		
,, Gregori,	,,		
,, Ambrosi,	,,		
,, Martine,	,,		
,, Nicholae,	,,		
,, Basili,	,,		
,, Germane,	,,		
,, Augustine,	,,		
,, Pauline,	,,		
,, Johannes,	,,		
,, Wilfride,	,,		
,, Willelme,	,,		
,, Cuthberte,	,,		
,, Swithune,	,,		
,, Sampson,	,,		
,, Edmunde,	,,		

The Structure of York and Sarum Prymers. (*The Litany.*) lxiii

York.		Sarum.	
Sancte Jeronime,	ora pro nobis.		
,, edwarde,[1]	,,		
,, Leonarde,	,,		
,, Benedicte,	,,		
,, Egidi,	,,		
,, Antoni,	,,		
,, Hillariou	,,		

Omnes sancti confessores, [orate *pro nobis*].
Omnes sancti monachi & heremite, [orate *pro nobis*].

Sancta Anna, ora *pro nobis*.[2]

Sancta maria magdalena, ora *pro nobis*,
Sancta maria egipciaca, [ora *pro nobis*].

Sancta Pelagia,	ora pro nobis.	Sancta anna,	ora pro nobis.
,, ffelicitas,	,,	,, katherina,	,,
,, Perpetua,	,,	,, barbara,	,,
,, Agatha,	,,	,, margareta,	,,
,, Agnes,	,,	,, scholastica,	,,
,, Cecilia,	,,	,, petronilla,	,,
,, Lucia,	,,	,, praxedis,	,,
,, Anastasia,	,,	,, sotheris,	,,
,, Sabina,	,,	,, prisca,	,,
,, Eufamea,	,,	,, tecla,	,,
,, ffides,	,,	,, editha,	,,
,, Karitas,	,,	,, affra,	,,
,, Spes,	,,	,, elizabeth,	,,
,, Katerina,	,,		
,, Margareta,	,,		
,, Juliana,	,,		
,, Scolastica,	,,		
,, Petronilla,	,,		
,, Astreberta,	,,		
,, Hilda,	,,		
,, Euerildis,	,,		
,, Etheldreda,	,,		

Omnes sancte uirgines,[3] orate *pro nobis*.
Omnes Sancti.[4]

---

[1] M omits.   [2] St. Anna omitted by W.   [3] '& vidue,' Sarum.
[4] 'et sancte dei,' Sarum.

The Structure of York and Sarum Prymers. (The Litany.)

York.	Sarum.
Propicius esto, parce nobis, domine.	
Ab omni malo, libera nos, domine.	
Ab insidiis diaboli, libera nos, domine.	
	A dampnatione perpetua, libera nos, domine.
	Ab inminentibus peccatorum nostrorum periculis, libera nos, domine.
A peste superbie, libera nos, domine.	Ab infestationibus demonum, libera nos, domine.
A carnalibus desideriis, libera nos, domine.	A spiritu fornicationis, libera nos, domine.
	Ab appetitu inanis glorie, libera nos, domine.
Ab omnibus inmundiciis mentis & corporis, libera nos, domine.	
A persecucione paganorum & omnium inimicorum nostrorum, libera nos, domine.	
Ab ira et odio, & omni mala uoluntate, libera nos, domine.	
A uentura ira, libera nos, domine.	Ab inmundis cogitationibus, libera nos, domine.
	A cecitate cordis, libera nos, domine.
	A fulgure & tempestate, libera nos, domine.
A subitanea & eterna morte, [libera nos, domine.]	A subitanea & improuisa morte, libera nos, domine.
Per misterium sancte incarnacionis tue, libera nos, domine.	
	Per natiuitatem tuam, libera nos, domine.
	Per sanctam circumcisionem tuam, libera nos, domine.
	Per baptismum tuum, libera nos, domine.
	Per ieiunium tuum, libera nos, domine.

The Structure of York and Sarum Prymers. (*The Litany.*) lxv

York.	Sarum.
	Per crucem & passionem tuam, libera nos, domine.
	Per pretiosam mortem tuam, libera nos, domine.
Per sanctam resurreccionem tuam, libera nos, domine.	Per gloriosam resurrectionem tuam, libera nos, domine.
	Per admirabilem ascencionem tuam, libera nos, domine.
	Per gratiam sancti spiritus paracliti, libera nos, domine.
A penis inferni, libera nos, domine.	In hora mortis succurre nobis domine, libera nos, domine.
	In die iudicii, libera nos, domine.
	Peccatores te rogamus, audi nos.
	Ut pacem & concordiam¹ nobis dones; te rogamus, audi nos.
	Ut misericordia et pietas tua nos semper custodiat. te rogamus, audi nos.
Ut sanctam ecclesiam tuam regere ac defensare digneris; te rogamus, audi nos.	
Ut dompnum apostolicum & omnes gradus ecclesie in sancta religione conseruare digneris²; te rogamus, audi nos.	
Ut archiepiscopum nostrum, et omnem congregacionem sibi commissam, in sancta religione conseruare digneris.³ te rogamus, audi nos.	
Ut regibus et principibus nostris pacem et ueram concordiam, atque uictoriam, donare digneris⁴; te rogamus, audi nos.	
	Ut episcopos & abbates nostros & omnes congregationes illis commissas, in sancta religione conseruare digneris; te rogamus, audi nos.

---

[1] The Sarum MS. omits '& concordiam.'
[2] episcopum for dompnum apostolicum in Sarum.   [3] This petition omitted by M.
[4] regi nostro for regibus in Sarum.

York.

Ut locum nostrum, & omnes habitantes in eo, uisitare & consolari digneris; te rogamus, audi nos.
Ut omnibus benefactoribus nostris, eterna bona retribuas;
[te rogamus, audi nos.]
Ut cunctum populum Christianum, precioso sanguine tuo redemptum, conseruare digneris;
te rogamus, audi nos.
Ut remissionem omnium peccatorum nostrorum nobis donare digneris;
te rogamus, audi nos.
Ut obsequium seruitutis nostre racionabile facias;
te rogamus, audi nos.

Ut animas nostras, & parentum nostrorum, ab eterna dampnatione eripias;
te rogamus, audi nos.

Ut misericordia & pietas tua nos semper custodiant;
te rogamus, audi nos.
Ut aeris temperiem bonam nobis dones;
te rogamus, audi nos.

Ut fructus terre dare & conseruare digneris;
te rogamus, audi nos.

Ut fratribus nostris & omnibus fidelibus infirmis, sanitatem mentis & corporis donare digneris;
te rogamus, audi nos.

Sarum.

Ut congregationes omnium sanctorum tuorum, in tuo seruitio conseruare digneris; te rogamus, audi nos.
Ut cunctum populum Christianum, precioso sanguine tuo redemptum, conseruare digneris;
te rogamus, audi nos.
Ut omnibus benefactoribus nostris sempiterna bona retribuas;
te rogamus, audi nos.

Ut oculos misericordie tue super nos reducere digneris;
te rogamus, audi nos.
Ut obsequium seruitutis nostre rationabile facias;
te rogamus, audi nos.
Ut mentes nostras ad celestia desideria erigas;
te rogamus, audi nos.

Ut miserias pauperum & captiuorum, intueri & releuare digneris;
te rogamus, audi nos.
Ut cunctis fidelibus defunctis, requiem eternam donare digneris;
te rogamus, audi nos.

The Structure of York and Sarum Prymers. (*The Litany.*) lxvii

York.	Sarum.
Ut ad gaudia eterna nos perducere digneris; *te rogamus, audi nos.*	
Ut nos exaudire digneris; te rogamus, audi nos.	
Fili dei, te rogamus, audi nos.	
Agnus dei qui tollis peccata mundi; parce nobis, domine.	
Agnus dei qui tollis peccata mundi; exaudi nos, domine.	
Agnus dei qui tollis peccata mundi; miserere nobis;	
Christe, audi nos.	
	Kyrieleison.
	Christeleison.
	Kyrieleison.
	Paternoster.
	Et ne nos inducas.
	Sed libera.
	Ostende nobis, domine, misericordiam tuam.
	Et salutare tuum da nobis.
	Et ueniat super nos misericordia tua, domine.[1]
	Salutare tuum secundum eloquium tuum.
Peccauimus, domine, cum patribus nostris.	
Iniuste egimus, iniquitatem fecimus.	
Domine, non secundum peccata nostra, facias nobis.	
Neque secundum iniquitates nostras, retribuas nobis.	
Ne memineris, domine, iniquitatum nostrarum antiquarum.	Oremus pro omni gradu ecclesie.
cito anticipent nos misericordie tue quia pauperes facti sumus nimis.	Sacerdotes tui induantur iusticiam, et sa[n]cti tui exultent.
Adiuua nos, deus salutaris noster.	Pro fratribus et sororibus nostris.
Et propter gloriam nominis tui, domine,	Saluos fac seruos tuos & ancillas tuas, deus meus, sperantes in te.

---

[1] M gives this and the next petition too.

lxviii *The Structure of York and Sarum Prymers.* (*The Litany.*)

York.
libera nos, & propicius esto peccatis nostris, propter nomen tuum.

Memor esto congregacionis tue. Quam possedisti ab inicio.

Sacerdotes tui induantur iusticiam. Et sancti tui exultent.

Domine, saluum fac regem. Et exaudi nos in die qua inuocauerimus te.

Saluum fac populum tuum, domine. [et benedic hereditati tue.]

Et rege eos, & ex[tolle illos usque in eternum].

Exurge, domine, adiuua nos. Et libera nos propter nomen tuum.

Domine, deus uirtutum, [conuerte nos]. Et ostende [faciem tuam, & salui erimus].

Domine, exaudi [orationem meam]. Et clamor meus [ad te ueniat].
Deus, cui proprium, etc. (see Part 1, p. 78).

Deus, in te sperancium fortitudo, adesto propicius inuocacionibus nostris; & quia sine te nichil potest mortalis infirmitas, presta auxilium gratie tue, ut in exequendis mandatis tuis & uoluntate tibi & accione placeamus.

Protector in te sperancium, deus, sine quo nichil est ualidum, nichil sanctum, multiplica super nos misericordiam tuam, ut, te rectore, te duce, sic transeamus per bona temporalia, ut non amittamus eterna.

Deus, cui omne cor patet, & omnis uoluntas loquitur, & quem nullum latet secretum, purifica, per inuocacionem sancti spiritus, cogitaciones

Sarum.
Pro cuncto populo catholico. Saluum fac populum tuum, domine, et benedic hereditati tue. Et rege eos, et extolle illos usque in eternum.

Domine, fiat pax in virtute tua; Et habundantia in turribus tuis.

Anime famulorum famularumque tuarum requiescant in pace. Amen.

Omnipotens sempiterne deus, qui facis mirabilia magna solus, pretende super famulos tuos, & super cunctas congregationes illis commissas,[1] spiritum gracie salutaris, et, ut in ueritate tibi complaceant, perpetuum eis rorem tue benedictionis infunde.

Deus, qui caritatis dona per graciam sancti spiritus tuorum cordibus fidelium infundis, da famulis & famulabus tuis, pro quibus tuam deprecamur clemenciam, salutem mentis et corporis, ut te tota uirtute diligant, & que tibi placita sunt, tota dilectione perficiant.

Deus a quo, etc. (see Pt. 1, p. 15).

Ineffabilem misericordiam tuam que-

---

[1] "famulum tuum archiepiscopum nostrum, & super cunctam congregacionem illi commissam" in York MSS.

The Structure of York and Sarum Prymers. (*The Litany.*) lxix

York.

cordis n*ost*ri, ut pe*rf*ecte te diligere & digne laudare mereamur.

Omnipotens sempit*er*ne deus, qui facis, etc. (see Sarum above).

Deus, qui caritatis, etc. (see Sarum above).

Adesto, d*omi*ne, supplicac*i*onibus nos*tri*s & uia*m* & actus famulo*rum* tuo*rum* i*n* salutis tue prosperitate dispone, ut int*er* om*ne*s huius uie & uite uarietates, tuo semp*er* protegantur auxilio.

Deus, a quo (see Pt. 1, p. 15).

Fideliu*m* deus (see Pt. 1, p. 36).

Omnium sancto*rum* intercessionib*us* q*ue*s*um*us, do*m*i*n*e, gra*cia* tua nos semper protegat, & *chris*tianis om*n*ib*us* uiuentibus atque defunctis m*isericord*iam tuam ubiq*ue* pretende, ut uiuentes ab o*m*nib*us* impugnac*i*onibus defensi tua opitulac*i*one saluentur, & defu*n*cti remissionem omni*um* suo*rum* merea*n*t*ur* accipe*re* pe*cc*atoru*m*.

Per *Christu*m [dominum nostrum. Amen.]

Sarum.

sumus, domine, nobis clementer ostende, ut simul nos a peccatis omnibus exuas, & a penis quas pro hiis meremur benignus eripias.

Fidelium deus, etc. (see Pt. 1, p. 36).

Pietate, etc. (see Pt 1, p. 51).

THE OFFICE FOR THE DEAD.[1]

Sarum Use.

Our text in Pt. 1 gives the **Sarum** Office, excepting that the V︷ and R︷ after the Magnificat should be transferred to the preceding psalm; and also that, it being impossible to establish the text of the concluding prayers of Placebo and Dirige as well as the conclusion of Matins commencing Libera me domine, those portions must await

---

[1] No reliance is to be placed on the use of Requiem, etc., after the Psalms in the Office for the Dead, though the York MS. M follows in a measure the plan shown under A, B, and C in the Table of Six Sarum Prymers.

lxx *The Structure of York and Sarum Prymers.* (*Placebo.*)

further investigation. It is clear that the concluding prayers of Placebo are not as a matter of course repeated at the end of Dirige.

York Use.[1]

Placebo.

The text of Pt. 1 gives us the Office for the Dead according to the Use of **York**, with the following exceptions.

The V̊ and R̊ after the Magnificat should be transferred to the preceding psalm, thus agreeing with **Sarum**.

The Anthem of the Magnificat reads:

    Tuam, deus, deposcimus pietatem, ut eis tribuere digneris lucidas & quietas mansiones.

The V̊s and R̊s after the psalm 'Lauda anima mea' read:

    Requiem eternam dona eis, domine.
    Et lux perpetua luceat eis.
    Credo uidere bona domini.
    In terra uiuencium.
    A porta inferi.
    Erue domine animas eorum.
    Requiescant in pace.
    Amen.[2]

The concluding prayers vary.[3]

Dirige.

FIRST NOCTURN.

The R̊ and V̊ before the first Lesson read:
    In memoria eter[na erunt iusti.
    Ab audicione mala non timebunt].

The V̊ of the second Lesson reads:
    Requiem eternam dona eis, domine.

---

[1] Text from MS. H.   [2] M misplaces the last two.
[3] The concluding prayers of Placebo are given by the 3 MSS. as follows:

H	W	M
Omnipotens sempiterne deus, cui nunc quam, etc.		
Deus, uenie largitor, etc.	Inclina, domine, aurem tuam (see Pt. 1, p. 55).	
	Quesumus, domine, pro tua pietate, etc.	
Deus, qui nos patrem (see Pt. 1, p. 58).	Miserere quesumus, domine, animabus, etc.	
	Fidelium deus (see Text, p. 36).	

The Structure of York and Sarum Prymers. (*Lauds.*) lxxi

SECOND NOCTURN.

The R̸ and V̸ before the 4th Lesson read :
Ne tradas bestiis animas confitentes tibi.
[Et animas pauperum tuorum ne obliuiscaris in finem.]

The R̸, V̸, and Repetition of the 6th Lesson read :
Libera me, domine, de uiis inferni; qui portas ereas confregisti, et visitasti infernum, et dedisti eis lumen, ut viderent te qui erant in penis tenebrarum.
Clamantes & dicentes, aduenisti, redemptor noster.
[Qui portas.]

THIRD NOCTURN.

The V̸ and R̸ before the 7th Lesson read :
Anime eorum in [bonis demorentur. Et semen eorum hereditet terram].

The R̸, V̸, and Repetition of the 8th Lesson read[1] :
Deus eterne, in cuius humana condicio potestate consistit, animas omnium fidelium defunctorum quesumus ab omnibus absolue peccatis. Ut penitencie fructum, quem uoluntas eorum optauit, preuenti morte non perdant.
Qui in cruce positus latronem sero penitentem suscepisti, eorum precamur pie peccata dele.
[Ut.]

The conclusion of matins Libera me, domine, etc. is given, as in our text, by all 3 MSS. down to the opening, Therefore what shall I? This is omitted, and the canticle concludes :
Audiui vocem de celo dicentem,
Beati [mortui qui in domino moriuntur].[2]

Lauds (of Dirige).

The Anthem of 'Ego dixi' reads :
Eruisti, domine, animam meam ne periret.
The V̸ and R̸ before the Benedictus read :
[A porta inferi.
Erue, domine, animas eorum.[3]]

---

[1] In H and W the Pater noster before the 1st, 4th, and 7th Lessons is often wanting.

[2] H has these last two lines on the margin, but in a contemporary hand : before them is inserted 'Libera me.'

[3] H omits this V̸ and R̸, also the Kyrie eleison, Christe eleison, Kyrie eleison, and Pater noster after the Benedictus, and the concluding V̸s and R̸s before the final prayers.

lxxii *Structure of York and Sarum Prymers.* *(Commendations.)*

After the psalm 'Exaltabo domine,' the MSS. read as follows:

H	M	W
		Requiem eternam.
		Credo uidere.
		A porta inferi.
Inclina, domine.		Domine, exaudi.
Quesumus, domine.		Dominus uobiscum.
Miserere quesumus, domine.		Animabus quesumus,
Animabus quesumus domine famulorum, etc.	Fidelium deus omnium. (Part 1, p. 36.)	domine, etc., as H. Requiescant in pace. Amen.

COMMENDATIONS.

Sarum Use.

Our text in Pt. 1 follows the Use of **Sarum**, if we add the prayer 'Misericordiam tuam domine.'

York Use.

Up to the commencement of the Psalm 'Domine probasti,' **York** Use follows our text. The psalm is, however, not given by any of the three MSS., but each concludes as follows:

H	M	W
Absolue quesumus, domine, animas famulorum, etc.	De profundis clamaui. Fiant aures, et cetera.	
Domine ihesu christe, qui, etc.		Requiem eternam. Credo uidere. A porta inferi.
Gaude uirgo mater christi, etc.	Domine, exaudi. Tibi, domine, commendamus, etc.	Absolue, etc., as H.
Deus, qui beatissimam uirginem, etc.	(See Part 1, p. 89.) Partem beate, etc.	

V.

Prymers Secundum Usum or Consuetudinem Anglie.

Prymers in which the Hours are described as above may be classed as following almost exactly the Sarum Use. The following gives the result of a collation of three MSS. of the above Use with the Sarum text laid down on p. lv etc. These MSS., excepting for its beauty Harl. 2846, have been, like those of Sarum, purposely selected at random. As in Sarum, the names of the saints in the Litany may vary in MSS. of this Use. One or two other slight variations occur, almost certainly only the result of accident. .

Brit. Mus. MS. 2 A IV.

The Litany.

The Collects at the end of the Litany vary from those of Sarum.

Dirige.

The V⁊ and R⁊ before the first Lesson differ from Sarum, and the V⁊ and R⁊ before the Benedictus in Lauds are omitted.

Commendations.

The V⁊ and R⁊ before the Ps. Domine probasti are omitted.

Brit. Mus. MS. Harl. 2846.

The Hours.

The Memorials of SS. Andrew, Stephen, and Laurence are omitted.

7 Psalms.

The Anthem is transferred to the conclusion of the 15 Psalms.

The Litany.

The prayer Deus a quo is omitted.

Commendations.

The V⁊ and R⁊ before Domine probasti are omitted.

lxxiv *Prymers Secundum Usum or Consuetudinem Anglie.*

Brit. Mus. MS. Sloane 2474.

The Litany.

The prayers Deus qui caritas, and Deus a quo, are transposed.

Dirige.

The V︦ and R︦ before the Lesson Spiritus meus read, Ne tradas &c.

The V︦ and R︦ before the Benedictus in Lauds read, Audiui vocem &c.

VI.

The Structure of Two Eleventh-Century Versions of the Hours of the Blessed Virgin Mary.

Where the Offices agree, the text is from MS. 2 B V. The varying size of the larger letters is not shown.

British Museum MS. Tib. A III., *commencing lf. 107 b.*	*British Museum MS. 2 B V*, *commencing lf. 1 b.*
uotiua laus in ueneratione *sanc*te marie uirg*inis*.	

[MATINS.]

| D*omi*ne, ad adiuuandu*m* me, festina. | \| D*omi*ne, labia mea aperies. |

D*eu*s, in adiutorium meu*m* intende.

Dom*i*ne, ad adiuuandu*m* me, festina.
Gloria patri [etc.].
Sicut erat [etc.].
Dom*i*ne, labia mea aperies.
Et os meu*m* adnuntiabit laudem tuam. III.
Dom*i*ne, quid multiplicati sunt.
    [In]vitatoriu*m*. Aue maria, gr*ati*a plena, dom*in*us tecum.
Venite, exultemus [etc.].

Quem terra [etc.].	**Ymnus.** Maria, m*a*ter d*omi*ni [etc.].
O gloriosa femina [etc.].	
An*tiphona.* Sp*iritu*s s*an*ctus in te descendit [etc.].	**A**n*tiphona.* Exaltata es, s*an*cta [etc.].

    P*salmus.* Domine d*omi*nus n*oste*r.

| **A**n*tiphona.* Uirgo uerbo concepit [etc.]. | **A**n*tiphona.* Dignare me laudare [etc.]. |

    P*salmus.* Domine, quis hab*itabit*.

| **A**n*tiphona.* Ecce, maria genuit nobis [etc.]. | **A**n*tiphona.* Sicut letantiu*m* omnium [etc.]. |

Psal**mus.** Fundamenta.

Benedicta tu.	V̄. Specie tua & pulchritudine tua.

Pater noster.

	Et ne nos [etc.].
Preces. Precibus & meritis [etc.].	Precibus & meritis [etc.].
Benedictio. Pater de celis deus [etc.].	**Benedictio.** Intus & [etc.].
Quas igitur tibi [etc.].	Ecce tu pulchra [etc.].

R̄. Sancta & immaculata uirginitas [etc.].
V̄. Benedicta tu in mulieribus [etc.].
Quia.

Benedictio. Beata interueniente maria [etc.].	Omni benedictione [etc.].
Lectio II. Recordare nostri [etc.].	**Lectio.** Que est ista que [etc.].

Tu autem.

R̄. Beata es maria, que dominum [etc.].	R̄. Super salutem & omnem [etc.].
V̄. Aue maria [etc.]. Genuisti.	V̄. Ualde eam nos oportet [etc.]. gaudent.
Benedictio. Intercessio sancte marie [etc.].	**Benedic** [.. ? ..]. Gratia sancti spiritus [etc.].
Lectio III. O maria [etc.].	**Lectio.** Pulchra es amica [etc.].

Tu autem.

R̄. Te laudant angeli [etc.].	R̄. Beata es, uirgo [etc.].
V̄. Ipsa [etc.]. Ut benedic.	V̄. Aue maria [etc.].

Te deum lau[damus, etc.].
In principio erat [etc.].
Te decet laus. Te decet ymnus [etc.].

Collecta. Famulorum tuorum [etc.].	**Collecta.** Deus, qui beate [etc.].

[LAUDS.]

Ad laudibvs.

Deus in adiutorium.

Domine, ad adiuuandum me, festina.

Gloria patri.

Deus misereatur nostri.

Antiphona. Post partum [etc.]. | Antiphona. Nigra sum, sed formosa [etc.].
Psalmus. Dominus regnauit.
Antiphona. Odor [etc.]. | Antiphona. Tota pulchra es [etc.].
Psalmus. Iubilate.
Antiphona. In odorem [etc.]. | Antiphona. Ortus conclusus [etc.].
Psalmus. Deus, deus meus.
Antiphona. Benedicta filia tua domino [etc.].
Psalmus. Benedicite.
Antiphona. Cum iocunditate [etc.]. | Antiphona. Felix namque [etc.].
Psalmus. Laudate.
Capitelum. Ego quasi [etc.]. | Capitulum. In omnibus requiem [etc.].
| Deo gratias.
R7. Sancta maria mater [etc.]. | R7. Adiuuabit eam [etc.].
V7. Et impetratam [etc.]. | V7. Deus in medio [etc.].
Gloria.
Ymnus. Aue maris stella [etc.]. | Ymnus. O quam glorifica [etc.].
V7. Speciosa facta est. | Antiphona. Diffusa est [etc.].
Antiphona. O gloriosa genitrix [etc.]. | In evangelio. Quomodo [etc.].
[Psalmus.] Benedictus dominus deus israhel.
Kyrrieleison.
Christeleison.
Kyrrieleison.

Ego dixi, domine, miserere mei. | Pater noster.
Conuertere. | Beata mater & innupta uirgo.
Fiat misericordia tua, domine. | Post partum uirgo.
Aue maria, gratia plena. | Specie tua & pulchritudine tua.
Post partum uirgo. | Aue maria, gratia plena.
Domine, exaudi orationem meam.
Concede, quesumus, misericors deus [etc.]. | Collecta. Concede nobis [etc.].
R7. Nos autem [etc.].
V7. Per signum [etc.].
Deus, qui pro nobis [etc.].
R7. Surrexit [etc.].
V7. In resurrectione [etc.].
Presta quesumus [etc.].

R̷. Ascendit deus [etc.].
V̷. Heua est [etc.].
　　Deus, cuius filius [etc.].
R̷. Spiritus sanctus [etc.].
V̷. Emitte spirituum [etc.].
　　Deus, cui omne cor patet [etc.].
R̷. Gloria tibi, trinitas [etc.].
V̷. Benedicamus [etc.].
Collecta. Omnipotens sempiterne deus, qui dedisti [etc.].
Antiphona. Saluator mundi [etc.].
V̷. Gaudet iusti [etc.].
Collecta. Concede, quesumus, omnipotens [etc.].

[PRIME.]

Ad Primam.
　　Deus, in adiutorium meum, intende.
Domine, ad adiuuandum me, festina.
　　Gloria patri.

Ymnus ad primam. Maria, mater domini [etc.].	**Ymnus ad primam.** A solis ortu [etc.].
Antiphona. Regali ex [etc.].	**A**ntiphona. Missus est gabriel [etc.].
Psalmus. Deus, in nomine tuo.	Psalmus. Confitemini domino.
Psalmus. Beati immaculati.	Psalmus. In quo corrigit.
Psalmus. Retribue seruo.	
Psalmus. Quicumque uult.	
Capitulum. In omnib[us, etc.].	Capitulum. In sion firmata sum [etc.].
	R̷. Adiuuabit eam deus uultu suo.
V̷. Beata mater [etc.].	V̷. Deus in medio [etc.].
	Deus uultu suo.
	Gloria patri.
	V̷. Diffusa [etc.].

　　Kyrrieleison.
　　Christeleison.

Kyrrieleison.
Pater noster.
| Et ne nos [etc.].
| Viuet anima mea.
| Erraui sicut ouis.
Credo in deum.
| Carnis resurrectionem.
Repleatur os meum laude tua.
[Domine], auerte faciem tuam a peccatis meis.
Cor mundum crea in me, deus.
Ne pro[i]icias me a facie tua.
Redde mihi letitiam salutaris tui.
Eripe me, domine, ab homine malo.
Eripe me de inimicis meis, deus meus.
Eripe me de operantibus iniquitatem.
Sic psallam.
Exaudi nos, deus, salutaris noster.
Deus, in adiutorium meum, intende.
Sanctus deus, sanctus, fortis, sanctus & immortalis.
Benedic, anima mea, dominum & omnia.
Benedic, anima mea, dominum, & noli.[1]
Qui propitiatur omnibus.
Qui redemit de interitu.
Qui coronat te in miseratione & misericordia.
Confiteor domino deo celi [etc.].
Misereatur & propitius [etc.].
Indulgentiam [etc.].
Conuerte nos, deus, salutaris noster.
Dignare, domine, die isto.
Miserere nostri, domine, miserere.
Fiat misericordia tua, domine, super nos.
| Beata mater & innupta uirgo.
| Post partum uirgo.
| Specie tua.
Aue maria.
Post partum. |
Domine, exaudi orationem meam.
Beate & gloriose [etc.]. | **Collecta.** Omnipotens sempiterne deus [etc.].

---

[1] For these last two lines MS. Tib., A III, reads "Benedic anima" only.

[TIERCE.]

Deus, in adiutorium meum.
Gloria patri.

Gabrihel [etc.].	**Ymnus ad tertiam.** Domus pudici pectoris [etc.].
Antiphona. Gaude, dei genitrix [etc.].	*Antiphona.* Aue maria [etc.].
	Psalmus. Legem pone.
Psalmus. Memento uerbi tui.	
Psalmus. Bonitatem fecisti.	
Capitulum. In sion firmata [etc.].	**Capitulum.** E[t] radicaui [etc.].
	R⁊. Diffusa [etc.].
V⁊. Specie tua [etc.].	V⁊. Propterea benedixit [etc.].
Intende.	V⁊. Dilexisti [etc.].

Kyrrieleison.
Christeleison.
Kyrrieleison.
Pater noster.

Preces. Ego dixi, domine. Aue maria. Beata mater. Post partum uirgo. Domine, exaudi.	Preces ut supra. Aue maria. Beata mater & innupta uirgo.
Collecta. Deus, qui salutis [etc.].	**Collecta.** Famulorum tuorum [etc.].

[SEXT.]

Ad VI.

Deus, in adiutorium meum, intende.
Gloria patri.

Ymnus. Maria celi [etc.].	**Ymnus ad sextam.** Quem terra [etc.].
Antiphona. Succurre, sancta genitrix [etc.].	*Antiphona.* Ne timeas, maria [etc.].
	Psalmus. Defecit.
Psalmus. Quomodo.	
Psalmus. Iniquos.	
Capitelum. E[t] radicaui [etc.].	Sicut cedrus [etc.].
	R⁊. Specie tua [etc.].
	V⁊. Intende [etc.].

Two Eleventh-Century Versions of the Hours. lxxxi

        V7. Adiuuabit eam deus [etc.].
Deus in medio eius. | Kyrrieleison.
        Christeleison.
        Kyrrieleison.
        Pater noster.
Ego dixi, domine. Aue maria. | Preces ut supra. Aue maria.
Beata mater. Domine, exaudi. | Beata mater.
Collecta. Concede, quesumus [etc.]. | Collecta. Deus, qui nos [etc.].

[NONE.]

Ad Nonam.
        Deus, in adiutorium meum.
        Gloria.

Ymnus. Maria virgo [etc.]. | **Ymnus ad VIIII.** Beata celi [etc.].

Antiphona. Rogamus [etc.]. | **Antiphona.** Spiritus sanctus [etc.].

        [Psalmus.] Mirabilia.
Psalmus. Clamaui.
Psalmus. Principes.
        Capitula. Sicut cinnamomum [etc.].
        | R7. Adiuuabit eam deus uultu suo.
        | V7. Deus in medio [etc.].
        V7. Diffusa est gratia [etc.].
        Kyrrieleison.
        Christeleison.
        Kyrrieleison.
        Pater noster.
Ego dixi, domine. Aue maria. | preces ut supra. Aue maria.
Beata mater. Domine, exaudi. | Beata mater.
        Collecta. Porrige nobis [etc.].

[EVENSONG.]

Ad vesperum.
Deus, in adiutorium meum.
Antiphona. Aue maria [etc.]. | **Antiphona ad vesperam.**
        | **Antiphona.** Benedicta tu [etc.].
        Psalmus. Dixit dominus domino meo.
Antiphona. Sancta [etc.]. | **Antiphona.** In odorem [etc.].

THE PRYMER.

Psalmus.   Letatus sum.
Antiphona.   Gaude, maria uirgo, cunctas [etc.].
Psalmus.   Nisi dominus.

Antiphona. Beata mater & in- | Antiphona.   Dignare me [etc.].
nupta [etc.].
Psalmus.   Memento.
Capitulum.   Ab initio [etc.].   Ego quasi [etc.].
Sancta maria, sucurre [etc.].   R7. Veni electa [etc.].
[?].   V7. Specie tua [etc.].
Sentiant.   quia.
                                       Gloria patri.
                                       quia.

Ymnus.   O quam [etc.].   Ymnus.   Aue, maris stella [etc.].
V7. Post partum [etc.].
Antiphona.   Virgo dei [etc.]. | Antiphona. Succurre,sancta[etc.].
Psalmus.   Magnificat.
Kyrrieleison.
Christeleison.
Kyrrieleison.

Pater noster.   Et ne nos.   Ego   Preces ut supra.   Aue maria.
dixi, domine.   Aue maria.   Beata mater.
Beata mater.   Post partum.
Domine, exaudi.
Collecta.   Concede [etc.].
                                       Deus qui [etc.].
                                       Benedicamus domino.
                                       Deo gratias.

Nos autem gloriari.   Ut supra.
Laudem dicite [etc.].
Letamini [etc.].
Collecta.   Infirmitatem [etc.].
Laudate dominum omnis.
De profundis.
Laudate.
Audiui uocem de celo.
pater.
Requiem.
A porta inferi.
Requiescant.

[COMPLINE.]

| A Completorium.

Conuerte nos, deus salutaris noster.
Deus, in adiutorium meum, intende.
| Gloria patri.
Psalmus. Cum inuocarem.
| Psalmus. In te, domine, speraui.
Psalmus. Qui habitat.
Psalmus. Ecce nunc.

Memento nostri, domine [etc.].
Ymnus. Christe [etc.].

Capitulum. Ecce [etc.].
V7. Sancta [etc.].

                    Ymnus. O quam [etc.].
                    Requiem ut supra.

                    Capitulum. Tu autem [etc.].
                    V7. Custodi nos [etc.].
                    Antiphona. Ecce completa [etc.].
                    Nunc dimittis seruum.

Kyrreleison.
Christeleison.
Kyrrieleison.
Pater noster.
| Et ne nos.
| In pace in idipsum.
Credo in deum.
| Carnis resurrectionem.
| **Preces.**

Benedicamus patrem.
Benedictus es in firmamento celi.
Benedicat & custodiat.
Dignare, domine, nocte ista.
Miserere nostri, domine.
Fiat misericordia tua, domine.
Aue maria.
Beata mater.
Post partum uirgo.
| Specie tua.
Domine, exaudi orationem meam.

Collecta. Protege [etc.].
Benedicat [etc.].

                    Collecta. Visita [etc.].
                    Collecta. Purifica [etc.].
                    Collecta. Da nobis [etc.].

VII.

The Structure of the Durham Prymer.
MS. Harl. 1804.

THE HOURS OF THE BLESSED VIRGIN MARY.

Matins.

Commences D*omi*ne labia, etc.; Et os meu*m*, etc.
The opening Deus in adiutorium meum, etc., to Alleluia inclusive; the **Invitatory**, Aue maria; the Venite (with the Invitatory interwoven); the Hymn,[1] Quem terra; the Psalms Domine dom*inu*s noster, Celi enarrant, and Domini est terra; a*ntiphona*, Benedicta tu; V⁊ Sicut, etc.; [R⁊] Odorem, etc.; Pater noster, etc.; Meritis, etc.; Jube, etc.; Alma, etc.; the first Lesson, Sancta maria, etc.; R⁊ Sancta et i*m*maculata, etc.; V⁊ Benedicta, etc.; R Q*ui*a, the second Lesson, Sancta maria piarum, etc.; R⁊ Beata, es maria, etc.; V⁊ Aue maria, etc.; R Genuisti. Iube d*omi*ne, etc.; In om*ni* tribulacione, etc.; the third Lesson, Sancta dei genitrix, etc.; R⁊ Felix namq*ue*, etc.; V⁊ Ora p*ro* populo, etc.; R Q*ui*a, etc.; Glo*ria* pat*ri*, etc.; Quia; the Te deum; a*ntiphona*, In prole mater, etc.

Lauds.

The opening Deus, etc.; **ps***almus*, Dominus regnauit; a*ntiphona*, Post partum, etc.; **ps***almus*, Iubilate deo; a*ntiphona*, Sancta dei genitrix, etc.; **ps***almus*, Deus deus meus; a*ntiphona*, In odore, etc.; **ps***almus*, Benedicite; a*ntiphona*, Benedicta a filio, etc.; **ps***almus*, Laudate dominum de celis (Cantate and Laudate too); a*ntiphona*, Ortus conclusus, etc.; **capitulum**, Beata es maria, etc.; R⁊ Sancta maria, mater christi, etc.; V⁊ Et impetratam, etc.; Sancta m*ari*a, Glo*ria* pa*tri*, Sanc*t*a maria; **ymnus**, O gloriosa dom*i*na; V⁊ Post partum, etc.; Dei genitrix, etc.; **ps***almus*, Benedictus do*minus*

---

[1] MS. has 'ps'.'

deus israel; a*ntiphona*, Uirgo dei genitrix, etc.; Concede nos; a*ntiphona*, Veni sancte sp*iritus*, etc; V̸ Emitte spiritum, etc.; [R̸] Et renouabis, etc.; or*acio*, Deus qui corda, etc., and the Memorial of the Passion.

Prime.[1]

Aue maria, etc.; *Christ*e audi nos.

The opening Deus, etc.; the Hymn Rex *christ*e, etc.; the Psalms Deus in nomine, Beatus uir, Quare fremuerunt, Uerba mea auribus, Laudate d*ominum* omn*es* gentes; a*ntiphona*, Sancta dei genitrix, etc.; Capitulum, Felix namq*ue*, etc.; R̸ Ih*es*u *christ*e fili, etc.; Ih*es*u *christ*e, etc.; qui de uirgine dignatus, etc.; Ih*es*u *christ*e, etc.; Gl*or*ia patri, etc.; Ih*es*u *christ*e, etc.; Aue maria, etc.; Benedicta, etc.; **oracio**, Concede misericors deus, etc.; [**oracio**], Sancti sp*iritus*, etc.; **Oracio**, Beati ioh*ann*is, etc.; **Oracio**, Da eterne, etc.; the Memorial of the Passion.

Tierce.

Aue maria, etc.; [Christe, etc.].

The opening Deus, etc., and the Hymn Rex, etc.; the Psalms Legem pone, Memor esto, and Bonitatem fecisti; a*ntiphona*, Dignare me laudare, etc.; cap*itulum*, Beata es maria q*ue* d*omin*um, etc.; R̸ Aue maria, etc.; Benedicta tu, etc.; Aue maria, etc.; Gl*or*ia patri, etc.; Aue maria, etc.; V̸ Post p*ar*tum, etc.; R̸ Dei genitrix, etc.; Or*acio*, Concede nos, etc.; **Oracio**, Deus qui corda, etc.; or*acio*, Ecclesiam tuam, etc.; **oracio**, Propiciare, etc.; the Memorial of the Passion.

Sext.

Aue maria, etc.; *Christ*e, etc.

The opening Deus, etc., and Hymn, Rex, etc.; the Psalms Defecit, Quomodo, and Iniquos; a*ntiphona*, Sub tuam, etc.; cap*itulum*, Maria uirgo semp*er* letare, etc.; R̸ Post partum, etc.; Post partum, etc.; V̸ Dei genitrix, etc.; Post partum, etc.; Gl*or*ia p*at*ri, etc.; Post partum, etc.; V̸ Speciosa, etc.; V̸ In deliciis, etc.; the Prayers Beate & gloriose, etc., Assit nobis, etc., Sit q*ue*sum*us* d*omi*ne, etc., Adiuuet nos, etc., and the Memorial of the Passion.

---

[1] Ad primam in dominica. But immediately succeeding this Prime office is that In ferialibus diebus ad primam, which is exactly the same, excepting that Beati immaculati and Retribue seruo take the place of Beatus uir, Quare fremuerunt, and Uerba mea auribus.

Structure of the Durham Prymer. (*Hours and* 7 *Psalms.*) lxxxvii

None.

Aue maria, etc.; *Christe*, etc.

The opening Deus, etc., and the Hymn, Rex, etc.; the Psalms Mirabilia, Clamaui, and Principes; a*ntiphona*, In prole mater, etc.; cap*itulum*, Te laudant angeli, etc.; ℞ Speciosa facta, etc.; Speciosa, etc.; In deliciis, etc.; Speciosa, etc.; Gl*or*ia pa*tri*, etc.; Speciosa, etc.; Dignare me, etc.; Da michi, etc.; the Prayers, Famulorum, etc.; Ure igne, etc.; Beati iohannis, etc.; Deus qui s*ancti*, etc.; and Uide d*omi*ne, etc.; the Memorial of the Passion.

Evensong.

Aue maria, etc.; Christe, etc.

The opening Deus, etc.; the Psalms Letatus sum, Ad te leuaui, Nisi quia, Qui confidunt, and In conuertendo; a*ntiphona*, Beata mater, etc.; cap*itulum*, Beata es maria, etc.; ℞ Sancta dei genitrix, etc.; Intercede, etc.; S*ancta* dei, etc.; Gloria patri, S*ancta* dei, etc.; ym*nus*, Aue maris stella; V7 Post partum, etc.; ℞ Dei gen*itrix*, etc.; the Magnificat. euang*elio*, Aue regina, etc.; or*acio*, Concede nos, etc.; a*ntiphona*, Ueni sancte sp*iritus*, etc.; V7 Emitte, etc.; [℞ Et renouabis, etc.]; the Prayer Deus qui corda, etc.; the Memorial of the Passion.

Compline.

Aue maria; *Christe*, etc.
Conuerte nos, etc.; Et auerte, etc.

The opening Deus, etc.; the Psalms Usquequo d*omi*ne, Iudica me, Sæpe expugnauerunt, and D*omi*ne non est; antip*hona*, Cum iocunditate, etc.; capitulu*m*, Sicut cynamomum, etc.; ℞ Aue maria, etc.; Aue maria, etc.; ℞ Benedicta, etc.; Aue maria, etc.; Gloria pa*tri*; Aue maria, etc.; ymp*nus*, Uirgo singularis, etc.; a*ntiphona*, Ecce ancilla, etc.; ffiat michi, etc.; Nunc dimittis; a*ntiphona*, Ecce completa est, etc.; the Prayers Deus qui de b*ea*te marie, etc.; Ure igne, etc.; Beati ioha*nn*is, etc.; Deus qui sancti, etc.; and Uide d*omi*ne, etc.; the Memorial of the Passion, the Recommendation, the Salue regina, with the addition O clemens, O pia, O dulcis maria salue, the Aue Maria, and the Prayer Om*ni*pote*ns* sempiterne deus, etc.

THE 7 PSALMS.

For the 15 Psalms, see Table of Contents, Introduction, p. xvii.

lxxxviii *The Structure of the Durham Prymer.* (*The Litany.*)

THE LITANY.

Collation with the Sarum, see p. lx.

A*ntiphona,* Ne reminiscaris do*mi*ne delicta no*s*tra vel parentum nostro*rum,* neq*ue* vindictam sumas de peccatis no*s*tris p*ro*pter nomen tuum.

The second Kyrieleison is not given. After S. Raphael, angeli et archangeli given. After Patriarchs and Prophets the saints' names read: petre, Paule, Andrea, Ioha*n*nes, Iacobe, Philippe, Bartholomee, Mathee, Thoma, Iacobe, Symon, Thadee, Mathia, Barnaba, Luca, Marce, ap*os*toli & euangeliste, discipuli do*mi*ni, innocentes, Stephane, Oswalde, Clemens, Alexander, Marcelle, Sixte, Laurenti, ypolite cum s. t, Corneli, Cipriane, Uincenti, Georgi, Dionisi cum s. t, Maurici c. s. t, Nichasi c. s. t, Eustachi c. s. t, ffabiane, Sebastiane, Grisogone, Quintine, Geruase, Prothasi, Ch*ris*tofore, Elphege, Thoma, Albane, Edmunde, Gorgoni, Oswyne, Cosma & damia, Marcelline & pet*er,* Blasi, m*ar*t*ires,* Cuthberte, Siluester, Marcialis, Hillari, Martine, Ambrosi, Augustine, Damase, Leo, Gregori, Augustine c. s. t, Athanasi, Basile, Taurine, Romane, Audoene, Nicholae, Remigi, Iuliane, Germane, Aidane, Cedda, Wilfride, Pauline, Dunstane, Iohannes, Will*elm*e, Edmunde, Swythune, Paule, Antoni, Hillarion, Machari, Ieronime, Benedicte, Carilephe, Maure, Columbane, Wandragesile, Boisile, Benedicte, Beda, Leonarde, Egide, Guthlace, Godrice, confessores, Maria magdalen*a,* ffides, ffelicitas, P*er*petua, Agatha, Agnes, Petrocinia, Cecilia, Lucia, Scolastica, ffides, Spes, Caritas, Genouefa, Tecla, Iuliana, Praxedis, Anastasia, Cristina, Prisca, Eufemia, Margareta, Katerina, Etheldreda, Hilda, Ebba, Brigida.

Then as Sarum (the first few words slightly varying), from Omnes sancte to Per misterium, etc., inclusive; then has, Per passionem et crucem tuam, Per gloriosam, etc., omitting all between of Sarum.

In place of Ut ep*iscopu*m, etc., are two supplications, Ut omnes grad*us* ecclesie in sancta religione conseruare digneris, and Ut ep*iscopu*m no*s*tr*um* & gregem sibi co*m*missum c. d, then Ut regibus et principibus no*s*tris pacem & vera*m,* and on as Sarum.

The supplication Ut mentes, etc., is placed before Ut fructus, etc.

Before Ut miserias our MS. inserts Ut regularibus disciplinis nos instruere digneris.

The Fili dei is repeated.

Before the first Kyrie our MS. has Ch*ris*te audi nos. After the

Structure of the Durham Prymer. (*Placebo and Dirige.*) lxxxix

second Kyrie the MS. concludes, Pater noster, Et ne nos, Et ueniat super.[1] Salutare. Esto nobis. A facie. Memor esto. Quam. Domine saluos. Et exaudi. Saluos fac. ffiat pax. Oremus pro fidelibus defunctis, Requiem. Domine exaudi. & clamor. Dominus vobiscum. Et cum; the prayers Deus cui proprium. Omnipotens sempiterne deus qui facis. Pretende. Deus a quo. A domo. Ecclesie tue. Quesumus omnipotens deus ut famulus. Rege quesumus. Familiam. Omnipotens. Adesto. Deus qui contritorum. Animabus. Deus qui. Deus qui laboribus.

THE OFFICE FOR THE DEAD.

Placebo.

psalmus, Dilexi; antiphona, Placebo; psalmus, Ad dominum; antiphona, Heu me; psalmus, Leuaui oculos; antiphona, Dominus custodit; psalmus, De profundis; antiphona, Si iniquitates; [psalmus], Confitebor; antiphona, Opera manuum; V̷ Requiem eternam; [R̷] Et lux; psalmus, Magnificat; antiphona, Audiui, Pater noster, A porta, Erue, Dominus vobiscum; 7 Prayers, Deus qui inter, etc.; Presta quesumus, Inclina domine, Deus venie, Deus cuius miseracione, Deus qui nobis patrem, Fidelium deus, Dominus vobiscum, Et cum, Requiescant. Amen.

Dirige.

FIRST NOCTURN.

psalmus, Uerba mea; antiphona, Dirige; psalmus, Domine ne in furore; antiphona, Conuertere; psalmus, Domine deus meus; antiphona, Ne quando; V̷ Requiem eternam; [R̷ Et lux]; lectio prima, Parce michi; R̷ Qui lazarum; V̷ Requiem; [R] Et locum; lectio ij', Tedet animam; R̷ Credo quod redemptor; V̷ Quem visurus; [R] Saluatorem; lectio iij', Manus tue fecerunt; R̷ Heu michi; V̷ Anima mea; [R] Dum.

SECOND NOCTURN.

[psalmus] Dominus regit me; antiphona, In loco; psalmus, Ad te domine; antiphona, Delicta; psalmus, Dominus illuminacio; antiphona, Credo videre; V̷ Anima mea; lectio iiij', Quantas habeo; R̷ Ne recorderis; V̷ Non intres; [R] Dum; lectio v', Homo natus; R̷ Domine quando veneris; V̷ Commissa mea;

---

[1] The 'etc.' will for the future be understood.

xc *Structure of the Durham Prymer. (Lauds of Dirige.)*

[R] Q*uia*; lec*tio* **vj**', Quis michi; R̸ Peccantem; V̸ Deus in nomine; [R] Q*uia*.

THIRD NOCTURN.

[ps*almus*], Expectans; a*ntiphona*, Complaceat; ps*almus*, Beatus qui intelligit; a*ntiphona*, Sana do*mine*; [ps*almus*], Quemadmod*um*; a*ntiphona*, Sitiuit; V̸ A porta; [R̸] Erue; lec*tio* **vij**', Spiritus meus; R̸ D*omine* secundum; V̸ Qui iniquitatem; [R] Ideo; lec*tio* [**viij**']; Pelli mee; R̸ Quomodo; V̸ Tibi soli; [R] Precor te; lec*tio* **ix**'[1], Quare de uulua.

The Conclusion of Matins. Libera me, etc.

R̸ Libera, Qui portas; V̸ Clamantes, Qui portas; a*ntiphona*, Audiui vocem, Pat*er* noster, Et ne nos; V̸ A porta; [R̸] Erue, D*omin*us vobiscum, Et cu*m*, **or' ut sup**r*a*.

Lauds.

[ps*almus*],[2] Miserere mei; a*ntiphona*, Exultabunt; ps*almus*, Te decet; a*ntiphona*, Exaudi do*mine*; ps*almus*, Deus deus meus; a*ntiphona*, Me suscepit; ps*almus*, Ego dixi; a*ntiphona*, Eruisti; ps*almus*, Laudate do*minum* de cel*is* (Cantate and Laudate too); a*ntiphona*, Omnis sp*iritus*; V̸ Requiem eternam; [R̸ Et lux]; ps*almus*, Benedictus; a*ntiphona*, Domine quod, Pater n*oster*, Et ne nos; V̸ A porta; [R̸] E*rue*, D*omin*us vobiscum.

---

[1] MS. has 'vj'.'   [2] MS. has 'an'.'

VIII.

TABLE SHOWING THE READING OF SIX SARUM PRYMERS.

This table furnishes some authority for the plan of the Sarum text laid down in the comparison of York and Sarum Prymers, p. lv. All six MSS. are Latin versions, the Hours in each being definitely stated to be according to the Use of Sarum. Where no variation is noted, the MSS. follow the reading of our text as given in Part I. The oft-recurring 'Domine exaudi orationem,' 'Ostende nobis,' &c., has not been noted, unless of distinct liturgical significance. The mark ——— indicates agreement with MS. A. The MSS. have been purposely selected at random.

A *Museum MS.* 2 A VIII. THE HOURS.	B *Museum MS.* Slo. 2683. THE HOURS.	C *Mus. MS.* Harl. 2976. THE HOURS.	D *Mus. MS.* Harl. 2985. THE HOURS.	E *Museum MS.* Slo. 2471. THE HOURS.	F *Museum MS.* Slo. 2565. THE HOURS.
Matins. The Pater noster, Hail Mary, and next Versicle and Response (all before the first lesson) are omitted.	The Hail Mary (before the first Lesson) is omitted.	As B.	As B.	As B.	As B.
The concluding Versicle and Response read, Ora pro nobis, sancta dei genitrix. Ut digni efficiamur promissionibus Christi.	————	————	————	————	————
Lauds. The Versicle and Response before the prayer 'Concede nos' read, Domine, exaudi orationem meam. Et clamor meus ad te veniat. No 'Benedicamus domino. Deo gratias,' after the prayer 'Concede nos.'	The Versicle and Response before the prayer 'Concede nos' read, 'Ostende nobis domine, misericordiam' tuam. Et salutare tuum da nobis. ————	As B.	————	As B.	As B.

xcii *Table showing the Reading of Six Sarum Prymers.*

A	B	C	D	E	F
After the Memorial of the Trinity follow the Memorials of the Holy Cross, SS. Michael, John the Baptist, Peter and Paul, Andrew, Thomas, Stephen, Laurence, Nicholas, Mary Magdalen, Katherine, and Margaret. The Memorial for Peace is not given. The concluding Glorious passion, etc., and Pater noster are not given.	The concluding Glorious passion, etc., is apparently purposely omitted; the Pater noster is not given.	No Glorious passion and no Pater noster, but in their place Benedicamus domino. Deo gratias.	As C.	No concluding Pater noster.	No concluding Pater noster.
Prime. The first Versicle after the Chapter is omitted. No concluding Pater noster.		Conclusion as before.			
Tierce. The first Response after the Chapter is omitted. No concluding Pater noster.		Conclusion as before.			
Sext. The first Response after the Chapter is omitted. No concluding Pater noster.		Conclusion as before.			

Table showing the Reading of Six Sarum Prymers. xciii

A	B	C	D	E	F
None. The first Response after the Chapter is omitted. No concluding Pater noster.	‖‖‖‖	Conclusion as before.	‖‖	‖‖	‖‖
Evensong. The Versicle and Response before the prayer 'Concede nos' read, 'Domine, exaudi orationem meam. Et clamor meus ad te veniat.' No concluding Pater noster.	‖‖‖‖‖‖‖‖‖	‖‖‖‖‖‖	‖‖‖‖‖‖‖‖‖	‖‖‖‖‖‖‖‖‖	‖‖‖‖‖‖‖‖‖
Compline. The Versicle and Response before the Nunc Dimittis read, 'Ecce ancilla domini. Fiat michi secundum verbum tuum.' No Versicle and Response before the prayer 'Gratiam tuam.'	‖‖‖‖‖‖‖‖‖‖	Conclusion as before.	‖‖‖‖‖‖	‖‖‖‖‖‖	‖‖‖‖‖‖
The Recommendation is placed between the Hour of the Cross and its Versicle and Response.		The Versicle and Response before the prayer 'Gratiam tuam,' read, 'Domine, exaudi orationem meam. Et clamor meus ad te veniat.'	As C.	As C.	As C.

xciv *Table showing the Reading of Six Sarum Prymers.*

A	B	C	D	E	F
No concluding Pater noster.	The Recommendation.	Conclusion as before.	As B.	As B.	As B.
The Salve Regina, the Hymn 'Virgo mater ecclesie,' etc., the Hail Mary, and the concluding Prayer 'Omnipotens sempiterne.'		As B.			
The 7 PSALMS conclude with the Anthem 'Ne reminiscaris .... peccatis nostris.'					
The 15 PSALMS conclude with the Anthem 'Parce domine .... irascaris nobis.'	Conclusion lost.				
THE LITANY. Differs from usual Sarum text.	As usual.	As B.	As B.	As B, but with an additional Collect.	As B.
Placebo. Requiem, etc., follows the Psalms Dilexi and Confitebor. The Versicle and Response 'A porta, etc., Krue, etc., appear after the Anthem of Confitebor instead of after that of the Magnificat.					

Table showing the Reading of Six Sarum Prymers.   xcv

A	B	C	D	E	F
The first Response of those at the conclusion is omitted.	The last Response of those at the conclusion is omitted.			Requiescant in pace, Amen, is inserted before the last Versicle and Response.	As C.
The final prayers are:— Deus, cui proprium, etc. Inclina, etc. Fidelium, etc.	Absolve, etc. Inclina, etc. Deus, qui nos patrem, etc. Fidelium, etc.	Deus, cui proprium, etc. Deus indulgentiarum, etc. Deus, cui proprium, etc. Deus qui inter, etc. Deus venie largitor, etc. Fidelium, etc.	As C.	Deus, cui proprium, etc. Absolve, etc. Inclina, etc. Deus qui nos patrem, etc. Fidelium, etc.	
Dirige. **1st Nocturn.** Requiem, etc., follows the first and third Psalms.	||| |||		
2nd Nocturn. Requiem, etc., follows each Psalm.	|||			
3rd Nocturn. Requiem, etc., follows each Psalm. The Versicle and Response after the Anthem of the Psalm Quemadmodum read, 'Ne tradas bestiis animas confitemini tibi. Et animas pauperum tuorum ne obliviscaris in finem.'	The concluding Versicle and Response read, Audivi, etc. No Pater noster before the 7th Lesson.	|||		

Table showing the Reading of Six Sarum Prymers.

A	B	C	D	E	F
Canticle of the Last Judgment. Apparently no construction of text possible in MSS.	—	—	—	—	—
Dirige (Lauds). Requiem, etc., follows the Psalms "Te decet" and "Ego dixi."	—	—	—	—	—
Of the concluding Versicles and Responses, the first two are not given. The concluding Prayers are:— Deus, cui proprium, etc. Inclina, etc. Fidelium, etc.	No Versicle and Response before the Benedictus.	Deus, cui proprium, etc. Deus cuius misericordie, etc. Omnipotens sempiterne deus, cui nunquam sine spe, etc. Omnipotens et misericors deus, etc. Inclina, etc. Animabus, etc.	As C.	Requiescant in pace, Amen, inserted before the last Versicle and Response. Deus, cui proprium, etc. Absolve, etc. Inclina, etc. Deus, qui nos patrem, etc. Fidelium, etc.	As C.
COMMENDATIONS. The concluding Versicles and Responses read, Requiem, A porta, Erue. The concluding Prayers are:— Tibi, etc. Misericordiam tuam, etc.	The first Versicle and Response omitted. The concluding Versicles and Responses are represented by 'V/ Requiem.'	As B. The last of the Versicles and Responses read, Domine, exaudi, etc., Et clamor, etc.	As C.	—	As B. As C.

PREFACE.

THE present volume supplies the text of the common mediæval Prayer-book. Mr. Warner considers the date of the MS. from which it has been taken to be about 1420-30. The particular MS. has been selected partly because, unlike many prymers whether in Latin or English, it contains only the indispensable contents of the book itself, with no additions of any kind; and partly because there is every reason to believe that the text is a good one.

In the Canticle of the Last Judgment, concluding the Matins of the Office for the Dead, it will be noticed that I have slightly altered the reading of the MS., the original text, however, being clearly shown. My alteration is not wholly satisfactory—the variation in the MSS. at this point is very remarkable.

Though I am responsible for the whole, Dr. Furnivall punctuated the volume, and added most of the foot-notes. To another gentleman I am indebted for the verse numbering. To Mr. Jenkinson, Librarian of Cambridge University, and to Mr. Scott of the British Museum, I am indebted for the facility with which I have been able to make use of the MS. To many Librarians also, in various places, and especially to all the officials in the Department of MSS. in the British Museum, I wish to express my grateful appreciation of their kindness, though the results of their assistance must be deferred till the appearance of the concluding Part of the work.

It will be borne in mind, that in accordance with the rules of our Society, all contractions have been expanded in *italics;* all words and letters in red ink in the original appear in **clarendon** type; and all additional matter not in the MS. (except the marginal verse numbers) is printed within square brackets [ ]. The collations with the Vulgate have been added to save the reader the trouble of referring constantly to the Latin text.

Preface.

The verse numbering of the Psalms refers to the Book of Common Prayer: those of the Lessons and Canticles follow the Vulgate.

STRUCTURE OF THE COMMON MEDIÆVAL PRYMER.

The following outline will enable the Reader to grasp the plan of the book. It should be mentioned that, in addition to the devotions enumerated, the Lesser Litany, that is, "Lord have mercy on us, Christ have mercy on us, Lord have mercy on us," the Lord's Prayer, Hail Mary, V̷'s and R̷'s (Versicles and Responses) occur here and there. In the Hours a short series of devotions, *Memorials,* may be present in Lauds, and the *Recommendation* (a few lines only) may occur at the end of Compline. It is almost certain that we must abandon the idea once entertained, that a critical text could be formed by collating a number of prymers. Such a course has been adopted for this edition; but the result is destructive, and very different to the one hoped for. Prymers which state in their text that they, or the Hours they contain, are according to the Use of Sarum, will be found to vary in the Hours and elsewhere, the variation, though slight, being clearly intentional, not the result of accident, and which the different dates of the MSS. do not, I think, explain.

The structure of Placebo and Lauds in the Office for the Dead, though at first sight apparently differing, is the same. Our text places a Versicle and Response after the Magnificat, they should almost certainly be placed before it; then, counting those psalms which follow each other with no intervening Anthem as one psalm, we find the structure of both offices alike.

THE HOURS.
MATINS.

The opening
The Venite
A Hymn
3 Psalms
Antiphon
V̷'s and R̷'s
The first Lesson, with its V̷'s and R̷'s
The second Lesson, with its V̷'s and R̷'s
The third Lesson, with its V̷'s and R̷'s
The Te Deum

Lauds.

The opening
8 Psalms (the Benedicite considered as one)
Antiphon, Chapter, Hymn, V̷ and R̷
The Benedictus, Antiphon, V̷ and R̷
The prayer 'Grant us,' etc., Antiphon, V̷ and R̷
3 Prayers, each with its Antiphon and V̷ and R̷
A Prayer: the Proper Antiphon of the Passion with its V̷ and R̷;
and the prayer 'Lord Jesu Christ,' etc.

The Hours of PRIME, TIERCE, SEXT, and NONE have each the same order of devotions, as follows:—

The opening
The Hymn 'Come, Holy Ghost,' etc.
3 Psalms
Antiphon, Chapter, V̷'s and R̷'s
The prayer 'Grant us,' etc.; the Proper Antiphon of the Passion, with its V̷ and R̷; and the prayer 'Lord Jesu Christ,' etc.

Evensong.

The opening
5 Psalms
Antiphon, Chapter, Hymn, V̷ and R̷
The Magnificat, Antiphon, V̷ and R̷
The prayer 'Grant us,' etc.; the Proper Antiphon of the Passion, with its V̷ and R̷; and the prayer 'Lord Jesu Christ,' etc.

Compline.

The opening
4 Psalms
Antiphon, Chapter, Hymn, V̷ and R̷
The Nunc Dimittis, Antiphon, V̷ and R̷
A Prayer; the Proper Antiphon of the Passion, with its V̷ and R̷;
and the prayer 'Lord Jesu Christ,' etc.

Concluding devotions.

THE SEVEN PENITENTIAL PSALMS.

THE FIFTEEN GRADUAL PSALMS.

THE LITANY.

THE OFFICE FOR THE DEAD (*as follows*).

Placebo (Vespers).

5 Psalms, each with its Antiphon
The Magnificat, with its Antiphon
A Psalm
V︦'s and R︦'s
Prayers

Dirige (Matins).

Consisting of 3 NOCTURNS; each composed of:—

3 Psalms, each with its Antiphon
3 Lessons, each with its R︦, V︦ and Repetition
    The Matins of Dirige then concludes with the Canticle of the Last Judgment.

Dirige (Lauds).

4 Psalms, three having Antiphons
Part of the 38th chapter of Isaiah, with its Antiphon
3 Psalms, Antiphon
The Benedictus, with its Antiphon
A Psalm
V︦'s and R︦'s
Prayers

COMMENDATIONS.

The psalms 'Beati immaculati' and 'Domine probasti'
V︦'s and R︦'s
One or two prayers

THE FACSIMILES.

The frontispiece is a reproduction, in full size, of the fly-leaf of the Museum MS. Prymer (Latin version), Sloane 2633. This facsimile is valuable—the piety evinced and homelike picture called up being of high interest. The Museum Catalogue describes the MS. as having been written in England in the middle of the 15th century.

A reproduction, in full size, from the Museum MS. prayer-book, Egerton 2019, lf. 142. A learned friend tells me that the small miniature within the D "is certainly a representation of Confession: the priest has his almuce over his head." The Museum Catalogue describes the MS. as having been written in France in the latter half of the 15th century.

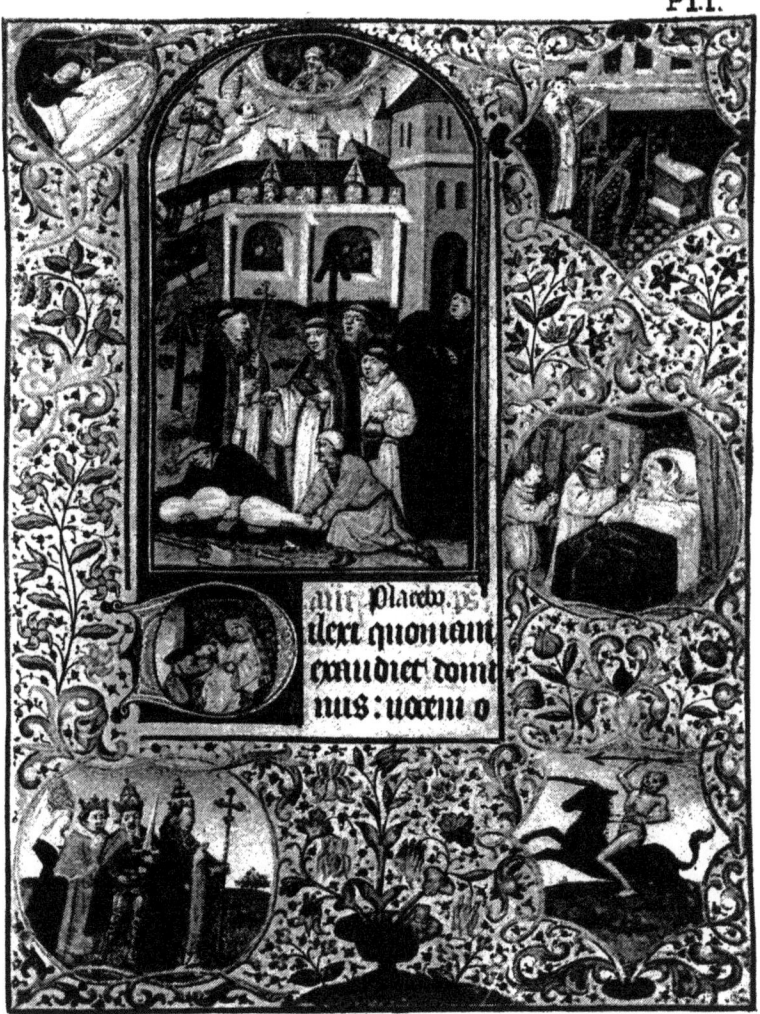

Pl.1.

[The Hours of the Blessed Virgin Mary.]

[MATYNS.]

Domine, labia mea aperies.

Lord, opene þou my lippis!
And my mouþ schal telle þi preisyng.
God, biholde þou in-to myn help!
Lord, haste þou to helpe me!
Glorie be to þe fadir, & to þe sone, & to þe holi goost!
As it was in þe bigynnyng, & now, & euere in-to þe worldis of worldis. amen!
Alleluya! Preise ʒe þe lord!
[Invitatorie] Hail, marie, ful of grace! þe lord is wiþ þee.

[psalm 95[1]]: Venite, exultemus.

1* Come ʒe, make we ful out ioie[2] to þe lord; herteli synge we[5] to god oure helþe[3]; [2] bifore occupie we[4] his face in knouleching; & herteli synge we[5] to him salmes.[6]
Hail, marie, ful of grace! þe lord is wiþ þee.

3 For god is a greet lord, and greet kyng aboue alle goddis. for þe lord schal not putte awey his puple; [4] for alle þe endis of erþe ben in his hond, & þe hiʒnessis of hillis[7] ben hise.
þe lord is wiþ þee.

5 For þe see is his, & he made it, & hise hondis formeden þe drie lond. [6] come ʒe, herie we, & falle we doun bifore god; wepe we bifore þe lord þat made us! [7] for he is oure lord

---

* None of the verses are numbered in the MS.; but the nos. are given for the reader's convenience in referring to other versions.
[1] 94 Vulgate.   [2] exultemus Vulgate.
[3] salutari V. (As all the Latin collations are from the Vulgate, the letter V will not be repeated after the rest of them.)   [4] praeoccupemus
[5–5] jubilemus   [6] in psalmis   [7] MS. hillis ben hillis ben

I. *Hours of the Blessed Virgin.*—1. *Matins.*

god; & we ben þe puple of his lesewe,[1] & þe scheep of his hond.

Hail, marie, ful of grace! þe lord is wiþ þee.

8 If ȝe han herde his vois to dai, nyle ȝe[2] make harde ȝoure hertis; as bi þe terryng to wrappe, bi[3] þe dai of temptacioun in desert; [9] where ȝoure fadris temptiden me; þei preueden[4] & siȝen my werkis.

þe lord is wiþ þee.

10 Fourti ȝeer y was offendid to þis generacioun, and y seide: 'euere þei erren in herte.' & þese men knewen not my weies; [11] to whiche[5] y swore in myn ire, 'þei schulen not entre[6] in-to my reste.'

Hail, marie, ful of grace! þe lord is wiþ þee.

Glorie be to þe fadir, & to þe sone, & to þe holi gost! As it was in þe beginnyng, & now, & euer in-to þe worldis of worldis. amen!

þe lord is wiþ þee.

Hail, marie, ful of grace! þe lord is wiþ þee.

Impnus: Quem terra.

The cloistre of marie beriþ him whom þe erþe, watris & heuenes worschipen, louten & prechen, þe which gouerneþ þe pre maner schap of þe world.

The wombe of þe maide beriþ him whom sunne, & moone, & alle þinges seruen bi tymes; fulfillid of grace of heuenes.

Blessid modir, bi goddis ȝifte! in whos wombe was closid, he þat is hiȝeste in alle craftis, & holdiþ þe world in his fist.

Sche is blessid & fulfillid of þe holi gost bi þe message of heuene; of whos wombe he þat is desirid to al folk was brouȝt forþ.

Glorie be to þee, lord, þat art borun of a maide! wiþ þe fadir & þe holi gost, in euerlastynge worldis. amen!

psalm [8]: Domine, dominus noster, quem.

1 Lord, þou art oure lord, þi name is ful[7] wondurful in al erþe! For þi greet doyng[8] is reisid aboue heuenes.

2 Of þe mouþ of ȝonge children not spekinge[9] & soukynge mylk, þou madist perfitli heriyng for[10] þin enemyes; þat þou distrie þe enemye & avengere.

---

[1] pascuae   [2] nolite   [3] in irritatione, secundum   [4] probaverunt me
[5] ut   [6] Si introibunt   [7] quam   [8] magnificentia   [9] infantium
[10] perfecisti laudem propter

I. Hours of the Blessed Virgin.—1. Matins.

3 For y schal see þin heuenes, þe werkes of þi fyngris; þe moone & þe sterris whiche þou hast foundid.

4 What is man þat þou art myndeful of him? eþer þe sone of a virgyn, for[1] þou visitist him?

5 Thou hast maad[2] him a litil lasse þan aungelis; þou hast corounned him wiþ glorie & honour, [6] & hast ordeyned[3] him aboue þe werkis of þin hondis.

Thou hast maad suget[4] alle þingis vndur hise feet; [7] alle scheep & oxis: feþermore &[5] þe beestis of þe feeld.

8 The briddis of þe eir, & fischis of þe see þat passen[6] bi paþþis of þe see.

9 Lord, þou art oure lord! þi name is ful wondurful in al erþe!
Glorie be to þe fadir [&c.].
As it was in þe biginnyng [&c.].

psalm [19[7]]: Celi enarrant.

1 Heuenes tellen out[8] þe glorie of god; & þe firmament telliþ þe werkis of hise hondis.

2 The dai telliþ out to þe dai a word; & þe nyȝt schewiþ kunnyng[9] to þe nyȝt.

3 No langagis[10] ben, neþer wordis; of whiche þe voicis of hem ben not herde.

4 The sown of hem ȝede out in-to alle erþe; & þe wordis of hem ȝeden out in-to þe endis of þe world.

5 In þe sunne he haþ set his tabernacle; & he as a spouse comynge forþ of his chaumbre.

He fulli ioiede[11] as a giaunt to renne his weie; [6] his goyng out was fro þe hiȝeste heuene.

And his goynge aȝen[12] was to þe hiȝeste þer-of; & noon is þat hidiþ him-silf fro his heete.

7 The lawe of þe lord is wiþ-out wem, & conuertiþ soulis; þe witnessyng of þe lord is feiþful, & ȝyueþ wisdom to litle children.

8 The riȝtfulnessis[13] of þe lord ben riȝtful, gladinge hertis; þe comaundement of þe lord is cleer, liȝtnynge[14] iȝen.

9 The hooli drede of þe lord dwelliþ in-to þe world[15]; þe domes of þe lord ben trewe, iustified in-to hem-silf.

[1] quoniam   [2] Minuisti   [3] constituisti   [4] subjecisti
[5] insuper et   [6] perambulant   [7] 18 V.   [8] enarrant
[9] scientiam   [10] loquelae   [11] Exultavit   [12] occursus   [13] Justitiae
[14] illuminans   [15] in saeculum saeculi

I. Hours of the Blessed Virgin.—1. Matins.

10 Desiderable more þan[1] gold & a ston myche preciouse,[2] & swettere þan hony & hony-combe.
11 For whi þi seruaunt kepiþ þo; myche ȝelding[3] is in þo to be kept.
12 Who vndurstondiþ trespassis? make þou me clene fro my pryuy synnes; [13] and of alien[4] synnes spare þi seruaunt.
  If þe forseid defautis ben not lord of me, þanne I schal be wiþouten wem; & y schal be clensid of þe most svnne.
14 And þe spechis of my mouþ schulen be þat þo plese[5]; & þenkynge[6] of myn herte euere in þi siȝt.
15 Lord, myn helpere, & myn aȝenbier!
  Glorie be to þe fadir [&c.].
  As it was [&c.].

psalm [24[7]]: Domini est terra.

1 The erþe & þe fulnesse þer-of is þe lordis; þe world[8] & alle þat dwellen þer-inne is þe lordis.
2 For he foundide it on þe sees; & made it redi on floodis.[9]
3 Who schal stie in-to þe hil of þe lord? eþer who schal stonde in þe hooli place of hym?
4 The innocent in hondis & in clene herte, which took[10] not his soule in veyn, neþer swore in gile to his neiȝbore.
5 This man schal take blessing of god; & merci of god, his helþe.
6 This is þe generacioun of men sekynge him; of men sekynge þe face of god of iacob.
7 Ȝe princis, take up ȝoure ȝatis! & ȝe euerlastynge ȝatis, be reisid! & þe king of glorie schal entre.
8 Who is þis kyng of glorie? þe lord stronge & myȝti, þe lord myȝti in batel.
9 Ȝe princis, take up ȝoure ȝatis! & ȝe euerlastynge ȝatis, be reisid! & þe king of glorie schal entre.
10 Who is þis kyng of glorie? þe lord of vertues; he is king of glorie.
  Glorie be to þe fadir [&c.].
  As it was in þe bigynnyng [&c.].

Antem: [Benedicta tu].

Blessid be þou among wymmen, & blessid be þe fruyt of þi wombe, ihesus! amen!

---

[1] more þan, super   [2] '& a ston myche preciouse' is repeated in the MS.
[3] retributio   [4] occultis...alienis   [5] ut complaceant   [6] meditatio
[7] 23 V.   [8] orbis terrarum   [9] super flumina præparavit   [10] accepit

I. *Hours of the Blessed Virgin.*—1. *Matins.*

V̄ Hooli modir of god, euere maide marie!

[R̄] Preie for us to oure lord god!

Pater noster: Oure fadir þat art in heuenes, halewid be þi name; come to þi kingdom; þi wille be don in erþe, and as it is in heuene; oure ech daies breed ȝyue us to-dai; and forȝyue us oure dettis, as & we forȝyuen to oure dettouris; and lede us not in-to temptacioun; but delyuere us from yuel. amen!

[Ave maria:] Hail, marie, ful of grace! þe lord is wiþ þee: blessid be þou among wymmen, & blessid be þe fruyt of þi wombe, ihesus! amen!

[V̄] **Et ne nos:** And lede us not in-to temptacioun;

[R̄] But delyuere us from yuel. amen!

V̄ Lord, comaunde us to blesse!

[R̄] Holi maiden of maidenes, preie for us to oure lord!

Leccio 1ᵃ: *Sancta maria virgo.*

Seynt marie, maide of maidenes, modir & douȝter of þe king of kingis! solace us þat we moun haue bi þee þe mede of heuenli kingdom, & wiþ goddis chosun regne wiþ-outen ende.

þou, lord, haue merci of us!

þanke we god!

[R̄]¹ Holi maidenhede, & wiþ-outen wem, y noot what preisyng y mai seie to þee, for him þat heuenes myȝte not take, þou bare in þi wombe.

[V̄] Blessid be þou among wymmen, & blessid be þe fruyt of þi wombe!

[Repeet] For him, þat heuenes myȝte not take, þou bare in þi wombe.

V̄ Lord, comaunde us to blesse!

[R̄] Preie for us wiþ meke þouȝt, maide marie!

Leccio ijᵃ: *Sancta maria, piarum.*

Seynt marie, mekest of alle meke wymmen! preie for us, holieste of alle holi wymmen, þat bi þee, maiden, he take oure preiers þat for us was born, & regneþ aboue heuenes, þat bi his charite oure synnes be forȝouun us.

---

¹ In the MS. the word Antem precedes the first Response after each of the three Lessons. With this exception, apart from additions in square brackets, and the substitution of misplaced letters, duly noted at foot of page when occurring, this edition should faithfully represent the MS. word for word.

þou, lord, haue merci of us!
þanke we god!
[R⁊] Blessid art þou, maide marie, þat bar oure lord! þou brouȝtest
forþ þe makere of þe world þat made þee, & þou bileuest¹
maide wiþ-outen ende.
[V⁊] Hail, marie, ful of grace! þe lord is wiþ þee.
[Repeet] þou brouȝtest forþ þe makere of þe world þat made þee,
& þou bileueuest¹ maide wiþ-outen ende.
V⁊ Lord, comaunde us to blesse!
[R⁊] Holi modir of god, be helpere to us!

Leccio iij[a]: Sancta dei genitrix q[ue].

Holi modir of god, þat worþili disseruedist to conseyue him
þat al þe world myȝte not holde! wiþ þi meke biseching
wasche awe oure giltis, þat we þat ben aȝenbouȝt moun stie
up to þe seete of endeles blis, þere þou dwellist wiþ þi sone
wiþ-outen tyme.
þou, lord, haue merci of us!
þanke we god!
[R⁊] Sikirli, maide marie, þou art holi, & worþi to haue al maner
preisinge; for of þee is risun þe sunne of riȝtwisnesse, oure
lord ihesu crist.
[V⁊] Preie for þe puple; bide for þe clergie; biseche for deuoute
wommans kynde! late alle fele þin help þat worþili maken
mynde of þee!
[Repeet] For of þee is risun þe sunne of riȝtwisnesse, oure lord
ihesu crist.
Glorie be to þe fadir, & to þe sone, & to þe holi gost!
þe sunne of riȝtwisnesse, oure lord ihesu crist.

psalm: te deum laudamus.

The, god, we preisen; lord, þee we knoulechen.
The, endeles fadir, euery erþe worschipiþ.
To þee alle aungelis, to þee heuenes & alle maner poweris,
To þee cherubyn and seraphyn, crien wiþ vois wiþ-oute ceessing:
Holi! Holi! Holi!
Lord god of oostis!
Heuenes & erþe ben ful of maieste of þi glorie.
The, þe glorious cumpeny of apostlis,

¹ remainest

The, þe preisable noumbre of prophetis,
Thee, preisiþ be whit oost of martris,
Thee, holi chirche knoulechiþ þorouȝ al þe world:
Fadir, of riȝt greet maieste;
And þi soþfast worschipful oneli sone;
And þe holi gost, oure confortour.
Thou, kyng of glorie, crist,
Thou art þe endeles sone of þe fadir!
Thou were not squoymous to take þe maidenes wombe to delyuere mankynde.
Whanne þou haddist ouercome þe scharpnesse of deeþ, þou openedist þe kingdom of heuenes to hem þat bileueden in þee.
Thou sittist on goddis riȝt side, in þe glorie of þe fadir.
We bileuen þat þou schalt come to be oure iuge; þerfor we biseche þee helpe þi seruauntis þat þou hast bouȝt wiþ þi precious blood.
Make hem to be rewardid wiþ seyntis in endeles blis!
Lord, make saaf þi puple, and blesse þin eritage!
Gouerne hem and make hem hiȝ wiþ-outen ende!
Bi ech dai we blessen to þee;
And we preisen þi name in-to þe world, & in-to þe world of world.
Lord, vouche-saaf to kepe us to dai wiþ-outen synne!
Haue merci of us, lord: haue merci of us!
Thi merci be maad vpon vs, lord: as we han hopide in þee.
In þee, lord, y haue hopid: late not me be schent wiþ-outen ende!

[Vȝ] Holi modir of god, euere maide marie,
[Rȝ] Preie for us to oure lord god!

IN LAUDIBUS.

Deus in adiutorium.

God, biholde þou in-to myn help.
Lord, haste þou to helpe me!
Glorie be to þe fadir [&c.].
As it was in þe bigynnyng [&c.].
Alleluya! Preise ȝe þe lord!

I. Hours of the Blessed Virgin.—2. Lauds.

psalm [93¹]: Dominus regnauit.

1 The lord haþ regned; he is cloþid wiþ fairnesse: þe lord is cloþid wiþ strengþe, & haþ gird him-silf.
2 For he made stidefast þe world, þat schal not be moued.
3 God! þi sete was maad redi fro þat tyme : þou art fro þe world.
4 Lord! þe floodis han reisid, þe floodis han reisid her vois.
Floodis reisiden her wawes; of þe voicis of many watris.
5 The reisyngis of þe see ben wondurful: þe lord is wonderful in hiȝ þingis.
6 Thi witnessingis ben able to be bileued gretli.² lord! holynesse bicomeþ þin hous in-to þe lengþe of daies.
Glorie be to þe fadir [&c.].
As it was in þe bigynnyng [&c.].

psalm [100³]: Iubilate deo.

1 Al erþe, synge ȝe herteli to god; serue ȝe þe lord in gladnesse! Entre ȝe in his siȝt, in ful out-ioiynge!
2 Wite ȝe þat þe lord him-silf is god; he made us, & not we maden us,
His puple & þe scheep of his lesewe.⁴ [3] entre ȝe in-to hise ȝatis in knouleching; entre ȝe in-to his porchis; knouleche ȝe to him in ympnes.⁵
Herie ȝe his name! [4] for þe lord is swete: his merci is wiþ-outen ende; & his treuþe is in generacioun & in-to generacioun.
Glorie be to þe fadir [&c.].
As it was in þe bigynnyng [&c.].

psalm [63⁶]: Deus, deus meus.

1 God, my god! y wake to þee ful eerli.⁷
2 Mi soule þirstide to þee; my flesch þirstide to þee ful many fold⁸:
In a lond forsakun, wiþ-out⁹ weie & wiþ-out watir; [3] so y apperide to þee in holi,¹⁰ þat y schulde se þi vertu & þi glorie.
4 For þi merci is betere þan lyues¹¹; my lippis schulen herie þee.
5 So y schal blesse þee in my liyf; & in þi name y schal reise myn hondis.

---

¹ 92 V. ² credibilia facta sunt nimis ³ 99 V. ⁴ pascuae
⁵ in confessione, atria ejus in hymnis; confitemini illi ⁶ 62 V.
⁷ ad te de luce vigilo ⁸ quam multipliciter ⁹ deserta, et invia
¹⁰ in sancto ¹¹ super vitas

I. *Hours of the Blessed Virgin.*—2. *Lauds.*

6 Mi soule be fillid as wiþ inner fatnesse & outmer fatnes[1]; and my mouþ schal herie wiþ lippis of ful out-ioiyng.[2]
7 So y hadde mynde of þee on my bed; in þe morntidis y schal þenke of þee, [8] for þou were myn helper,
And in þe keueryng of þi wyngis y schal make ful out-ioie: [9] my soule cleuyde aftir þee; þi riȝthond took me vp.
10 Forsoþe! þei souȝten in veyn my liyf: þei schulen entre in-to þe lower þingis[3] of erþe; [11] þei schulen be bitakun in-to þe hondis of swerd; þei schulen be maad þe partis of foxis.
12 But þe king schal be glad in god; & alle men schulen be preisid þat sweren in him; for þe mouþ of hem þat speken wickid þingis is stoppid.

[Psalm 67[4]: Deus misereatur.]

1 God, haue merci on us and blesse us! liȝtne he his chere on vs, & haue merci on vs!
2 That we knowe þi weie in erþe; þin helþe[5] in alle folkis.
3 God! puplis knouleche to þee[6]; alle puplis knouleche to þee.[6]
4 Heþene men,[7] be glade & make fulli ioie, for þou demest puplis in equyte, & dressist heþene men[7] in erþe.
5 God, puplis knouleche to þee; [6] þe erþe ȝaf his fruyt.
God, oure god, blesse us! [7] god blesse us! & alle þe costis of erþe drede him.
Glorie be to þe fadir [&c.].
As it was in þe bigynnyng [&c.].

psalm: Benedi[ci]te, omnia opera domini, domino.

57 Alle werkis of þe lord, blesse ȝe þe lord! [8]herie ȝe, & ouerhiȝe ȝe[9] him in-to þe worldis![8]
58 Aungelis of þe lord, blesse ȝe to þe lord! [59] ȝe heuenes, blesse to þe lord!
60 Alle watris þat ben aboue heuenes, blesse ȝe to þe lord! [61] alle vertues of þe lord, blesse ȝe to þe lord!
62 The sunne & mone, blesse ȝe to þe lord! [63] þe sterris of heuene, blesse ȝe to þe lord!

---

[1] adipe et pinguedine [2] labiis exultationis [3] inferiora [4] 66 V.
[5] salutare [6] confiteantur tibi [7] gentes
[8—8] This latter half of the verse is left out of all the subsequent verses, except nos. 74, 83, 88. [9] laudate et superexaltate

I. Hours of the Blessed Virgin.—2. Lauds.

64 Reyn & dew, blesse ȝe to þe lord !· [65] wyndis of god, blesse ȝe to þe lord !
66 Fier & swellynge heete, blesse ȝe to þe lord ! [67] coold & somer, blesse ȝe to þe lord !
68 Dewes & hoor frost, blesse ȝe to þe lord ! [69] frost & coold, blesse ȝe to þe lord !
70 Iyse & snow, blesse ȝe to þe lord ! [71] nyȝtis & daies, blesse ȝe to þe lord.
72 Liȝt & derknesse, blesse ȝe to þe lord ! [73] leitis[1] & cloudis, blesse ȝe to þe lord.
74 The erþe, blesse to þe lord ! herie & ouerhiȝe it him[2] in-to þe worldis !
75 Hillis, boþe more & lasse, blesse ȝe to þe lord ! [76] alle þat buriounnen[3] in erþe, blesse ȝe to þe lord !
77 Wellis,[4] blesse ȝe to þe lord : [78] sees & floodis,[5] blesse ȝe to þe lord !
79 Whalis, & alle þingis moued[6] in watris, blesse ȝe to þe lord ! [80] alle foules[7] of heuene, blesse ȝe to þe lord !
81 Alle kynde of bestis & wandrynge,[8] blesse ȝe to þe lord ! [82] & mennes sones, blesse ȝe to þe lord !
83 The folk of israel, blesse to þe lord ! herie & ouerhiȝe it him in-to þe worldis !
84 Prestis of þe lord, blesse ȝe to þe lord : [85] seruauntis of þe lord, blesse ȝe to þe lord !
86 Spiritis & soulis of iust men, blesse ȝe to þe lord ! [87] hooli & meke men of herte, blesse ȝe to þe lord !
88 Anany, aȝarie, misael, blesse ȝe to þe lord ! herie ȝe, & ouerhiȝe ȝe him in-to þe worldis !
    The fadir, & þe sone, & þe hooli gost; herie we, & ouerhiȝe we him wiþ-outen ende !
    Blessid art þou, lord, in þe firmament of heuene ; & worþi to be heried, & glorious, & ouerhiȝed in-to þe worldis !

    psalm [148]: **Laudate do**mi**num, de cel**is.

1 Ȝe of [heuene], herie þe lord ! herie ȝe him in hiȝ þingis[9] !
2 Alle hise aungelis, herie ȝe him : alle hise vertues, herie ȝe him !

---

[1] fulgura   [2] superexaltet eum   [3] universa germinantia   [4] fontes
[5] flumina   [6] quae moventur   [7] volucres
[8] omnes bestiae et pecora [tame bestis, cxlviii, 10, in next psalm]   [9] excelsis

3 Sunne & moone, herie ȝe him! alle sterris & liȝt, herie ȝe him!
4 Heuenes of heuenes, herie ȝe him! and þe watris þat ben aboue heuenes, [5] herie þe name of þe lord!
 For he seide, & þingis weren maad; he commaundide, & þingis weren maad of nouȝt.[1]
6 He ordeynede þo þingis in-to þe world[2]; he settide a comaundement, & it schal not passe.
7 Ȝe of erþe, herie þe lord! dragouns and alle depþis of watris[3];
8 Fier, hail, snow, iys, spiritis of tempestis, þat don his word;
9 Mounteynes & alle litle hillis; trees berynge fruyt, & alle cedris;
10 Wilde beestis & alle tame bestis[4]; serpentis & feþerid briddis;
11 The kingis of erþe & alle puplis; þe princis & alle iugis of erþe;
12 Ȝonge men & virgyns, elde men wiþ ȝongere, herie þe name of þe lord! for þe name of him aloon is enhaunsid.[5]
 His knouleching[6] be on heuene & erþe; [13] & he haþ enhaunsid þe horn of his puple.
 An ympne be to alle hise seyntis, to þe children of israel, to a puple neiȝing[7] to him!

[psalm 149]: **Cantate domino.**

1 Synge ȝe to þe lord a newe songe! his heriyng be in þe chirche of seyntis.
2 Israel, be glade in him þat made him; & þe douȝtris of sion, make ful out-ioie[8] in her kyng!
3 Herie þei his name in a queer! seie þei salm[9] to him in a tympan & sautre.
4 For þe lord is wel plesid in his puple; & he haþ reisid mylde men in-to helpe.
5 Seyntis schulen make ful out-ioie in glorie; þei schulen be glade in her beddis.
6 The ful out-ioiyng of god in þe þrote of hem; & swerde scharpe in ech side[10] in þe hondis of hem;
7 To do veniaunce in naciouns; blamyngis in puplis;
8 To bynde þe kingis of hem in stockis; & þe noble men of hem in irun manyclis;
9 That þei make in hem doom writun: þis is glorie to alle hise seyntis.

---

   [1] et creata sunt   [2] Statuit ea in aeternum   [3] abyssi
   [4] bestiae, et universa pecora   [5] exaltatum   [6] Confessio
   [7] appropinquanti   [8] exultent   [9] psallant   [10] gladii ancipites

psalm [150]: Laudate dominum in sanctus eius.

1. Herie ȝe þe lord in hise seyntis! herie ȝe him in þe firmament of his vertu!
2. Herie ȝe him in hise vertues! herie ȝe him bi[1] þe multitude of hise gretnesse!
3. Herie ȝe him in þe sown of trumpe! herie ȝe him in a sautre & harp!
4. Herie ȝe him in tympan & queer[2]! herie ȝe him in stryngis & orgun!
5. Herie ȝe him in cymbalis sownynge wel! herie ȝe him in cymbalis of iubilacioun! [6] ech[3] spirit, herie þe lord!

Glorie be to þe fadir [&c.].
As it was in þe bigynnyng [&c.].

Antem: O admirabile!

O, þou wondurful chaunge! þe makere of mankynde, takynge a bodi wiþ a soule, of a maide vouchide-saaf be bore, & so, forþ-goynge man, wiþ-outen seed, ȝaf to us his god-hede.

[Capitile] Maria virgo, semper letare.

Marie, maide, euere be glade, þat disseruydist to bere crist, makere of heuene & of erþe; for of þi wombe þou brouȝtest forþ þe saueour of þe world. þanke we god!

Impnus: O gloriosa domina.

O þou ioieful womman, hiȝe aboue þe sterris, him þat made þee of nouȝt, wiseliche þou ȝaf souke wiþ þin hooli tete. That sorie eue dide awey, þou ȝeldist wiþ hooli fruyt. þou art maad wyndowe of heuene, þat soreuful men entre as sterris. Thou art wiket of þe hiȝ king, & þe greet ȝate of liȝt þat schyneþ briȝt. folkis raunsoned, reioice[4] ȝe [of] þe liyf ȝouun bi a maide.

Glorie be to þee, lord, þat art born of a maide, wiþ þe fadir & þe holigost, in-to þe world wiþ-outen ende. amen!

Vȝ God chees hir, & bifore chees hir;
[Rȝ] And he makiþ hir to dwelle in his tabernacle.

Benedictus dominus deus israel.

Blessid be þe lord god of israel! for he haþ visitid & maad redempcioun of his puple.

---

[1] secundum   [2] choro   [3] omnis   [4] enjoy

I. *Hours of the Blessed Virgin.*—2. *Lauds.*

69 And he haþ rerid[1] to us an horn of helþe, in þe hous of dauiþ, his child:
70 As he spak bi þe mouþ of hise hooli profetis, þat weren fro þe world[2]:
71 Helþe fro oure enemyes, & fro þe hond of alle men þat hatiden us:
72 To do merci wiþ oure fadris; & to haue mynde of his holi testament;
73 The greet ooþ[3] þat he swore to abraham oure fadir; to ȝyue himsilf to us,
74 That we wiþ-outen drede, delyuerid fro þe hond of oure enemyes, serue to him,
75 In holynesse & riȝtwisnesse bifore him, in alle oure daies.
76 And þou, child, schalt be clepid þe prophete of þe hiȝeste; for þou schalt go bifore þe face of þe lord, to make redi hise weies.
77 To ȝyue science of helþe[4] to his puple, in-to remissioun of her synnes;
78 Bi þe inwardnesse[5] of þe merci of oure god; in þe which he, spryngynge vp fro an hiȝ,[6] haþ visitid us;
79 To ȝyue liȝt to hem þat sitten in derknessis & in þe schadewe of deeþ; to dresse[7] oure feet in-to þe weie of pees.

Glorie be to þe fadir [&c.].
As it was in þe bigynnyng [&c.].

Antem: [O gloriosa dei genitrix].

O, þou glorious modir of god, euere maide marie, þat disseruedist to bere þe lord of alle þingis! and þou, maiden, alone to ȝyue souke to þe king of aungelis! þou piteuous, we bisechen þee, haue mynde of vs, & praie euer to crist for us, þat we, holpen bi þi preieris, moun disserue to come to þe king-dom of heuenes.

V̄ Lord god of vertues, conuerte us,
[R̄] And schewe vs þi face, & we schulen be saf.

Orisoun: concede nos!

Graunt us þi seruauntis, lord god, we preien þee, þat we moun be ioieful euere-more in helþe of soule & of bodi; &, þorouȝ þe bisechyng of þe glorious, euerlastynge maide marie, we

---

[1] erexit [2] a saeculo [3] jusjurandum [4] scientiam salutis
[5] per viscera [6] oriens ex alto [7] ad dirigendos

moun be delyuerid of þis sorewe þat we han now; and vse[1] fulliche þe ioie wiþ-outen ende; bi oure lord ihesu crist, þi sone, þat lyueþ & regneþ wiþ þee, in oonhede of god þe holigost, bi alle worldis of worldis. amen!

Blesse we þe lord!
þanke we god!

Antem: veni, sancte!

Come, holigost! fulfille þe hertes of þi trewe seruauntis, & liȝtne þe fier of þi loue in hem!

[V̄] Sende out þi gost, & þei schulen be maad!
[R̄] And þou schalt make newe þe face of þe erþe.

Orisoun: Deus, qui corda.

God, þat tauȝtest þe hertes of þi trewe seruauntis bi liȝtnyng of þe holi goost, graunte us to sauere riȝtfulnesse in þe same gost, & to be ioieful euere more of his hooli confort; bi crist oure lord. amen!

Antem: [Libera nos].

Blessid trinite, delyuere us, saue us, & iustifie us!
[V̄] Blessid be þe name of þe lord!
[R̄] from þis now & in-to þe world.

Orisoun: Omnipotens, sempiterne!

Almyȝti, euerlastinge god, þat ȝauest us, þi seruauntis, in knouleching of trewe feiþ to knowe þe ioie of þe endeles trinite, & in þe myȝt of þe maieste to worschip þe oonhede, we bisechen, bi þe sadnesse[2] of þat selue bileue, we be kept & defendid of alle aduersites, bi crist oure lord. amen!

Antem: [Omnes sancti].

Alle halewene of god þat ben felowes to þe citeseynes of heuene, praie ȝe for us to oure lord!
[V̄] Riȝtful men, be glade & bliþe in oure lord;
[R̄] And make ȝe fulli ioie, alle þat ben of riȝtful herte.

Orisoun: Omnium sanctorum.

We biseche þee, almyȝti god, þat bi þe meritis of þi modir & maide marie, & of alle halewene, we be defendid from alle yuelis, so þat þorouȝ her preieris we moun lyue peisibli in þi worschip, bi crist oure lord. amen!

---

[1] possess, enjoy   [2] stedfastness

Antem: [Da pacem].

Lord! ȝyue vs pees in oure daies, for þer is noon þat fiȝtiþ for us but þou oure god;

V̥ Lord, late pees be maad in þi vertu;

[R̥] And plente in þi touris.

Orisoun: deus a quo.

God, of whom ben hooli desiris, riȝtful counselis and iust dedes, ȝyue to þi seruauntis þat pees þat þe world mai not ȝyue, so þat oure hertes be ȝouun to kepe þin hestis, and drede of oure enemyes be takun from vs, so þat oure tymes be peisible in þi proteccioun, bi oure lord ihesu crist, þi sone, þat lyueþ wiþ þee, & regneþ god bi alle worldis of worldis. amen!

Blesse we þe lord!
þanke we god!

Patris sapiencia.

The wisdom of þe fadir,
    þe treuþe of þe hiȝ king,
God and man was takun
    In þe morenyng.

Of hise knowun disciplis
    Soone he was forsak;
Sold & put to peyne,
    Mankynde saaf to make.

V̥ We worschipe þee, crist, & blesse to þee;
[R̥] ffor bi þi deeþ þou hast aȝenbouȝt þe world.

Orisoun: Domine ihesu criste!

Lord ihesu crist, goddis sone of heuene, sette þi passioun, þi cros and þi deeþ, bitwixe þi iugement & oure soulis, now & in our of oure deeþ; & vouche-saaf to ȝyue to lyuynge men merci and grace in þis liyf here; and to hem þat ben deed, forȝyuenesse & reste; to þe chirche & to þe rewme, pees & acoord; & to us synful men, liyf & glorie wiþ-outen ende; þou þat lyuest & regnest god bi alle worldis of worldis. amen!

þe glorious passioun of oure lord ihesu crist, brynge vs to þe ioie of paradis. amen!

Pater noster; Oure fadir [etc.].

[PRIME.]

Deus in adiutorium.

God, biholde þou in to myn help!
Lord, haste þou to helpe me!
Glorie be to þe fadir [&c.].
As it was in þe bigynnyng [&c.].
Alleluya! Preise ȝe þe lord!

Impnus: veni creator.

Come, holigost, oure maker, visite þou þe þouȝtis of þi seruauntis; & fulfille wiþ þi souereyn grace þe hertis þat þou hast maad! Haue mynde, þou makere of helþe, þat sum tyme þou took liknesse of oure bodi, & were borun of þe vnwemmed maide. Marie, ful of grace, modir of merci, defende us from oure enemy, & take us up in our of deeþ! Glorie be to þee, lord, þat art borun of a maide, wiþ þe fadir & þe holi gost, in euerlastynge worldis. amen!

[psalm 54[1]]: deus in nomine tuo.

1 God, in þi name make þou me saaf; & in vertu deme þou me!
2 God, here þou my preier; wiþ eeris perseyue þou þe wordis of my mouþ!
3 For aliens han rise aȝenes me, & stronge men souȝten my liyf; & þei settiden not god bifore her siȝt.
4 For lo, god helpiþ me; & þe lord is vptakere of my soule.
5 Turne þou awey yuelis to myn enemyes; & lese þou hem in þi treuþe!
6 Wilfuli y schal make sacrifice to þee; &, lord, y schal knouleche to þi name, for it is good;
7 For þou delyueridist me fro alle tribulacioun; & myn iȝe dispiside on myn enemyes.

Glorie be to þe fadir [&c.].
As it was in þe bigynnyng [&c.].

psalm [117[2]]: laudate dominum.

1 Alle heþen men,[3] herie ȝe þe lord! alle puplis, herie ȝe him!
2 For his merci is confermed on vs; & þe treuþe of þe lord dwelliþ wiþ-outen ende.

---

[1] 53 Vulgate   [2] 116 Vulgate   [3] gentes

I. *Hours of the Blessed Virgin.*—3. *Prime.*

Glorie be to þe fadir [&c.].
As it was [&c.].

psalm [118[1]]: Confitemini.

1. Knouleche ȝe[2] to þe lord, for he is good; for his merci is wiþ-outen ende.[3]
2. Israel, seie now, for[4] he is good; for his merci is wiþ-outen ende.[3]
3. The hous of aaron, seie now, for he is good; for his merci is wiþ-outen ende.
4. Thei þat dreden þe lord, seie now; for his merci is wiþ-outen ende.
5. Of tribulacioun, y inwardli clepide[5] þe lord; & þe lord herde me in largenesse.[6]
6. The lord is an helpere to me; y schal not drede what a man schal do to me.
7. The lord is an helpere to me; & y schal dispise myn enemyes.
8. It is betere[7] for to triste in þe lord, þan for to triste in man.
9. It is betere for to hope in þe lord, þan for to hope in princis.
10. Alle folkis cumpassiden me; & in þe name of þe lord it befelde,[8] for y am avengid on hem.
11. Thei cumpassynge, cumpassiden me: in þe name of þe lord, for y am avengid on hem.
12. Thei cumpassiden me as bees; & þei brenten out[9] as fier doþ among þornes; & in þe name of þe lord, for y am avengid on hem.
13. I was hurtlid & turned vp so doun,[10] þat y schulde falle doun; & þe lord took me up.
14. The lord is my strengþe & myn heryng[11]; & he is maad to me in-to heelþe.
15. The vois of ful out-ioiyng[12] and of heelþe, be in þe tabernaclis of iust men!
16. The riȝt hond of þe lord haþ do vertu; þe riȝt hond of þe lord enhaunside me; þe riȝt hond of þe lord haþ do vertu.
17. I schal not die, but y schal lyue; & y schal telle þe werkis of þe lord.

[1] 117 Vulgate   [2] Confitemini   [3] in saeculum   [4] quoniam
[5] De tribulatione invocavi   [6] latitudine   [7] Bonum
[8] et in nomine Domini   [9] exarserunt   [10] Impulsus eversus sum
[11] laus   [12] Vox exultationis

18   *I. Hours of the Blessed Virgin.*—3. *Prime.*

18 The lord, chastisynge, haþ chastisid me; and he ȝaf not me to deeþ.
19 Opene ȝe to me þe ȝatis of riȝtfulnesse; & y schal entre bi þo; & y schal knouleche to þe lord. [20] þis ȝate is of þe lord, & iust men schulen entre bi it.
21 I schal knouleche to þee, for þou herdist me, & art maad to me in-to heelþe.
22 The stoon whiche bilderis repreueden, þis is maad in-to þe heed of þe corner.
23 This þing is maad[1] of þe lord, & it is wondurful bifore oure iȝen.
24 This is þe dai which þe lord made; make we ful out ioie, & be glade þer-inne.
25 A, lord, make þou me saaf! a, lord, make þou wel prosperite! [26] blessid is he þat comeþ in þe name of þe lord!
    We blessiden ȝou of þe hous of þe lord; [27] god is lord, & haþ ȝoue liȝt to vs.
    Ordeyne ȝe a solempne dai in þicke puplis,[2] til to þe horn of þe auter.
28 Thou art my god, & y knouleche[3] to þee; þou art my god, & y schal enhaunce þee.
    I schal knouleche[3] to þee, for þou herdist me; and þou art maad to me in-to helþe.
29 Knouleche ȝe to þe lord, for he is good; for his merci is wiþ-outen ende.
    glorie be to þe fadir [&c.].
    As it was in þe biginning [&c.].

Antem: [O admirabile].

O þou wondurful chaunge! þe makere of mankynde, takynge a bodi wiþ a soule, of a maide vouchide saaf be bore, & so, forþ goynge man, wiþ-outen seed, ȝaf to us his god-hede.

Capitile: [In omnibus requiem].

In alle þingis y souȝte reste; and in þe eritage of þe lord y schal dwelle. þanne þe makere of alle þingis seide to me; & he þat made me restide in my tabernacle. þanke we god!

[V̄] Hail, marie, ful of grace! þe lord is wiþ þee.
[R̄] hail, marie, ful of grace! þe lord is wiþ þee.
[V̄] Blessid be þou among wymmen, and blessid be þe fruyt of þi wombe!

---

[1] factum est istud   [2] condensis   [3] confitebor

[℞] þe lord is wiþ þee.
[℣] Glorie be to þe fadir, and to þe sone, and to þe hooli goost!
[℞] Hail, marie, ful of grace! þe lord is wiþ þee.
[℣] Hooli modir of god, euere maide marie,
[℞] Preie for us to oure lord god!

Orisoun: Concede nos.

Graunte us, þi seruauntis, lord god, we preien þee, þat we moun be ioieful euere more in heelþe of soule & of bodi; & þorouȝ þe bisechyng of þe glorious euerlastinge maide marie, we moun be delyuerid of þis sorewe þat we han now, & vse fulliche þe ioie wiþ-outen ende, bi oure lord ihesu crist, þi sone, þat lyueþ & regneþ wiþ þee, in oonhed of god þe holigost, bi alle worldis of worldis. amen!

Blesse we þe lord!
þanke we god!

Hora prima.

 Ihesu, at oure of pryme,
  Was led to fore pilat;
 Wiþ false witnessyng
  Michel accused for hate;

 Buffetid; hise hondis weren boundun;
  þei spaten in his face;
 þus þei biseien foule,
  Oure lord, king of grace.

℣ We worschipe þee, crist, & blesse to þee;
[℞] Ffor bi þi deeþ þou hast aȝenbouȝt þe world.

Orisoun: Domine ihesu christe!

Lord ihesu crist, goddis sone of heuene, sette þi passioun, þi cros & þi deeþ, bitwixe þi iugement & oure soulis, now & in our of oure deeþ; & vouche saf to ȝyue to lyuynge men, merci & grace in þis liyf here; & to hem þat ben deed, forȝyuenesse & reste; to þe chirche & to þe rewme, pees & acoord; & to us synful men, liyf & glorie wiþ-outen ende; þou þat lyuest and regnest god, bi alle worldis of worldis. amen!

þe glorious passioun of oure lord ihesu crist, brynge us to þe ioie of paradis. amen!

Pater noster; Our fadir [&c.].

[TIERCE.]

Deus in adiutorium.

God, biholde þou in to myn help!
Lord, haste þou to helpe me!
Glorie be to þe fadir [&c.].
As it was in þe bigynnyng [&c.].
Alleluya! Preise 3e þe lord!

Impnus: Veni, creator spiritus!

Come, holi gost, oure makere! visite þou þe þou3tis of þi seruauntis, & fulfille wiþ þi souereyn grace þe hertis þat þou hast maad. Haue mynde, þou makere of heelþe, þat sum tyme þou took liknesse of oure bodi, & were borun of þe vnwemmed maide. Marie, ful of grace, modir of merci, defende us from oure enemy, and take us vp in our of deeþ! Glorie be to þee, lord, þat were born of a maide, wiþ þe fadir & þe hooli goost, in wor[l]dis wiþ-outen ende. amen!

psalm [120¹]: ad dominum cum tribularer.

1 Whanne y was set in tribulacioun,² y criede to þe lord, & [he] herde me.
2 Lord, delyuere þou my soule fro wickid lippis, & fro a gileful tunge.
3 What schal be 3ouun to þee, eþer what schal be leid to þee, to a gileful tunge?
Scharpe arowis of þe my3ti; wiþ colis þat maken desolat.
4 Allas to me! for my dwellyng³ in an alien lond is maad longe. y dwellide wiþ men dwellynge in cedar: [5] my soule was myche a comelyng.⁴
6 Y was peisible wiþ hem þat hatiden pees. whan y spak to hem, þei a3enseiden⁵ me wiþ-outen cause.
Glorie be to þe fadir [&c.].
As it was in þe bigynnynge [&c.].

psalm [121⁶]: Leuaui occulos.

1 I reiside myn i3en to hillis, fro whennes help schal come to me.
2 Myn help is of þe lord, þat made heuene & erþe.
3 The lord 3yue not þi foot in-to mouynge; neþer he nappe⁷ þat kepiþ þee!

---

¹ 119 Vulgate   ² tribularer   ³ incolatus meus
⁴ *incola*, alien, stranger: 'homelyng,' native.
⁵ impugnabant   ⁶ 120 Vulgate   ⁷ dormitet

I. Hours of the Blessed Virgin.—4. Tierce.

4 Lo! he schal not nappe, neþer slepe,[1] þat kepiþ israel.
5 The lord kepiþ þee; þe lord is þi proteccioun aboue þi riʒt honde.
6 The sunne schal not brenne þee bi dai; neþer þe moone bi nyʒt.
7 The lord kepiþ þee fro al yuel; þe lord kepe þi soule!
8 The lord kepe þi goyng-in & þi goynge-out; fro þis now, & in to þe world![2]

Glorie be to þe fadir [&c.].
As it was in þe bigynnyng [&c.].

psalm [122[3]]: letatus sum.

1 I am glade in þese þingis þat ben seid to me: we schulen go in-to þe hous of þe lord.
2 Oure feet weren stondinge in þi forʒerdis,[4] þou ierusalem.
3 Ierusalem which is bildid as a citee: whos part taking þer-of, is in-to þe same þing.
4 For þe lynagis,[5] þe lynagis of þe lord stieden þidur; þe witnessyng of israel to knouleche to þe name of þe lord.
5 For þei saten þere on seetis in doom; setis on þe house of dauiþ.
6 Preie ʒe þo þingis þat ben to þe pees of ierusalem; & habundaunce be to hem þat louen þee.
7 Pees be maad in þi vertu, & habundaunce in þi touris.
8 For[6] my briþeren & my neiʒboris, y spak pees of þee;
9 For[6] þe hous of oure lord god, y souʒte goodis to þee.

Glorie be to þe fadir [&c.].
As it was in þe bigynnyng [&c.].

Antem: [Quando natus].

Whanne he was born wondurfulliche of a maide, þanne was fulfillid holi writ. þou cam doun as reyn in-to a flees, for to make saaf mankynde: þee we preisen, oure god.

Capitile: [Ab initio].

Fro þe biginnyng & bifore worldis, y was maad; & y schal not ende vn-to world þat is to come; & in hooli wonyng y seruede bifore him. þanke we god!

[V̄] Hooli modir of god, euere maide marie!
[R̄] Hooli modir of god, euere maide marie!
[V̄] Preie for us to oure lord god,
[R̄] Euere maide marie!

---

[1] dormitabit neque dormiet   [2] in saeculum   [3] 121 Vulgate   [4] atriis
[5] tribus   [6] Propter

[V͞] Glorie be to þe fadir & to þe hooli goost!
[R͞] Hooli modir of god, euere maide marie,
[V͞] Aftir þi child-beryng þou leftist[1] maide wiþ-outen wem.
[R͞] Modir of god, preie for us!

Orisoun: concede nos.

Graunte us, þi seruauntis, lord god, we preien þee, þat we mai be ioieful euere more in heelþe of soule & of bodi; & þorouȝ þo bisechinge of þe glorious euerlastinge maide marie, we moun be deliuerid of þis sorewe þat we han now, & vse fulliche þe ioie wiþ-outen ende, bi oure lord ihesu crist, þi sone, þat lyueþ & regneþ wiþ þee in oonhede of god þe holi goost, bi alle worldis of worldis. amen!

Blesse we þe lord!
Þanke we god!

[Crucifige clamitant.]

At vndren þe false iewis
Crieden with hiȝ vois,
"Delyuere vs baraban,
And do þis on þe cros!"
A scharp coroun of þornes
þei diden on his heed;
And dide him bere his cros.
þere he schulde be deed.

V͞ We worschipe þee, crist, & blesse to þee;
[R͞] Ffor bi þi deeþ þou hast aȝenbouȝt þe world.

Orisoun: Domine ihesu criste!

Lord ihesu crist, goddis sone of heuene, sette þi passioun, þi cros & þi deeþ, bitwixe þi iugement & oure soulis, nowe & in our of oure deeþ; and vouche-saf to ȝyue to lyuynge men, merci & grace in þis liyf here; & to hem þat ben deed, forȝyuenesse & reste; to þe chirche & to þe rewme, pees & a-coord; and to us synful men, liyf & glorie with-outen ende; þou þat lyuest and regnest god bi alle worldis. amen!

þe glorious passioun of oure lord ihesu crist, brynge us to þe ioie of paradis. amen!

pater noster: Oure fadir þat art [&c.].

---

[1] remainedst

[SEXT.]
Deus in adiutoriu*m*.

God, biholde þou in-to myn help!
Lord, haste þou to helpe me!
Glorie be to þe fadir [&c.].
As it was in þe bigy*n*nyng [&c.].
Alleluya! Preise ȝe þe lord!

Impn*us*: veni creator!

Come, holi goost, oure makere, visite þou þe þouȝtes of þi seruau*n*tis, & fulfille wiþ þi souereyn grace þe hertes þat þou hast maad! Haue þou mynde, þou makere of helpe, þat su*m* tyme þou took liknesse of oure bodi, & were born of þe vnwe*m*med maide. Marie, ful of grace, modir of merci, defende us from oure enemy, and take us up in our [of] deeþ! Glorie be to þee, lord, þat were boru*n* of a maide, wiþ þe fadir & þe holi goost, in worldis wiþ-outen ende! amen!

p*salm* [123[1]]: Ad te leuaui oc*u*los meos.

1 To þee y haue reisid myn iȝen, þat dwellist in heuenes.
  2 Lo, as þe iȝen of þe seruau*n*tis ben in þe bond of her lordis!
As þe iȝen of þe hand-maide ben in þe handis of hir ladi; so oure iȝen be to oure lord god, til he haue merci on us.
3 Lord, haue þou merci on us! haue þou merci on us! for we ben myche fillid wiþ dispisynge;
4 For oure soule is myche fillid; we ben maad schenschip[2] to hem þat ben habu*n*daunt wiþ richessis, and dispisyng to proude men.

Glorie be to þe fadir [&c.].
As it was in þe bigy*n*nyng [&c.].

p*salm* [124[3]]: Nisi q*u*ia do*min*us.

1 Israel, seie now, but for[4] þe lord was in us; but for[5] þe lord was in us;
Wha*n*ne men risiden aȝen*es* us, [2] in hap[5] þei swolewid us al quyk.
Wha*n*ne þe woodnes of hem was wrooþ aȝen*es* us; [3] in hap[6] watir hadde sopun us up.[6]

---

[1] 122 Vulgate.   [2] opprobrium   [3] 123 Vulgate   [4] nisi quia
[5] forte   [6] absorbuisset nos

Oure soule passide þorouȝ a stronde; [4] in hap oure soule hadde
passid þorouȝ a watir vnsuffrable.
5 Blessid be þe lord, þat ȝaf not us in taking to þe teeþ of hem!
6 Oure soule, as a sparewe, is delyuerid fro þe snare of hunteris.
The snare is brokun; & we ben delyuerid.
7 Oure help is in þe name of þe lord, þat made heuene & erþe.
Glorie be to þe fadir [&c.].
As it was in þe bigynnyng [&c.].

[Ps. 125[1]]: **Qui confidunt.**

1 Thei þat tristen in þe lord, ben as þe hil of sion: he schal not
be moued wiþ-outen ende, þat dwelliþ [2] in ierusalem.
Hillis ben in þe cumpas[2] of it; & þe lord is in þe cumpas[2] of his
puple, fro þis tyme, now, & in to þe world.[3]
3 For þe lord schal not leue þe ȝerde[4] of synneris on þe part[5] of
iust men; þat iust men holde not forþ her hondis to wickidnesse.
4 Lord, do þou wel to good men, & of riȝtful herte!
5 But þe lord schal lede hem þat [bowen] in-to obligaciouns,[6] wiþ
hem þat worchen wickidnesse: pees be on israel!
Glorie be to þe fadir [&c.].
As it was in þe bigynnyng [&c.].

Antem: [Rubum quem].

Bi þe buysch þat moises siȝ vnbrent, we knowen þat þi preisable
maidenhede is kept. modir of god, preie for us!

Capitile: Et sic in sion.

And so in sion y was fastned; and in an halewid citee also y
restide, & in ierusalem my power. þanke we god!
[V̄] Aftir þi child bering, þou leftist maide wiþ-outen wem.
[R̄] Aftir þi child beryng, þou leftist maide wiþ outen wem.
[V̄] Modir of god, preie for us!
[R̄] þou leftest maide wiþ-outen wem.
[V̄] Glorie be to þe fadir, & to þe sone, & to þe holigost!
[R̄] Aftir þi child-beryng, þou leftist maide wiþ-outen wem.
[V̄] þou art maad faire & softe
[R̄] In þi delicis, hooli modir of god.

---

[1] 124 Vulgate   [2] circuitu   [3] saeculum   [4] virgam   [5] super sortem
[6] Declinantes autem in obligationes.

Orisoun: Concede nos.

Graunte us þi seruauntis, lord god, we preien þee, þat we moun be ioieful euer-more in heelþe of soule & of bodi; and þorouȝ þe bisechinge of þe glorious euerlastynge maide marie; we mai be delyuerid of þis sorewe þat we han now, & vse fulliche þe ioie wiþ-outen ende, bi oure lord ihesu crist, þi sone, þat lyueþ wiþ þee, & regneþ in oonhed of god þe holigost, bi alle worldis of worldis. amen!

Blesse we þe lord!
þanke we god!

[Hora sexta.]

At myddai, oure lord ihesu
   Was nailed on þe rode,
Bitwixe twey þeeues hangid;
   His bodi ran al on blood.

Hym þirstide for peyne;
   þei ȝauen him drynke galle.
Al þis peyne he suffride,
   Ffro deeþ to bie us alle.

V̷ We worschipe þee, crist, & blesse to þee,
[R̷] Ffor bi þi deeþ þou hast aȝen bouȝt þe world.

Domine ihesu criste!

Lord ihesu crist, goddis sone of heuene, sette þi passioun, þi cros & þi deeþ, bitwixe þi iugement & oure soulis, now & in our of oure deeþ; and vouche saaf to ȝyue to lyuynge men, merci & grace in þis lyif here; & to hem þat ben deed, for-ȝyuenesse & reste; to þe chirche & to þe rewme, pees & acoord; & to us synful men, liyf & glorie wiþ-outen ende; þou þat lyuest & regnest, god, bi alle worldis of worldis, amen!

þe glorious passioun [of] oure lord ihesu crist, brynge us to þe ioie of paradis! amen!

Pater noster: Oure fadir [&c.].

[NONE.]
Deus in adiutorium.

God, biholde þou in to myn help!
   Lord, haste þou to helpe me!
   Glorie be to þe fadir [&c.].

As it was in þe bigynnyng [&c.].
Alleluya! Preise ȝe þe lord!

Impn*us*: veni creator.

COme, holi goost, oure makere, visite þou þe þouȝtes of þi seruau*n*tis; & fulfille wiþ þi souereyn grace, þe hertis þat þou hast maad! Haue mynde, þou makere of helpe, þat sum tyme þou took liknesse of oure bodi, & were born of þe vnwe*m*med maide. Marie, ful of grace, modir of merci, defende us from oure enemy, & take us up in our of deeþ! Glorie be to þee, lord, þat were born of a maide, wiþ þe fadir & þe holigost, in worldis wiþ-outen ende! amen!

psalm [126¹]: In co*n*ue*r*tendo.

1 Whanne þe lord turned þe caitifte² of sion we weren maad as confortid.
2 Tha*n*ne oure mouþ was fillid wiþ ioie, & oure tu*n*ge wiþ ful out-ioiyng.
3 Tha*n*ne þei schulen seie among heþen men³: 'þe lord magnefied to do wiþ hem.'
4 The lord magnefiede to do wiþ us; we ben maad glade.
5 Lord, turne þou oure caitifte,² as a stronde in þe souþ!
6 Thei þat sowen in teeris, schulen repe in ful out-ioiyng.
7 Thei goynge, ȝede*n* & wepten, sendynge her seedis;
But þei comynge, schule*n* come wiþ ful out-ioiynge, berynge her handfuls.

Glorie be to þe fadir [&c.].
As it was in þe bigy*nn*yng [&c.].

psalm [127⁴]: Nisi do*m*inus edificaue*r*it.

1 But if þe lord bilde þe hous, þei þat bilden it han trauelid in veyn.
2 But if þe lord kepe þe citee, he wakiþ⁵ in veyn þat kepiþ it.
3 It is veyn to ȝou to rise bifore þe liȝt: rise ȝe aftir þat ȝe han sette, þat eten þe breed of sorewe.
Wha*n*ne he schal ȝyue sleep to his loued, [4] lo þe eritage of þe lord, is sones⁶: þe mede is þe fruyt of wombe.
5 As arowis ben in þe hond of þe myȝti; so þe sones of hem þat ben schaku*n*.⁷

---

¹ 125 Vulgate   ² captivitatem   ³ inter gentes   ⁴ 126 Vulgate
⁵ vigilat   ⁶ ecce hereditas Domini, filii.   ⁷ excussorum

6 Blessid is þe man þat haþ fillid his desir of þo: he schal not be schent[1] whanne he schal speke to hise enemyes in þe ȝate.
Glorie be to þe fadir [&c.].
As it was in þe bigynnyng [&c.].

psalm [128[2]]: Beati omnes.

1 Blessid ben alle men þat dreden þe lord; þat gon in hise weies!
2 For þou schalt ete þe trauelis of þin hondis: þou art blessid, & it schal be wel to þee.
3 Thi wiyf as a plenteuous vyne in þe sides of þin hous;
4 Thi sones as þe newe spryngyngis[3] of olyue trees in þe cumpas of þi boord.
5 Lo, so a man schal be blessid þat drediþ þe lord!
6 The lord blesse þee fro sion; & se þou þe goodis of ierusalem, in alle þe daies of þi liyf!
7 And se þou þe sones of þi sones: & se þou pees on israel!
Glorie be to þe fadir [&c.].
As it was in þe bigynnyng [&c.].

Antem: [Germinauit radix].

The rote of iesse haþ burioned; a sterre is risun of iacob; a maide haþ borun oure saueour. þee we preisen, oure god!

capitile: Et radicaui.

And y haue rotid me in a worschipful puple; & his eritage in-to þe parties of my god[4]; and my wiþ-holding[5] is in þe fulnesse of seyntis. þanke we god.

[Vy] Thou art maad fair & softe,
[Ry] þou art maad fair & softe.
[Vy] In þi delicis, hooli modir of god,
[Ry] And softe.
[Vy] Glorie be to þe fadir, & to þe sone, & to þe holigost!
[Ry] þou art maad fair & softe.
Vy Hooli maide, vouche saaf þat y worschipe þee!
[Ry] Ȝyue to me vertu aȝenes þin enemyes!

Orisoun: Concede nos.

Graunte us þi seruauntis, lord god, we preien þee, þat we moun be ioieful euer more in helþe of soule & of bodi; &

---

[1] non confundetur [2] 127 Vulgate [3] novellae
[4] in parte Dei [5] detentio

þoronȝ þe bisechyng of þe glorious euerlastynge maide marie, we moun be delyuerid of þis sorewe þat we han now, & vse fulliche þe ioie wiþ-outen ende, bi oure lord ihesu crist, þi sone, þat lyueþ wiþ þee, & regneþ in onhede of god þe holi gost, bi alle worldis of worldis. amen!

Blesse we þe lord!
þanke we god!

Hora nona.

At noon diede oure lord ihesu,
   þat was of myȝtes moost;
He criede 'heli' to his fadir,
   And so he lefte his gooste.

A spere in to his side
   Was þrillid of a kniȝt;
And þanne þe erþe quakede;
   þe sunne wiþ-drowe his liȝt.

V̷ We worschipe þee, crist, & blesse to þee,
[R̷] Ffor bi þi deeþ þou hast aȝenbouȝt þe world.

Orisoun: Domine ihesu criste!

Lord ihesu crist, goddis sone of heuene, sette þi passioun, þi cros & þi deeþ, bitwixe þi iugement & oure soulis, now & [in] our of oure deeþ; and vouche saaf to ȝyue to lyuynge men, merci & grace in þis liyf here; & to hem þat ben deed, forȝȝuenesse & reste; to þe chirche & to þe rewme, pees & acoord; & to us synful men, liyf & glorie wiþ-outen ende: þou þat lyuest & regnest god, bi alle worldis of worldis. amen!

þe glorious passioun of oure lord ihesu crist, brynge us to þe ioie of paradis! amen!

Pater noster: Oure fadir [&c.].

HERE BIGYNNEþ EUESONG.

Deus in adiutorium.

God, biholde þou in to myn help!
   Lord, haste þou to helpe me!
   Glorie be to þe fadir [&c.].
As it was in þe bigynnyng [&c.].
Alleluya!   Preise ȝe þe lord!

Psalmes.

[1][Ps. 122.] **Letatus sum in hiis**: I am glade in þese þingis [&c.].
[Ps. 123.] **Ad te leuaui oculos**: To þee y haue rei [&c.].
[Ps. 124.] **Nisi quia dominus erat**: But for þe lord was [&c.].
[Ps. 125.] **Qui confidunt in domino**: Thei þat tristen in þe [&c.].
[Ps. 126.] **In conuertendo dominus**: Whanne þe lord turned [&c.].

Antem: [Post partum].

Aftir þi child-berynge, þou leftist maide wiþ-outen wem. modir of god, preie for us!

Capitile: Beata es, virgo.

Blessid art þou, maide marie, þat bar oure lord; þou brouȝtist forþ þe makere of þe world, þat made þee; & þou bileuest[2] maide wiþ-outen ende. þanke we god!

Impnus: Aue maris stella, dei mater!

Hail, sterre of þe see, holi modir of god! and þou, euer maide, holi ȝate of heuene, Takyng þat word 'hail' of gabrielis mouþ, sette us alle in pees! chaungynge þe name of eue, Louse þe bondis of gilti men! profere liȝt to blynde men; do awey oure yuelis, & axe alle goodis! Schewe þat þou art oure modir! take he, bi þee, oure preier, þat for us was bore. & suffride to be þi sone! Maide, þou art aloon deboner among us alle! make us vnbounde of synnes, & be chast & deboner! Ȝyue us clene liyf; make redi a siker weie, so þat we, seynge god, be glade euer more! Preisyng be to god þe fadir; worschip to þe hiȝeste crist, & to þe hooli gost; oon worschip to hem þre. amen!

V⁊ Grace is ȝouun in þi lippis;
[℟] þerfor god haþ blessid þee wiþ-outen ende.

psalm: Magnificat.

46 Mi soule magnefieþ þe lord;
47 And my spirit haþ gladid in god, myn heelþe;
48 For he haþ biholde þe mekenesse of [his] hand maidun[3]; for lo, of þis alle generaciouns schulen seie þat y am blessid.
49 For he þat is myȝti haþ don to me grete þingis; & his name is hooli.
50 And his merci is fro [kynrede into] kynredis[4] to men þat dreden him.

---

[1] All these are one earlier in the Vulgate.
[2] remainest [3] ancillae suae [4] a progenie in

I. Hours of the Blessed Virgin.—7. Evensong.

51 He made my3t in his arme; he scateride proude men wiþ þe þou3t[1] of his herte.
52 He sette doun[2] my3ti men fro sete, & enhaunside meke men.
53 He haþ fulfillid hungry men wiþ goodis; & he haþ lefte riche men voide.
54 He, hauynge mynde of his merci, took up[3] israel, his child.
55 As he haþ spekun to oure fadris; to abraham & to his seed in-to þe worldis.[4]

Glorie be to þe fadir [&c.].
As it was in þe bigynnyng [&c.].

Antem: [Sancta maria, succurre].

Seynte marie, socoure wrecchis; helpe feerful, and refresche þe soreuful! Preie for þe puple; bide for þe clergie; biseche for deuoute wommanes-kynde!

V̄ Lord, schewe us þi mercy,
[℞] And 3yue us þin heelþe!

[Orisoun]: concede nos.

Graunte us þi seruauntis, lord god, we preien þee, þat we moun be ioieful euer more in heelþe of soule & of bodi; & þorour þe bisechyng of þe glorious euerlastynge maide marie, we moun be delyuerid of þis sorewe þat we han now, & vse fulliche þe ioie wiþ-outen ende, bi oure lord ihesu crist, þi sone, þat lyueþ & regneþ wiþ þee in oonhede of god þe holi gost, bi alle worldis of worldis. amen!

Blesse we þe lord!
þanke we god!

[De cruce deponitur.]

Fro cros, crist was takun doun
 At euesong tyme, we fynde;
Power of resureccioun
 Was hid in goddis mynde.
Þe medicyn of liyf, bi storie,
 Took sithe deeþ out of toun.
Allas! þe coroun of glorie
 Was þus cast vpsedoun.

V̄ We worschipe þee, crist, and blesse to þee;
[℞] Ffor bi þi deeþ þou hast a3enbou3t þe world.

---

[1] mente   [2] Deposuit   [3] suscepit   [4] in saecula

I. *Hours of the Blessed Virgin.*—8. *Compline.*

Orisoun: Domine ihesu criste.

Lord ihesu crist, goddis sone of heuen, sette þi passioun, þi cros & þi deeþ, bitwixe þi iugement & our soulis, now & in our of oure deeþ; & vouche saaf to ȝyue to lyuynge men, merci & grace in þis liyf here; & to hem þat ben deed, for-ȝyuenesse & reste; to þe chirche & to þe rewme, pees & acoord; & to us synfu[l] men, liyf & glorie wiþ-outen ende; þou þat lyuest & regnest god, bi alle worldis of worldis. amen!

þe glorious passioun of oure lord ihesu crist brynge us to þe ioie of paradis! amen!

pater noster: Oure fadir [&c.].

HERE BIGYNNEÞ COMPLYN.

[V] God, oure helpe, conuerte þou us,
[R] And turne awey þin ire from vs!

God, biholde þou in-to myn help!
Lord, haste þou to helpe me!
Glorie be to þe fadir [&c.].
As it was in þe bigynnyng [&c.].
Alleluya! Preise ȝe þe lord!

psalm [13[1]]: vsquequo.

1 Lord, hou longe forȝitest þou me in-to þe ende? hou longe turnest þou a-wey þi face fro me?
2 Hou longe schal y sette counsel in my soule? sorewe in myn herte bi dai?

Hou longe schal myn enemy be reisid on[2] me? [3] my lord god, biholde þou, & here þou me!

Liȝtne þou myn iȝen, lest ony tyme y slepe in deeþ; [4] lest ony tyme myn enemy seie 'y hadde þe maistri aȝenes him.'

Thei þat trublen me schule haue ioie if y schal be stired; [5] for-soþe y hopide in þi merci.

[3] Myn herte schal fulli haue ioie in þin helpe; [6] y schal synge to þe lord þat ȝyueþ goodis to me; & y schal seie salm[4] to þe name of þe hiȝeste lord.

Glorie be to þe fadir [&c.].
As it was in þe bigynnyng [&c.].

---

[1] 12 Vulgate [2] super [3] MS. has O [4] psallam

I. Hours of the Blessed Virgin.—8. Compline.

[psalm 43[1]]: Iudica me, deus.

1 God, deme þou me, & departe[2] þou my cause fro a folk not hooli! delyuere þou me fro a wickid man & gileful!
2 For þou art god, my strengþe. whi hast þou put me abak[3]? & whi go y soreuful, while þe enemy turmentiþ me?
3 Sende out þi liȝt & þi treuþe! þo[4] ledden me forþ & brouȝten in-to þin holi hil, & in-to þi tabernacle.
4 And y schal entre to þe auter of god, to god þat gladiþ my ȝougþe. God, my god, y schall knouleche to þee in an harp. [5] my soule, whi art þou sorie; & whi trublist þou me?
6 Hope þou in god; for ȝit y schal knouleche to him; he is þe heelþe of my chere, and my god.
Glorie be to þe fadir [&c.].
As it was in þe biginning [&c.].

[psalm 129[5]]: Sepe expugnauerunt.

1 Israel, seie now: 'ofte þei fouȝten aȝenes me fro my ȝougþe;
2 Ofte þei fouȝten aȝenes me fro my ȝougþe; & soþeli þei myȝten[6] not to me;
3 Synneris forgiden[7] on my bak; þei maden longe[8] her wickidnesse.
4 The iust lord schal bete þe nollis[9] of synneris.
5 alle þat haten sion be schent & turned abak!
6 Be þei maad as þe hey of hous-coppis,[10] þat driede up bifore þat it be drawun up[11]; [7] of which hey, he þat schal repe, schal not fille his hond; & he þat gedere handfuls, schal not fille his bosum.
8 And þei þat passiden forþ,[12] seiden not, 'þe blessyng of þe lord be wiþ ȝou! we blessiden ȝou in þe name of þe lord.'
Glorie be to þe fadir [&c.].
As it was in [&c.].

psalm [131[13]]: Domine non est.

1 Lord, myn herte is not enhaunsid,[14] neþer myn iȝen ben reisid.
2 Neþer y ȝede in grete þingis, neþer in meruelis aboue me.
3 If y felide not mekeli, but enhaunside my soule. As a child wened on his modir, so ȝelding[15] be in my soule!
4 Israel, hope in þe lord, fro þis tyme now, and in-to þe world!

---

[1] 42 Vulgate   [2] discerne
[3] repulisti   [4] ipsa   [5] 128 Vulgate   [6] potuerunt   [7] fabricauerunt
[8] prolongauerunt   [9] cervices   [10] tectorum   [11] evellatur
[12] praeteribant   [13] 130 Vulgate   [14] exaltatum   [15] retributio

I. Hours of the Blessed Virgin.—8. Compline.

Glorie be to þe fadir [&c.].
As it was [&c.].

Antem: [Cum iocunditate].

Wiþ gladnesse, halewe we þe mynde of blessid marie, þat sche preie for us to oure lord ihesu crist.

[Capitile: Sicut cynamomum.]

As canel & bawme swete smellynge, y ȝaf odour; as tried myrre, y ȝaf swetnesse of smelling. þanke we god!

Impnus: virgo singularis.

Maide, þou art aloon deboner among alle! make us unbounde of synnes, & be chast & deboner. Ȝyue us clene liyf. make redi a siker weie, so þat we, seynge god, be glade euere more. Preisyng be to god þe fadir; worship to þe hiȝeste crist & to þe holigost; oon worschip to hem þre! amen!

V̅ God chees hir, & bifore chees hir;
[R̅] And he makiþ hir to dwelle in his tabernacle.

psalm: Nunc dimitis seruum tuum, domine.

29 Now, lord, þou leuest þi seruaunt: aftir þi word, in pees;
30 For myn iȝen han seyn þin helþe,
31 Which þou hast maad redi to-fore þe face of alle puplis.
32 Liȝt and¹ reuelacioun of heþen men, & glorie to þi puple israel.

Glorie be to þe fadir [&c.].
As it was in þe bigynnyng [&c.].

Antem: [Glorificamus te.]

We glorifien þee, modir of god, for of þee is crist born. make saaf alle men þat glorifien þee.

V̅ Lord god of vertues, conuerte us.
[R̅] And schewe þi face, & we schulen be saaf.

Oracio: Gratiam tuam quesumus.

Lord, we bisiche þee, sende þi grace in-to oure hertis, þat we, bi þe message of þe aungel, knowe þe incarnacioun of þi sone crist, and be brouȝt bi his passioun to þe glorie of his resureccioun; bi þe silf ihesu crist, þi sone, oure lord; þat wiþ þee lyueþ & regneþ in oonhede of god þe holigost, bi alle worldis of worldis. amen!

¹ ad

[Hora completorii.]

At our of comepelyn
  þei leiden hym in graue,
þe noble bodi of ihesu,
  þat mankynde schal saue.

With spicerie he was biried,
  Hooli writ to fulfille.
þenke we sadli on his deeþ;
  þat schal saue us from helle.

V̷ We worschipe þee, crist, & blesse to þee.
[R̷] Ffor bi þi deeþ þou hast aȝenbouȝt¹ þe world.

Oracio: Domine ihesu criste.

Lord ihesu crist, goddis sone of heuene, sette þi passioun, þi cros & þi deeþ bitwixe þi iugement and oure soulis, now & in oure of oure deeþ; and vouche-saf to ȝyue to lyuynge men, merci & grace in þis liyf here; & to hem þat ben deed, forȝy[ue]nesse & reste; to þe chirche & to þe rewme, pees & acord; and to us synful men, liyf & glorie wiþ-outen ende; þou þat lyuest & regnest god, bi alle worldis of worldis. amen!

þe glorious passioun of oure lord ihesu crist brynge vs to þe ioie of paradis! amen!

pater noster: Oure fadir [&c.].

[Antem]: Salue regina!

Hail, quene, modir of merci, oure liyf, oure swetnesse & oure hope, hail! to þee we crien, exiled sones of eue; to þee we siȝen, gronynge in þis valey of teeris; þer-for turne to vsward þi merciful iȝen, & schewe to us ihesu, þe blessid fruyt of þi wombe, aftir þat we ben passid hennes. O þou deboner, O þou meke, O þou swete maide marie, hail!

Hail, marie, ful of grace! þe lord is wiþ þee. blessid be þou among wyme[n], & blessid be þe fruyt of þi wombe, ihesus! amen!

[Orisoun]: Omnipotens sempiterne.

Almiȝti endeles god, þat art worchinge wiþ þe holi gost, wondurfulli þou madist redi þe bodi & þe soule of þe moost

---
¹ MS. aȝen aȝenbouȝt

I. Hours of the Blessed Virgin.—Concluding Devotions.

blessid modir & [maide] marie, to disserue to be maad a worþi wonyng for þi sone. graunte þat we be delyuerid, bi hir meke preier, of yuelis þat we han now, and of sudeyn deeþ and endeles, bi crist oure lord. amen!

[Antem]: Aue regina celorum!

Hail, quene of heuenes, modir of þe king of aungelis! O marie, flour of virgines, as þe rose or þe lilie, make preiers to þi sone, for þe helþe of alle cristen men!
Hail, marie, ful of grace! [&c.].

Orisoun: Mer[i]tis & preci[bus].

Bi þe meritis & preieris of his meke modir, blesse us þe sone of god þe fadir! amen!

psalm [130[1]]: De profundis.

1 Lord, y criede to þee fro depþis; lord, here þou my vois!
2 Thyne eeris be maad ententif in-to þe vois of my bisechyng!
3 Lord, if þou kepist[2] wickidnessis, lord, who schal susteyne?
4 For merci[3] is at þee; and, lord, for þi lawe y abode[4] þee.
5 Mi soule susteynede in his word; [6] my soule hopide in þe lord. Fro þe moruntide kepyng[5] til to þe nyȝt; [7] israel, hope in þe lord! For whi,[6] merci is at þe lord; & plenteuous redempcioun is at[7] him;
8 And he schal aȝenbie israel fro alle wickidnessis þer-of.

Lord, haue merci of us!
Crist, haue merci of us!
Lord, haue merci of us!

pater noster: Oure fadir [&c.].
[V͡] And lede us not in-to temptacioun,
[R͡] But delyuere us from yuel.
[V͡] Endeles reste, ȝyue hem, lord;
[R͡] And euerlastinge liȝt, liȝtne to hem!
[V͡] From þe ȝate of helle,
[R͡] Lord, delyuere her soulis!
[V͡] I bileue to se þe goodis of þe lord;
[R͡] In þe lond of lyuynge.
[V͡] Lord, here my preier,
[R͡] And my cry come to þee!

---
[1] 129 Vulgate. MS. De profundus   [2] observaveris   [3] propitiatio
[4] sustinui   [5] custodia   [6] quia   [7] apud

[Oracio: Fidelium deus.]

Lord, þat art maker & aȝenbier of alle feiþful men, ȝyue þou, & graunte, remissioun & forȝyuenesse of alle synnes, to þe soulis of alle feiþful men þat ben deed, so þat þei mowe haue þe forȝyuenesse þat þei euere desirede; bi crist, oure lord. amen!

[V̷] Reste þei in pees!
[R̷] Amen!

Here enden matyns, euesong, and compelyn.

& HE[RE] BIGYNNEN ÞE SEUENE SALMES.

[I.] psalm [6]: **Domine, ne in furore.**

1. Lord, repreue þou not [me] in þi stronge veniaunce[1]; neþer chastise[2] þou me in þin ire!
2. Lord, haue þou merci on me, for y am siyk! lord, make þou me hool,[3] for alle my bones ben trublid.
3. And my soule is trublid gretli; but þou, lord, hou longe?
4. Lord, be þou conuertid, & delyuere my soule! make þou me saaf, for þi merci!
5. For noon is in deeþ which is myndeful of þee; but in helle, who schal knouleche to þee?
6. I trauelide[4] in my weilyng; y schal wasche my bed bi ech niȝt; y schal moiste[5] my bedstre[6] wiþ my teeris.
7. Myn iȝe is disturblid of woodnesse[7]; y wexe elde among alle myn enemyes.
8. Alle ȝe þat worchen wickidnesse, departe fro me; for þe lord haþ herd þe vois of my wepyng.
9. The lord haþ herde my bisechyng; þe lord haþ resseyued my preier.
10. Alle myn enemyes be aschamed, and be disturblid gretli: be þei turned to-gider, & be þei aschamed full swifteli!

Glorie be to þe fadir [&c.].
As it was in þe biginning [&c.].

[II.] psalm [32[8]]: **Beati quorum.**

1. Blessid ben þe,[9] whose wickidnessis ben forȝouun, & whos synnes ben hilid.
2. Blessid is þe man to whom þe lord arettid[10] not synne; neþer gile is in his spirit.
3. For y was stille[11]; my bones wexiden elde, while y criede al dai.
4. For bi dai & niȝt þin hond was maad greuous[12] on me; y am turned in my wrecchidnesse, while þe þorn is set in.[13]

---

[1] in furore [2] corripias [3] sana me [4] Laboravi [5] moist *repeated in MS.* [6] lectum [7] a furore [8] 31 Vulgate. [9] Beati [10] imputavit [11] tacui [12] gravata est [13] configitur

II. The Seven Penitential Psalms.

5 I made my synne knowun to þee; & y hidde not myn vnriʒt-fulnesse.
6 I seide, 'y schal knouleche aʒenes me myn vnriʒtfulnesse to þee, lord';[1] & þou hast forʒouun þe wickidnesse of my synne.
7 For þis þing, ech hooli man schal preie to þee in couenable[2] tyme. Neþeles, in þe greet flood of many watris, þo schulen not neiʒe to þee.
8 Thou art maad my refuyt fro tribulacioun þat cumpasside me; þou, my fulli ioiynge,[3] delyuere me fro hem þat cumpassen me!
9 I schal ʒyue vndurstonding to þee, & schal teche þee in þis weie in which þou schalt go; y schal make stidefast myn iʒen on þee.
10 Nile ʒe[4] be maad as an hors & mule, to whiche[5] is noon vndur-stonding? Lord, constreyne þou þe chekis of hem wiþ a bernacle & bridel,[6] þat neiʒen[7] not to þee.
11 Many betyngis ben of þe synner; but merci schal cumpasse him þat hopiþ in þe lord.
12 ʒe iust men, be glad, & make fulli ioie[8]; and alle ʒe riʒtful men of herte, haue glorie!

Glorie be to þe fadir [&c.].
As it was in þe biginning [&c.].

[III.] psalm [38[9]]: **Domine, ne in furore.**

1 Lord, repreue þou not me in þi stronge vengeaunce[10]; neþer chastise þou me in þin ire!
2 For þyne arowis ben ficchid in me, & þou hast conferned þin hond on me.
3 Noon helþe is in my flesch, fro þe face of þin ire; no pees is to my bones, fro þe face[11] of my synnes.
4 For my wickidnessis ben gon ouer myn heed as an heuy birþun; þo ben maad greuouse on me.
5 Myn heelid woundis weren rotun, & ben brokun,[12] for þe face of myn vnwisdom.
6 I am maad a wrecche, and y am bowid doun[13] til in-to þe ende; al dai y entride soreuful;

---

[1] injustitiam meam Domino [2] opportuno [3] exultatio mea [4] Nolite
[5] quibus [6] In camo et freno [7] approximant [8] exultate
[9] 37 Vulgate. [10] in furore [11] a facie
[12] Putruerunt et corruptae sunt cicatrices meae [13] curvatus

II. *The Seven Penitential Psalms.*

7 For my leendis ben fillid wiþ scornyngis, and heelþe is not in my flesch.

8 I am turmentid, & maad lowe ful gretli; y roride for þe weilyng of myn herte.

9 Lord! al my desir is bifore þee; & my weilyng is not hid fro þee.

10 Myn herte is disturblid in me; my vertu forsook me; and þe liȝt of myn iȝen, & it is not wiþ me.

11 Mi frendis & my neiȝboris neiȝiden & stoden aȝenes me,

12 And þei þat weren bisidis[1] me stoden a-fer; & þei diden violence þat souȝten my liyf.

And þei þat souȝten yuelis to me, spaken vanitees, & þouȝten gilis al dai.

13 But y, as a deef man, herde not; & as a doumbe man not openynge his mouþ.

14 And y am maad as a man not herynge, & not hauynge repreuyngis in his mouþ.

15 For, lord, y hopide in þee; my lord god, þou schalt here me.

16 For y seide, 'lest eny tyme myn enemyes haue ioie on me,' & þe while my feet ben moued, þei spaken greet þingis on me.

17 For y am redi to betingis[2]; & my sorewe is euere in my siȝt.

18 For y schal telle my wickidnesse; and y schal þenke[3] for my synne.

19 But myn enemyes lyuen, & ben confermyd on me; & þei ben multiplied þat haten me wickidli.

20 Thei þat ȝelden yuelis for goodis, bacbitiden me, for y suede goodnesse.

21 Mi lord god, forsake þou not me! go þou not awey fro me!

22 Lord god of myn helþe, biholde þou in-to[4] myn help!

Glorie be to þe fadir [&c.].

As it was in þe bigynning [&c.].

[IV.] psalm [51[5]]: **Miserere mei, deus!**

1 God, haue þou merci on me! bi [6]þi greet merci,
 And bi[6] þe mychelnesse of þi merciful doyngis, do þou awey my wickidnes!

2 More,[7] waische þou me fro my wickidnesse, and clense me fro my synne!

3 For y knouleche my wickidnes; & my synne is euere aȝenes me.

---

[1] juxta [2] ego in flagella paratus sum [3] cogitabo [4] Intende in
[5] 50 Vulgate. [6-6] secundum [7] Amplius

II. *The Seven Penitential Psalms.*

4 I haue synned to þee aloon; & y haue don yuel bifore þee, þat þou be iustified in þi wordis, & ouercome whan þou art demed.

5 For, lo! y was conseyued in wickidnessis; and my modir conseyuede me in synnes.

6 For, lo! þou louedist treuþe; þou hast schewid me þe vnserteyn þingis & pryue þingis¹ of þi wisdom.

7 Lord! sprynge² þou me wiþ isope, & y schal be clensid; waische þou me, & y schal be maad whiyt more þan snowe.

8 ȝyue þou ioie & gladnesse to myn heryng; & bones maad meke schulen ful out make ioie.³

9 Turne awei þi face fro my synnes; & do a-wey alle my wickidnessis!

10 God! make þou a clene herte in me; & make þou newe a riȝtful spirit in myn entrailes.

11 Caste þou not me awey fro þi face; & take þou not fro me þin hooli spirit!

12 ȝyue þou⁴ to me þe gladnesse of þin helþe; & conferme þou me wiþ þe principal spirit!

13 I schal teche wickid men þi weies, & vnfeiþful men schulen be conuertid to þee.

14 God! þe god of myn helþe! delyuere þou me fro bloodis, & my tunge schal ioiefuli synge⁵ þi riȝtfulnesse.

15 Lord! opene þou my lippis, & [my] mouþ⁶ schal telle þi preisyng.

16 For if þou haddist wolde sacrifice, y hadde ȝoue: treuli þou schalt not delite in brent sacrificis.

17 Sacrifice to god is a spirit trublid⁷: god! þou schalt not dispise a contrit herte, & maad meke.

18 Lord! do þou benyngneli in þi good wille to sion; þat þe wallis of ierusalem be bildid.

19 Thanne þou schalt take plesauntli⁸ þe sacrifice of riȝtfulnesse, offringis & brent sacrificis; þanne þei schulen putte calues on þin auter.

Glorie be to þe fadir [&c.].
As it was in þe bigynnyng [&c.].

¹ occulta   ² Asperges   ³ exultabunt   ⁴ Redde   ⁵ exultabit
⁶ os meum.   ⁷ humiliatum   ⁸ acceptabis

II. *The Seven Penitential Psalms.*

[V.] p*salm* [102¹]: Do*m*i*ne,* **exaudi!**

1 Lord, here þou my p*r*eier; and my cry come to þee!
   2 Turne not awey þi face fro me! in what euer dai y am trublid, bowe dou*n* þi*n* eere to me!
   In what euer dai y schal inwardli clepe þee, here þou me swifteli!
3 For my daies han failid as smoke; & my bones drieden up as critou*n*s.²
4 I am smytu*n* as hey, & myn herte driede up; for y haue forȝite my breed.
5 Of þe vois of my weilyng, my boon cleuyde to my flesch.
6 I am maad liyk a pellican of wildirnesse; y am maad as a nyȝt-crowe in an hous.
7 I wakide,³ and y am maad as a solitarie sparewe in þe roof.
8 Al dai myn enemyes dispiseden me; and þei þat preiside*n* me, sworen aȝen*es* me.
9 For y eet aischis as brede, and y medlid my drynk wiþ weping,
10 Fro þe face of þe ire of þin indignaciou*n*; for þou reisinge me, hast hurtlid me dou*n*.
11 Mi daies bowiden awey as schadewe; & y wexide drie as hey.
12 But, lord, þou dwellist wiþ-outen ende; & þi memorial i*n* genera-ciou*n*, & in-to generaciou*n*.
13 Lord! þou, risynge up, schal haue merci on sion; for þe tyme to haue merci þer-of comeþ; for þe tyme comeþ.
14 For þe stones þer-of plesiden þi seruau*n*tis; & þei schulen haue merci on þe lond þer-of.
15 And, lord, heþen men schulen drede þi name; & alle kingis of erþe schulen drede þi glorie.
16 For þe lord haþ bildid sion; and he schal be seyn in his glorie.
17 He bihede on þe preier of meke men; and he dispisede not þe preier of hem.
18 Be þese þingis writu*n* in a-noþir generaciou*n*; & þe puple þat schal be maad, schal preise þe lord.
19 For he bihelde fro his hiȝ holi place; þe lord lokide fro heuene in-to erþe,
20 For to here þe weilyngis of feterid men,⁴ and for to vnbynde þe sones of slayn men;
21 That þei telle in sion þe name of þe lord; and his preisyng in ier*u*salem,

---

¹ 101 Vulgate.   ² cremium   ³ Vigilavi   ⁴ gemitus compeditorum

II. The Seven Penitential Psalms.

22 In gaderyng to-gidere puplis in to oon, and kingis, þat þei serue þe lord.
23 It aunsweride to him[1] in þe weie of his vertu: telle þou to me þe fewnesse of my daies!
24 Aȝenclepe þou not me in þe myddil of my daies; þi ȝeeris ben in generacioun, and in-to generacioun.
25 Lord! þou foundidist þe erþe in þe biginnynge; & heuenes ben þe werkis of þin hondis.
26 Tho[2] schulen perische, but þou dwellist parfitli; & alle schulen wexe eld as a cloþ.
27 And þou schalt chaunge hem as an hilyng,[3] & þo schulen be chaungid; but þou art þe same þi silf, & þi ȝeeris schulen not faile.
28 The sones of þi seruauntis schulen dwelle; & þe seed of hem schal be dressid in-to þe world.
Glorie be to þe fadir [&c.].
As it was in þe biginning [&c.].

[VI.] psalm [130[4]]: De profundis.

1 Lord! y criede to þee fro depþis; lord, here þou my vois!
2 Thyne eeris be maad ententif in-to þe vois of my biseching!
3 Lord, if þou kepist wickidnessis; lord, who schal susteyne?
4 For merci is at þee; &, lord, for þi lawe y abode þee.
5 Mi soule susteynede in his word; [6] my soule hopide in þe lord.
Fro þe morwetid keping til to þe niȝt, [7] israel, hope in þe lord!
For whi, merci is at þe lord; & plenteuouse redempcioun is at him.
8 And he schal aȝenbie israel fro alle þe wickidnessis[5] þerof.
Glorie be to þe fadir [&c.].
As it was in þe biginnige [&c.].

[VII.] psalm [143[6]]: Domine exaudi.

1 Lord, here þou my preier; wiþ eeris perseyue þou my biseching; in þi treuþe, here þou me in þi riȝtfulnesse!
2 And entre þou not in-to doom wiþ þi seruaunt; for ech man lyuynge schal not be maad iust in þi siȝt.
3 For þe enemy pursuede[7] my soule; he made lowe my liyf in erþe;

---

[1] Respondit ei   [2] Ipsi   [3] opertorium   [4] 129 Vulgate. MS. De profundus
[5] iniquitatibus   [6] 142 Vulgate.   [7] persecutus est

II. *The Seven Penitential Psalms.*

He haþ set me in derk placis, as þe deed men of þe world. [4] and my spirit was aunguyschid[1] on me; myn herte was disturblid in me.

5 I was myndeful of elde daies; y biþouȝte in alle þi werkis; y biþouȝte in. þe dedis of þin hondis.

6 I helde forþ myn hondis to þee; my soule as erþe wiþout watir to þee.

7 Lord, here þou me swifteli; my spirit failide.
Turne þou not awey þi face fro me; & y schal be liyk to hem þat gon doun in to þe lake.

8 Make þou eerli þi merci herd to me, for y hopide in þee.
Make þou knowun to me þe weie in which y schal go; for y reiside my soule to þee.

9 Delyuere þou me fro myn enemyes! lord! y fledde to þee. [10] teche þou me to do þi wille; for þou art my god.
Thi good spirit schal lede me forþ in-to a riȝtful lond. [11] lord! for þi name, þou schalt quykene me in þin equyte;
Thou schalt lede my soule out [of][2] tribulacioun; [12] & in þi name þou schalt scatere alle myn enemyes;
And þou schalt lese alle hem þat trublen my soule, for y am þi seruaunt.

Glorie be to þe fadir [&c.].
As it was in þe biginninge [&c.].

[1] anxiatus est   [2] de

HERE BIGINNEN ÞE FIFTENE SALMES.

[I. Ps. 120.[1]] **Ad dominum cum tribularer**: Whanne y was set [etc.].
[II. Ps. 121.] **Leuaui oculos me[os]**: I reiside myn iȝen [etc.].
[III. Ps. 122.] **Letatus sum in hiis**: I am glade in þese [etc.].
[IV. Ps. 123.] **Ad te leuaui oculos**: To þee y haue reiside [etc.].
[V. Ps. 124.] **Nisi quia dominus**: Israel, seie now [etc.].
[VI. Ps. 125.] **Qui confidunt in domino**: Thei þat tristen in þe lord [etc.].
[VII. Ps. 126.] **In conuertendo dominus**: Whanne þe lord turnede [etc.].
[VIII. Ps. 127.] **Nisi dominus edificauerit**: But if þe lord bilde [etc.].
[IX. Ps. 128.] **Beati omnes qui**: Blessid ben alle [etc.].
[X. Ps. 129.] **Sepe expugna[uerunt]**: Israel, seie now [etc.].
[XI. Ps. 130.] **De profundus**: Lord, y criede to þee [etc.].
[XII. Ps. 131.] **Domine non est**: Lord, myn herte is not [etc.].
Glorie be to þe fadir [&c.].
As it was in þe bigynnyng [&c.].

[XIII.] psalm [132[2]]: **Memento, domine, dauid.**

1 Lord, haue þou mynde on dauiþ, & of al his myldenesse;
2 As he swoor to þe lord, he made a vowe to god of iacob:
3 I schal not entre in to þe tabernacle of myn hous; y schal not stie in to þe bed of my restyng;
4 I schal not ȝyue sleep to myn iȝen, & napping[3] to myn iȝe-liddis, & reste to my templis, [5] til y fynde a place to þe lord, a tabernacule to god of iacob.
6 Lo! we herden þat ark of testament in effrata; we founden it in þe feldis of wode.

---

[1] All these numbers are one earlier in the Vulgate.
[2] 131 Vulgate.
[3] dormitationem

III. *The Fifteen Gradual Psalms.*

7 We schulen entre in-to þe tabernacule [of] hi*m*,¹ we schulen worschipe [in] þe place² where hise feet stoden.
8 Lord! rise þou in-to þi rest; þou & þe ark of þin halewyng.
9 Thi prestis be cloþed wiþ riȝtfulnesse; & þi seyntis make ³ful out
ioie in ful out ioiyng³
10 For dauiþ þi seruau*n*t, turne not awey þe face of þi crist.
11 The lord swoor treuþe to dauiþ; & he schal not make hi*m* veyn:
[12] 'of þe fruyt of þi wombe y schal sette on þi seete.
13 'If þi sones schulen kepe my testament, & my witnessingis, þese
whiche y schal teche hem;
'And þe sones of hem til in-to þe world, þei schulen sit on þi
seete.'
14 For þe lord chees sion; he chees [it]⁴ in-to dwelling to himsilf:
15 'This is my reste in-to þe world of world; y schal dwelle here,
for y chees it.
16 'I, blessynge, schal blesse þe widewe of it; y schal fille wiþ loues
þe pore men of it;
17 'I schal cloþe wiþ heelþe þe p*r*estis þer-of; & þe holi men þer-of
⁵schulen make ful out-ioie in ful out-ioiyng.⁵
18 'Thidur y schal brynge forþ þe horn of dauiþ; y made redi a
lanterne to my crist.
19 'I schal cloþe hise enemyes wiþ schame; but myn halewyng
schal floure out⁶ on hi*m*.'
Glorie be to þe fadir [&c.].
As it was i*n* þe bigy*n*ny*n*ge [&c.].

[XIV.] ps*alm* [133⁷]: **Ecce, quam bonu***m***.

1 LO, hou good & hou merie it is, þat briþeren dwelle to-gidere
in oon!
2 As oynement in þe heed, þat goiþ dou*n* to þe beerd, in-to þe beerd
of aaron,
That goiþ dou*n* in-to þe coler of his cloiþ; [3] as þe dewe of
hermon þat [goiþ] dou*n*⁸ in-to þe hil of sion.
4 For þere þe lord sente blessyng, & liyf in-to þe world.
Glorie be to þe fadir [&c.].
As it was in þe bigi*n*ning [&c.].

¹ ejus   ² in loco   ³⁻³ exultent   ⁴ elegit eam
⁵⁻⁵ exultatione exultabunt   ⁶ efflorebit   ⁷ 132 Vulgate.
⁸ descendit

III. The Fifteen Gradual Psalms.

[XV.] psalm [134¹]: **Ecce nunc.**

1 LO, now, blesse ȝe þe lord; alle þe seruauntis of þe lord!
2 ȝe þat stonden in þe hous of þe lord; in þe forȝerdis of þe hous of oure god.
3 In niȝtis, reise ȝe ȝoure hondis in-to holi þingis, & blesse ȝe þe lord!
4 The lord blesse þee fro sion; which lord made heuene & erþe.
Glorie be to þe fadir [&c.].
As it was in þe bigynnynge [&c.].

Here enden þe fiftene salmes.

[1] 133 Vulgate.

IV. *The Litany.*

AND HERE BIGYNNEþ þE LETANIE.

Antem: [Ne reminiscaris].

Lord! haue þou no mynde of oure giltis, neþer of oure kynred; ne take no veniaunce of oure synnes, for þi name, lord! spare, lord, spare to þe puple, þat wiþ þi preciouse blood bouʒtest þe world aʒen! be not wrooþ to us wiþ-outen ende!

Lord, haue merci of us!
Crist, haue merci of us!
Lord, haue merci of us!
Crist, here us!
God, fadir of heuene, haue merci of us!
God þe sone, þat bouʒtest þe world, haue merci of us!
God þe holi gost, haue merci of us!
Holi trinite, oon god, haue merci of us!

Seynt Marie,	preie for us!
Holi modir of god,	preie for us!
Holi virgyn of virginis,	*preie for us!*
Seynt Michael,	*preie for us!*
Seynt gabriel,	preie for us!
Seynt raphael,	*preie for us!*
Alle holi aungelis & arcaungels,	*preie ʒe for us!*
Alle ordris of holi spiritis,	*preie ʒe for us!*
Seynt Ioon batist,	preie for us!
Alle holi patriarkis & profetis,	*preie ʒe for us!*
Seynt petre,	*preie for us!*
Seynt poul,	*preie for us!*
Seynt andreu,	*preie for us!*
Seynt Ioon,	*preie for us!*
Seynt philippe,	*preie for us!*
Seynt Iames,	*preie for us!*
Seynt bartolomeu,	*preie for us!*

Seynt Matheu,	*preie for us!*
Seynt symounde,	*preie for us!*
Seynt Iudee,	*preie for us!*
Seynt Mathie,	*preie for us!*
Seynt thomas,	*preie for us!*
Seynt bernard,	*preie for us!*
Seynt tadee,	*preie for us!*
Seynt luyk,	*preie for us!*
Seynt Mark,	*preie for us!*
Alle holi apostls & euauⁿgelistis,	*preie for us!*
Alle holi disciplis of oure lord,	*preie for us!*
Alle holi innocentis of oure lord,	*preie for us!*
Seynt steuene,	*preie for us!*
Seynt lyne,	*preie for us!*
Seynt clete,	*preie for us!*
Seynt clement,	*preie for us!*
Seynt ciprian,	*preie for us!*
Seynt laurence,	*preie for us!*
Seynt vincent,	*preie for us!*
Seynt george,	*preie for us!*
Seynt ffabiane,	*preie for us!*
Seynt sebastiane,	*preie for us!*
Seynt cosma,	*preie for us!*
Seynt damyane,	*preie for us!*
Seynt denys,	*preie for us!*
Seynt eustas & þi felowis,	*preie ȝe for us!*
Seynt thomas,	*preie for us!*
Seynt Cristofre,	*preie for us!*
Alle holi martires,	*preie ȝe for us!*
Seynt siluestre,	*preie for us!*
Seynt hillari,	*preie for us!*
Seynt Martyn,	*preie for us!*
Seynt Ambrose,	*preie for us!*
Seynt Austyn,	*preie for us!*
Seynt Ierom,	*preie for us!*
Seynt gregorie,	*preie for us!*
Seynt Nicolas,	*preie for us!*
Seynt cutberd,	*preie for us!*
Seynt swithyn,	*preie for us!*
Seynt benete,	*preie for us!*

IV. *The Litany.*

Seynt leonard,	preie for us!
Seynt gilis,	preie for us!
Seynt dunston,	preie for us!
Alle holi confessours,	preie ʒe for us!
Seynt marie maudelen,	preie for us!
Seynt marie egipcian,	preie for us!
Seynt agace,	preie for us!
Seynt agneis,	preie for us!
Seynt Lucie,	preie for us!
Seynt kateryne,	preie for us!
Seynt Margarete,	preie for us!
Seynt Iulian,	preie for us!
Seynt cristyne,	preie for us!
Seynt peronel,	preie for us!
Seynt radegounde,	preie for us!
Seynt freswide,	preie for us!
Alle holi virgynes,	preie ʒe for us!
Alle maner seyntis,	preie ʒe for us!

Lord, be good-liche, & spare us!
From alle yuelis; lord, delyuere us!
From alle temptacions of þe deuel; lord, delyuere us!
From endeles dampnacion; lord, deliuere us!
From vnclennesse of bodi & soule; lord, delyuer us!
From þe spirit of leccherie; lord, delyuere us!
From wraþþe, & hate, & al yuel wille; lord, delyuere us!
From vnclene þouʒtis; lord, deliuere us!
Be þin incarnacioun; lord, deliuere us!
Bi þi passioun; lord, delyuere vs!
Bi þi resureccioun; lord, delyuere us!
Bi þin assencion; lord, delyuere us!
Bi þe grace of þe holigost; lord, delyuere us!
In þe dai of doom; lord, deliuer us!
We synful preien þee to here us!
That þou ʒyue us pees; we preien þee to here us!
That þi merci & þi pitee kepe us; we preien þee to here us!
That þou gouerne & kepe þi chirche; we preien þee to here us!
That þou ʒyue pees to oure kingis & princis; we preien þee to here us!
That þou kepe oure bischopis in holi religioun; we preien þee to here us!

That þou kepe alle cristen soulis from endeles dampnacioun; we
    preien þee to here us!
That þou vouche-saaf to ȝyue us fruytis of þe erþe; we preien
    þee to here us!
Lombe of god, þat doist awey synnes of þe world; haue mer[ci]
    of us & ȝyue us pees!
Crist, here us!
Lord, haue merci of vs!
Crist, haue merci of us!
Lord, haue merci of us!
Pater noster [&c.].
And lede us not in-to temptacioun,
But delyuere us from yuel.   amen!
And þi merci come vpon us, lord;
Thyn heelþe, aftir þi speche!
Be to us, lord, a tour of strengþe
Fro þe face [of] oure enemy!
Pees be maad in þi vertu!
And plente in þi toures!
Lord god of vertues, conuerte us,
& schewe þi face, & we schulen be saaf.

Oracio: deus cui proprium.

God! to whom it is proprid to be merciful euere, & to spare,
take oure preier, & late þe merci of þi pitee assoile hem
þat ben boundun wiþ þe cheyne of synnes, bi crist, oure lord.
amen!

[Oracio]: Ecclesie tue.

Lord! be þou plesid wiþ þe preieris [of] þi chirche, & graunte
þat alle errours & aduercitees be distried, bi crist, oure lord.
amen!

[Oracio]: Vre, igne sancti spiritus!

LOrd! we bisecche þee þat þou brenne oure lendis & oure
herte wiþ þe fire of þe holigoost, þat we mowe serue to þee
wiþ chast bodi, & plese to þee wiþ clene herte; bi crist, oure
lord.   amen!

[Oracio]: Omnipotens sempiterne!

Almyȝti god wiþ-outen ende, þat art endeles helpe of alle þat
bileuen in þee, here oure preier for alle men & wymmen,

IV. The Litany.

for whiche we bisechen to þi goodnesse; & graunte hem
helþe of bodi & soule, so þat whanne þei ben hool, þei moun
ȝelde þankyngis to þee in þi chirche; bi crist, oure lord.
amen!

[Oracio]: Pietate tua q*uesumus*, d[*omine*].

FOr þi pitee, lord, we biseche þee vnbynde þe bondis of[1]
alle oure synnes; And þorouȝ þe preier of þe glorious euerlastynge maide marie, wiþ alle þi seyntis;: kepe us þi
seruauntis, & oure king, & alle cristen puple, in alle holynesse; & alle þat bi kynred of blood, or bi homelynesse, or
bi preier, be oned wiþ us, clense hem of alle vices, & liȝtne
hem wiþ vertues! pees & helþe ȝyue to us; & putte from
us oure enemyes, boþe þo þat we sen & þo þat we moun
not se. Ȝyue þi charite to oure frendes & to oure enemyes;
& helþe to alle siyk; & to alle cristen, quyke & deed, graunte
liyf & endeles reste, bi crist, oure lord.   amen.

Here endiþ þe letanie.

[1] MS. of of.

AND HERE BIGYNNEþ PLACEBO [OR VESPERS OF THE OFFICE FOR THE DEAD].

psalm [116¹]: **Dilexi** quoniam.

1 I louede þe lord; for þe lord schal here þe vois of my preier.
2 For he bowide doun his eere to me; & ²y schal inwardli clepe him² in my daies.
3 The sorewis of deeþ cumpassiden me; and þe perelis of helle founden me.
4 I foond tribulacioun & sorewe; & ³y clepide inwardli³ þe name of þe lord:
'Thou, lord, delyuere my soule!' [5] þe lord is merciful & iust; & oure god doiþ merci.⁴
6 And þe lord kepiþ litil children; y was mekid, & he delyueride me.
7 Mi soule, turne þou in-to þi reste, for þe lord haþ do wele to þee;
8 For he haþ delyuerid my soule fro deeþ, myn iȝen fro wepingis, my feet fro fallynge doun.
9 I schal plese þe lord in þe cuntre of hem þat lyuen.⁵
Antem: I schal plese þe lord in þe cuntre of hem þat lyuen.

psalm [120⁶: Ad] **dominum** cum **tribularer**.

1 Whanne y was set in tribulacioun, y criede to þe lord, and he herde me.
2 Lord, delyuere þou my soule fro wickid lippis, & fro a gileful tunge!
3 What schal be ȝouun to þee, eþer what schal be leid to þee, to a gileful tunge?
Scharpe arowis of þe myȝti, wiþ colis þat maken desolat.
4 Allas to me! for my dwellyng in an alien lond is drawe alonge⁷; y dwellide with men dwellynge in cedar; [5] my soule was myche a comelyng.⁸

---

¹ 114 Vulgate. ²⁻² invocabo ³⁻³ invocavi ⁴ miseretur
⁵ in regione vivorum ⁶ 119 Vulgate. ⁷ prolongatus est
⁸ incola

6 I was peisible wiþ hem þat hatiden pees. whanne y spak to hem, þei aȝenseiden me wiþouten cause.[1]

Antem: Woo is me! for my dwelling is drawe alonge.

psalm [121[2]]: Leuaui oculos.

1 I reiside myn iȝen to þe hillis, fro whennes help schal come to me.
2 Myn help is of þe lord, þat made heuene & erþe.
3 The lord ȝyue not þi foot in-to mouyng; neþer he nappe[3] þat kepiþ þee!
4 Lo, he schal not nappe, neþer slepe,[4] þat kepiþ israel.
5 The lord kepiþ þee; þe lord is þi proteccioun aboue þi riȝt hond.
6 The sunne schal not brenne þee bi dai, neþer þe moone bi nyȝt.
7 The lord kepe þee from al yuel! þe lord kepe þi soule!
8 The lord kepe þi goyng in & þi goyng out, from þis tyme now, & in-to þe world!

Antem: The lord ke[pe] þee from al yuel! þe lord kepe þi soule!

psalm [130[5]]: De profundis.[6]

1 Lord, y criede to þee from depþis; lord, here þou my vois!
2 Thyne eeris be maad ententif, in-to þe vois of my bisechyng.
3 Lord! if þou kepist wickidnessis; lord! who schal susteyne?
4 For merci[7] is at þee; &, lord, for þi lawe y abode þee.
5 Mi soule susteynede in his word; [6] my soule hopide in þe lord. Fro þe moruntide keping til to þe niȝt, [7] israel, hope in þe lord! For whi, merci[8] is at þe lord; & plenteuouse redempcioun is at him.
8 And he schal aȝenbie israel, fro alle þe wickidnessis þer-of.[9]

Antem: Lord! if þou kepist wickidnessis; lord! who schal susteyne?

psalm [138[10]]: Confitebor.

1 Lord, y schal knouleche to þee in al myn herte, for þou herdist þe wordis of my mouþ.
Mi god, y schal synge to þee in þe siȝt of aungelis; [2] y schal worschipe to þin hooli temple, and y schal knouleche to þi name,

---

[1] impugnabant me gratis   [2] 120 Vulgate.   [3] dormitet
[4] dormitabit neque dormiet   [5] 129 Vulgate.   [6] profundus MS.
[7] propitiatio   [8] misericordia   [9] ejus   [10] 137 Vulgate.

V. The Office for the Dead.—1. Placebo or Vespers.

On þi mercy & þi treuþe; for þou hast magnefied þin holi name aboue al þing.

3 In what-euer day y schal inwardli clepe þee, here þou me! þou schalt multiplie vertu in my soule.

4 Lord! alle þe kyngis of erþe knouleche to þee, for þei herden alle þe wordis of þi mouth.

5 And synge þei in þe weies of þe lord, for þe glorie of þe lord is greete.

6 For þe lord is hiȝ, & biholdiþ meke þingis, & knoweþ afer hiȝ þingis.[1]

7 If y schal go in þe myddis of tribulacioun, þou schalt quykene me; & þou strecchidist forþ þin hond on[2] þe ire of myn enemyes, & þi riȝthond made me saaf.

8 The lord schal ȝelde for me. lord! þi merci is wiþouten ende[3]; dispise þou not þe werkes of þin hondis.

Antem: Lord! dispise þou not þe werkis of þin hondis.

psalm: **Magnificat.**

46 Mi soule magnefieþ þe lord;
47 And my spirit haþ gladid in god, myn helþc.[4]
48 For he haþ biholde þe mekenesse of his hond-maidun; for, lo, of þis,[5] alle generaciouns schulen seie þat y am blessid.[6]
49 For he þat is myȝti haþ don to me grete þingis; & his name is holi.
50 And his merci is fro kynredis in to kynredis,[7] to men that dreden him.
51 He made myȝt in his arm; he scateride proude men with þe þouȝt[8] of his herte.
52 He sette doun myȝti men fro seete; & enhaunside meke men.
53 He haþ fulfillid hungri men wiþ goodis; & he haþ lefte riche men voide.
54 He, hauynge mynde of his merci, took up israel, his child.
55 As he haþ spokun to oure fadris; to abraham & to his seed in-to þe worldis.

Antem: I herde a vois from heuen seiynge, 'blessid ben deed men þat dien in þe lord.'

V⁊ Ffrom þe ȝate of helle,
[R⁊] Lord, delyuere her soulis!

---

[1] humilia .. et alta a longe. [2] super [3] in saeculum [4] salutari
[5] ex hoc [6] MS. bles blessid [7] a progenie in progenies [8] mente

V. The Office for the Dead.—1. Placebo or Vespers.

Lord, haue merci of us!
Crist, haue merci of us!
Lord, haue merci of us!
Pater noster: Oure fadir [&c.].

psalm [146[1]]: Lauda, anima mea.

1. Mi soule, herie þou þe lord! y schal herie þe lord in my liyf; y schal synge[2] to my god as longe as y schal be.
2. Nile ȝe[3] triste in princis, neþer in þe sones of men, in whiche is noon heelþe.
3. The spirit of him schal go out, & he schal turne aȝen in-to his erþe: in þat dai alle þe þouȝtis of hem schulen perische.
4. He is blessid, of whom þe god of iacob is his helpe; his hope is in his lord god, [5] þat made heuene & erþe, þe see, & alle þingis þat ben in þo.[4]

Which kepiþ treuþe in to þe world; [6] makeþ doom to hem þat suffren wronge; ȝyueþ mete to hem þat ben hungri.

7. The lord vnbyndiþ feterid men; þe lord liȝtneþ blynde men.
8. The lord reisiþ men hurtlid doun[5]; þe lord loueþ iust men.
9. The lord kepiþ comelyngis[6]; he schal take up a modirles child[7] & a widewe; and he schal distrie þe weies of synneris.
10. [The lord schal regne in to þe worldes; þe god of syon in alle generaciouns & in to generacioun.]

[V̸] Endeles reste, ȝyue hem lord,
[R̸] And euerlastynge liȝt liȝtne to hem!
[V̸] From þe ȝate of helle,
[R̸] Lord, delyuere her soulis!
[V̸] I bileue to se þe goodis of þe lord
[R̸] In þe lond of lyuynge men.
[V̸] Lord, here þou my preier,
[R̸] And my cry come to þee!

Orisoun: Inclina, domine.

Lord! bowe þou þin eere to oure preieris, wiþ whiche we biseche loweliche þi merci; þat þou sette þe soulis of þi seruauntis, boþe of men & wymmen, þat þou hast comaundid to passe out of þis world, in þe cuntre of pees and of liȝt; & comaunde þat þei be felowis of þin halewene; bi crist, oure lord. amen!

---

[1] 145 Vulgate. [2] psallam [3] Nolite [4] eis [5] erigit elisos
[6] advenas [7] pupillum

ffor fadir and modir: Deus, qui patrem & matrem.

God, þat comaundid us to worschipe fadir & modir, haue merci of þe soulis of my fadir & of my modir, and forȝyue hem alle her synnes; & make us to lyue wiþ hem in þe blisse wiþ-outen ende. amen!

ffor a cor present: Deus, cui proprium.

God, to whom it is proprid to haue merci & to spare euer more, loweliche we biseche þee þat þou set þe soule of þi seruaunt, which þou hast comaundid to dai to passe out of þis world, be not take in-to þe hondis of oure enemy; ne forȝite it not in-to þe ende, but comaunde it to be takun up of holi aungelis, & to be ladde in-to þe cuntre of lif, so for þat he hopide & bileuede in þee. late him disserue to be euer glade in þe cumpeny of þin halewene. amen!

ffor a soul in mynde dai: Deus, indulgenciarum.

Lord god of forȝyuenesse, graunte þou to þe soule of þi seruaunt, whos ȝeris mynde we maken to dai, a seete of refreschinge blisse of reste & clerene of liȝt. amen!

HERE BIGINNEÞ DIRIGE.

[FIRST NOCTURN.]

psalm [5]: verba mea.

1 Lord, parseyue þou my words wiþ eeris! vndurstonde þou my cry!
2 Mi king & my god! ȝyue þou tent to þe vois of my preier!
For, lord, y schal preie to þee; [3] here þou eerli[1] my vois!
Eerli[1] y schal stonde nyȝ þee, & y schal se, [4] for þou art god not willinge wickidnesse.
Neþer an yuel-willid man[2] schal dwelle bisidis þee; [5] neþer vniust men schulen dwelle bifore þin iȝen.
Thou hatist alle þat worchen wickidnesse; [6] þou schalt lese alle þat speken lesyng.

[1] mane   [2] maliguus

V. The Office for the Dead.—2. Dirige (Matins 1st Nocturn).

The lord schal holde abhominable, a manquellere & gileful man.
7 But, lord, in þe multitude of þi merci, y schal entre in-to þin hous; y schal worschipe þee at þin hooli temple in þi drede.[1]
8 Lord, lede þou forþ me in þi riȝtfulnesse; for[2] myn enemyes, dresse þou my weie in þi siȝt![3]
9 For whi, treuþe is not in her mouþ; her herte is veyn.
10 Her þrote is an opyn sepulcre; þei diden gilefuli wiþ her tungis: god, [11] deme þou hem!
Falle þei doun fro her þouȝtis; up þe multitude of her wickidnessis, caste þou hem doun; for, lord, þei han terrid þee to ire.[4]
12 And alle þat hopen in þee be glade; þei schulen make fulli ioie wiþ-outen ende; & þou schalt dwelle in hem,
And alle þat louen þi name schulen haue glorie in þee; [13] for þou schalt blesse a iust man.
Lord! þou crouned us, as wiþ þe schelde of þi good wille.
Antem: Mi lord god, dresse þou my weie in þi siȝt!

psalm [6]: Domine, ne in furore tuo.

1 Lord, repreue þou not me in þi stronge veniaunce,[5] neþer chastise þou me in þin ire.
2 Lord, haue þou merci on me, for y am siyk! lord, make þou me hool; for alle my bones ben trublid!
3 And my soule is trublid greetli; but þou, lord, hou longe?
4 Lord, be þou conuertid, & delyuere my soule! make þou me saaf, for[6] þi merci!
5 For noon is in deeþ which[7] is myndeful of þee; but in helle, who shal knouleche to þee?
6 I trauelide[8] in my weilyng; y schal wasche my bed bi ech nyȝt; y schal moiste my bed-stree[9] wiþ my teeris.
7 Myn iȝe is disturblid of woodnesse[10]; y wexe elde among alle myne enemyes.
8 Alle ȝe þat worchen wickidnesse, departe fro me; for þe lord haþ herd þe vois of my weping.
9 The lord haþ herd my bisechyng; þe lord haþ resseyued my preier.

---

[1] timore tuo   [2] propter   [3] Verse 8 is repeated in the MS.
[4] irritaverunt te   [5] ne in furore tuo arguas me   [6] propter   [7] qui
[8] Laboravi   [9] stratum   [10] a furore

10 Alle myn enemyes be aschamed¹ & be disturblid gretli: be þei turned to gidere; & be þei aschamed¹ ful swifteli!

Antem: Lord, be þou conuertid, & delyuere my soule; for þer is no man in deeþ þat medefuli haþ mynde of þee.

[psalm 7]: *Domine deus meus! in te speraui.*

1 Mi lord god, y haue hopid in þee; make þou me saaf fro alle men þat pursuen me; & delyuere þou me!

2 Lest eny tyme he, as a lioun, rauysche my soule, þe while non is þat aȝenbieþ, neþer to make saaf.²

3 Mi lord god, if y dide þis þing³; if wickidnesse is in myn hondis,

4 If y ȝeldide to men ȝeldinge⁴ to me yueles, falle y, bi disseruynge, voide⁵ fro myn enemyes.

5 Myn enemy pursue⁶ my soule, and take; & defoule my liyf in erþe, & brynge my glorie in-to dust.

6 Lord! rise þou up in þin ire; & be þou reisid in þe coostis⁷ of myn enemyes;

And, my lord god, rise þou up in þe comaundement which þou hast comaundid; [7] & þe synagoge of puplis schal cumpasse⁸ þee.

And for þis, go þou aȝen an hiȝ. [8] þe lord demeþ puplis.

Lord! deme þou me bi my riȝtfulnes, & bi myn innocense on me.

9-10 The wickidnesse of synneris be endid⁹; & þou, god, sekynge þe hertis & reynes, schalt dresse¹⁰ a iust man.

11 Mi iust help is of þe lord, þat makiþ saaf riȝtful men in herte.

12 The lord is a iust iuge, strong, & pacient; wher he is wroþ bi alle daies?¹¹

13 If ȝe ben not conuertid, he schal florische his swerd; he haþ bent his bouwe, & maad it redi.

14 And þer-in he haþ made redi vessels¹² of deeþ; he haþ fulli maad redi his arowis wiþ brennynge þingis.

15 Lo, he haþ conseyued sorewe; he peynfulli brouȝte forþ vnriȝtfulnesse, & childide¹³ wickidnesse.

16 He openyde a lake, & diggide it out; & he felde¹⁴ in-to þe diche which he made.

¹ Erubescant ² neque qui salvum faciat ³ istud
⁴ reddidi retribuentibus ⁵ inanis ⁶ Persequatur ⁷ finibus
⁸ circumdabit ⁹ Consumetur ¹⁰ diriges
¹¹ numquid irascitur per singulos dies ¹² vasa ¹³ peperit ¹⁴ incidit

V. *The Office for the Dead.*—2. *Dirige (Matins 1st Nocturn).*

17 His sorewe schal be turned in-to his heed[1]; & his wickidnesse schal come doun in-to his necke.

18 I schal knouleche to þe lord bi[2] his riȝtfulnesse; and y schal synge to þe name of þe hiȝeste lord.

Antem: Lest eny tyme he take my soule as a lioun, whiles þer is noon to aȝenbie, neþer to make saf.

V͡7 Ffrom þe ȝate of helle,

[R͡7] Lord, delyuere her soulis!

Pater noster: Oure fadir [&c.].

leccio .1ᵃ. Parce michi, domine! [Job vii. 16—21.]

16 LOrd, spare þou me, for my daies ben not[3]! [17] what is man, for þou magnefiest him? eþer what settest þou þin herte towardis him? [18] þou visitist him eerli; and sodeynli þou preuest him. [19] hou longe sparest þou not me, neþer suffrest[4] þat y swolewe my spotele? [20] y haue synned, o þou keper of men, what shal y do to þee? whi hast þou set me contrarie to þee? & y am maad greuouse[5] to my silf? [21] whi doist þou not awey[6] my synne? & whi takest þou not a-wey[7] my wickidnesse? lo, now, y slepe in poudur; and if þou sekest me eerli, y schal not abide.[8]

R͡7 I bileue[9] þat myn aȝenbier lyueþ; & y schal rise out of þe erþe in þe laste dai[10]; & in my flesche y schal se god, my sauyour.

V͡7 Whom y my silf schal se, beynge not anoþir,[11] & myn iȝen schulen biholde him.

[Repeet] And in my fleisch, y schal see god, my saueour.

Leccio iiᵃ: Tedet animam. [Job x. 1—7.]

1 It anoieþ my soule of my lyif; y schal lette[12] my speche aȝenes me, y schal speke in þe bitternesse of my soule. [2] y schal seie to god, 'nyle[13] þou condempne me; schewe þou to me whi þou demest me so. [3] wheþer it semeþ good to þee, if þou falseli chalengist & oppressist me, þe werk of þin hondis, & if þou helpe þe counseil of wickid men.[14] [4] wheþer

---

[1] caput [2] Confitebor Domino secundum [3] nihil [4] dimittis me
[5] gravis [6] non tollis [7] non aufers [8] subsistam [9] Scio
[10] et in novissimo die de terra surrecturus sum; et rursum circumdabor pelle mea. [11] et non alius [12] dimittam [13] Noli [14] impiorum

V. *The Office for the Dead.*—2. *Dirige (Matins 2nd Nocturn).*

fleischli iȝen ben to þee? eþer as a man seeþ, also þou schalt
se? [5] wheþer þi daies ben as þe daies of man; & þi ȝeeris
ben as mannes tymes, [6] þat þou enquere my wickidnesse,
& enserche[1] my synne, [7] & wite þat y haue do no wickid
þing, siþen no man is, þat mai delyuere fro þyn hond?'

℞ Thou þat reisidist aȝen stynkynge laȝer fro his graue; þou,
lord, graunte hem reste & places of forȝyuenesse!

V̄ Thou þat art to come to deme þe quyke & þe dede, & þe
world bi fier!

[Repeat] Thou, lord, graunte hem reste, & place of forȝyuenesse!

lecc*io* iij[a]: **Man***us* **tue.** [Job x. 8—12.]

8 Thyne hondis maden me, & han formed me al in cumpas[2]; &
þou castist me doun so sodeynli! [9] y biseche þee haue
þou mynde þat þou madist me of cley, & schalt brynge me
aȝen in-to poudur. [10] wheþer þou hast not softid[3] me as
mylk; and hast cruddid me to-gideres[4] as chese? [11] þou
hast cloþid me wiþ skyn & flesch; & þou hast ioyned me
to-gideres wiþ bones & synewes. [12] þou hast ȝoue liyf and
merci to me; & þi visitacioun haþ kept[5] my spirit.

℞ Lord, whanne þou schalt come to deme þe erþe, where schal
y hide me fro þe face of þi wraþþe? for y haue synned ful
myche in my liyf.

V̄ I drede my trespassis, & y am aschamed to-fore þee: whanne
þou schalt come to iugement, nyle þou condempne me.

[Repeat] Ffor y haue synned ful myche in my liyf.

[SECOND NOCTURN.]

p*salm* [23[6]]: **Domi***n***us regit me.**

1 The lord gouerneþ me, and no þing schal faile to me; [2] in
þe place of pasture, þere [he] haþ set[7] me.

He nurschide[8] me on þe watir of refresching; [3] he conuertid
my soule.

He ledde me forþ on þe paþþis of riȝtfulnesse, for[9] his name.

4 For whi,[10] þouȝ y schal go in þe myddis of schadewe of deeþ, y
schal not drede yuelis; for[11] þou art wiþ me:

Thi ȝerde & þi staf, þo[12] han confortid me.

[1] scruteris   [2] plasmaverunt me totum in circuitu   [3] mulsisti
[4] coagulasti   [5] custodivit   [6] 22 Vulgate.   [7] collocavit   [8] educavit
[9] propter   [10] Nam   [11] Quoniam   [12] ipsa

V. *The Office for the Dead.*—2. *Dirige (Matins 2nd Nocturn).*

5 Thou hast maad redi a boord¹ in my siȝt, aȝenes hem þat trublen me;
Thou hast maad fat myn heed wiþ oile; & my cuppe fillynge gretli is ful cleer.²

6 And þi merci schal sue me in alle þe daies of my liyf;
And þat y dwelle in þe hous of þe lord, in-to þe lengþe of daies.

Antem: He haþ set me in place of pasture.

psalm [25³]: **Ad te [domine] leuaui.**

1 Lord, to þe y haue reisid my soule. my god! y triste in þee; be y not aschamed!
Neþer myn enemyes scorn me; [2] for alle men þat suffren þee schulen not be schent.⁴
Alle men doynge wickid þingis to veynli,⁵ be þei schent!

3 Lord, schewe þou þi weies to me; & teche þou me þi paþþis!

4 Dresse⁶ þou me in þi treuþe, and teche þou me; for þou art god my saueour, & y suffride⁷ þee al dai.

5 Lord, haue þou mynde of þi merciful doyngis, & of þi mercies, þat ben fro þe world.⁸

6 Haue þou not mynde of þe trespassis of my ȝougþe, & on myn vnkunnyngis!⁹
Thou, lord, haue mynde on me bi þi merci; for þi goodnesse!

7 The lord is swete & riȝtful; for þis cause he schal ȝyue a lawe to men trespassynge¹⁰ in þe weie.

8 He schal dresse deboner men in doom¹¹; he schal teche mylde men hise weies.

9 Alle þe weies of þe lord ben merci & treuþe, to men sekynge his testament & his witnessyngis.

10 Lord, for þi name þou schalt do merci to my synne; for it is myche.

11 Who is a man þat drediþ þe lord? he ordeyneþ to him a lawe in þe weie which he chees.

12 His soule schal dwelle in goodis; & his seed schal enerite þe lond.

13 The lord is sadnesse¹² to men þat dreden him; & his testament is þat it be schewid to hem.

---
¹ mensam   ² inebrians, quam praeclarus est!   ³ 24 Vulgate.
⁴ sustinent te non confundentur   ⁵ supervacue   ⁶ Dirige   ⁷ sustinui
⁸ a saeculo   ⁹ ignorantias   ¹⁰ delinquentibus   ¹¹ Diriget mansuetos in judicio
¹² Firmamentum

14 Myn iȝen ben euere to þe lord, for he schal breide awey¹ my feet fro þe snare.
15 Biholde þou on me, & haue þou merci on me, for y am oon aloon² & pore!
16 The tribulaciouns of myn herte ben multiplied: delyuere þou me of my nedis!³
17 Se þou my meke-nesse & my trauel⁴; & forȝyue þou alle my trespassis!
18 Biholde þou myn enemyes, for þei ben multiplied; & þei haten me bi wickid hatrede.
19 Kepe þou my soule, & delyuere þou me! be y not aschamed, for y hopide in þee.
20 Innocent men & riȝtful clyueden to me, for y suffride⁵ þee.
21 God delyuere þou, israel, fro alle hise tribulaciouns!

Antem: Lord, remmembre þou not þe trespassis of my ȝougþe, and myn ignorauncis!

psalm [27⁶]: Dominus illuminacio.

1 The lord is my liȝtnyng and myn heelþe; whom schal y drede?
The lord is defender of my liyf; for whom schal y tremble?
2 The while noieful men neiȝen to me, for to ete my fleschis,
Myn enemyes þat trubliden me, þei weren maad sike, & felden doun.
3 Thouȝ castels stonden to-gidere aȝenes me, myn herte schal not drede.
Thouȝ batel riseþ aȝenes me, in þis þing y schal haue hope.
4 I axide of þe lord o þing; y schal seke þis þing; þat y dwelle in þe hous of þe lord in alle þe daies of my liyf,
That y se þe wille of þe lord, & þat y visite his temple.
5 For he hidde me in his tabernacle; in þe dai of yuelis, he defendide me in þe hid place of his tabernacle.
He enhaunside me in a stoon; [6] and now he enhaunside myn heed ouer myn enemyes.
7 I cumpasside & offride in his tabernacle a sacrifice of criynge; y schal synge,⁷ & y schal seie salm to þe lord.
8 Lord, here þou my vois, bi which y criede to þee! haue þou merci on me, & here me!

¹ evellet ² quia unicus ³ de necessitatibus meis ⁴ laborem
⁵ quia sustinui ⁶ 26 Vulgate
⁷ Circuivi et immolavi ... vociferationis; cantabo

9 Myn herte seide to þee, my face souȝte þee; lord, y schal seke efte þi face!
10 Turne þou not awey þi face fro me! bowe þou not awey[1] in ire fro þi scruaunt!
11 Lord, be þou myn helper! forsake þou not me! & god, myn helpe, dispise þou not me!
12 For my fadir & my modir han forsakun me; but þe lord haþ take me.[2]
13 Lord, sette þou a lawe to me in þi weie, & dresse þou me in þe paþþe, for[3] myn enemyes!
14 Bitake þou not me in-to þe soulis of hem þat trublen me; for wickid witnessis han rise aȝenes me, & wickidnesse liede[4] to it-silf.
15 I bileue to se þe godis of þe lord, [5]in þe lond of þe lord, in þe lond of hem þat lyuen.[5]
16 Abide þou þe lord, & do manli[6]! & þin herte be confortid, & suffre þou[7] þe lord.

Antem: I bileue to se þe godis of þe lord, in þe lond of hem þat lyuen.

V̄ Riȝtful men schulen be in endeles mynde;
[R̄] þei schulen not drede of yuel heryng.

Pater noster: Oure fadir [&c.].

leccio iiij[a]: **Quantas habeo.** [Job xiii. 23—28.]

23 Hou grete synnes & wickidnessis haue y! schewe to me my felonyes & trespassis![8] [24] whi hidest þou þi face, & demest me, þin enemy? [25] þou schewist þi power aȝenes a leef which is rauyschid[9] wiþ þe wynde, & þou pursuest drie stobil; [26] for þou writist bitternessis aȝenes me, & wolt waste me wiþ þe synnes of my waxinge age.[10] [27] þou hast set my foot in a stok,[11] and þou hast kepte[12] alle my paþþis, & þou hast biholde[13] þe steppis of my feet; [28] & y schal be wastid as rotenesse, & as a cloþ which is etun of a mouȝte.[14]

R̄ Woo is me, lord! for y haue synned ful myche in my lif. what schal y, wrecche, do? whidur schal y flee, but to þee,

---

[1] ne declines [2] assumpsit me [3] dirige ... propter
[4] mentita est [5] MS. wrong. in terra viventium V. [6] viriliter
[7] sustine [8] iniquitates et peccata [9] rapitur
[10] adolescentiae [11] nervo [12] observasti [13] considerasti
[14] tinea

my god? haue merci on me, whanne þou schalt come in þe laste dai!

V̌ Mi soule is gretli trublid; but þou, lord, socoure þou it.

[Repeet] Whanne þou schalt come in þe laste dai.

leccio vᵃ: Homo nat*us* de muliere. [Job xiv. 1—6.]

1 A man þat is born of a womman, lyueþ schort tyme, & is fillid wiþ many wrecchidnessis. [2] which[1] goiþ out & is defoulid as a flour, & fleeþ as a schadewe, & dwelliþ neuer parfitli in þe same staat. [3] and gessist þou[2] it worþi to opene þin iȝen on siche a man, & to brynge him into doom wiþ þee? [4] who mai[3] make him clene þat is conseyued of vnclene seed? wheþer not þou þat aloon?[4] [5] þe daies of a man ben schorte; þe noumbre of his moneþis ben at þee;[5] þou hast set[6] hise termes, þe whiche moun not be passid. [6] þer-for go þou awey fro him a litil, þat he haue reste, til þe mede disirid come; [7] & his dai is as þe dai of an hirid man.[7]

Ř Lord, reherce þou not my synnes whanne þou schalt come to deme þe world bi fier!

V̌ Mi lord god, dresse þou my weie in þi siȝt,

[Repeet] Whanne þou schalt come to deme þe world bi fier!

[8] Leccio vjᵃ: [Quis michi hoc tribuat]. [Job xiv. 13—16.]

13 Who mai graunte to me þis, þat þou defende me in helle, & hide me til þi greet veniaunce[9] passe, & þat þou ordeyne me a tyme in which þou haue mynde of me? [14] gessist þou not[10] þat a deed man schal lyue aȝen? / Alle þe daies in whiche y trauele[11] now, y abide til my chaungyng come. [15] þou schalt clepe me, & y schal answere þee; þou schalt strecche þi riȝt hond to þe werk of þin hondis. [16] sikirli[12] þou hast noumbrid my steppis; but, lord, spare þou my synnes!

Ř Lord, nyle þou deme me aftir my dede! y haue do no þing worþi in þi siȝt. þerfor y bisech þi maieste, þat þou, god, do awey my wickidnesse.

---

[1] qui [2] ducis [3] MS. mai mai. [4] Nonne tu qui solus es?
[5] apud te [6] MS. se set. constituisti [7-7] sicut mercenarii, dies ejus
[8] The heading *Quare de vulua* is given wrongly in the MS. [9] furor tuus
[10] Putasne [11] milito [12] quidem

V. The Office for the Dead.—2. Dirige (Matins 3rd Nocturn).

V7 More-ouer, god, wasche þou me fro myn vnriȝtfulnesse, & clense þou me of my trespas! for y haue synned to þee aloon.
[Repeet] þerfor y biseche þi maieste, þat þou, god, do awey wickidnesse.

[THIRD NOCTURN.]

psalm [40[1]]: **Expectans, expectaui.**

1 I, abidinge, abode þe lord; & he ȝaf tent to me.
And he herde my preieris; [2] & he ledde me out fro þe lake of wrecchidnesse, & fro þe filþe of drast.[2]
And he ordeynede my feet on a stoon; & he dresside my goyngis.[3]
3 And he sente[4] in-to my mouþ a new songe, a song to oure god.
4 Many men schulen se, & schulen drede, & schulen haue hope in þe lord.
5 Blessid is þe man of whom þe name of þe lord is his hope; and he bihelde not in-to vanytees & in-to false woodnessis.[5]
6 Mi lord god, þou hast maad þi meruelis many; & in þi þouȝtis, noon is þat is liyk þee.
7 I telde[6] & y spak; & þei ben multiplied aboue noumbre.
8 Thou noldest sacrifice & offryng; but þou madist parfitli[7] eeris to me.
9 Thou axidist not [8]brent sacrifice and sacrifice for synne:[8] þanne y seide: 'lo, y come!'
10 In þe heed of þe book it is writun of me, þat y schulde do þi wille. my god, y wilnede also to do þi lawe in þe[9] myddis of myn herte.
11 I telde[6] þi riȝtfulnessis[10] in a greet chirche: lo! y schal [not] refreyne[11] my lippis: lord, þou wistist!
12 I hidde not þi riȝtfulnesse[10] in myn herte; y seide þi treuþe & þin heelþe;
13 I hidde not þi merci & þi treuþe, fro a myche[12] counseil.
14 But þou, lord, make not fer[13] þi merciful doyngis fro me! þi mercy & þi treuþe euere token me up.[14]
15 For whi, yuelis of whiche is no noumbre cumpassiden me; my wickidnessis token[15] me, and y myȝte not þat y schulde se.

---

[1] 39 Vulgate.   [2] ? draft. de luto faecis.   [3] direxit gressus meos   [4] immisit   [5] insanias   [6] Annuntiavi   [7] perfecisti   [8-8] holocaustum et pro peccato   [9] MS. in þe in þe   [10] justitiam   [11] non prohibebo   [12] multo   [13] ne longe facias   [14] susceperunt me   [15] comprehenderunt

V. *The Office for the Dead.*—2. *Dirige* (*Matins* 3rd *Nocturn*).

Tho ben mutiplied aboue þe heeris of myn heed, and myn herte forsook me.
16 Lord, plese it to þee þat þou delyuere me! lord, biholde þou to helpe me!
17 Be þei schent & aschamed to-gidere, þat seken my liyf, to take awey it!
Be þei turned abak, & be þei aschamed, þat wolen yuelis to me!
18 Bere þei her confusioun anoon, þat seien to me, [1]'wel! wel!' þat is in scorun.[1]
19 Alle þat seken þee, be fulli ioieful & be glad on þee! & seie þei þat louen þin heelþe, 'þe lord be magnefied euer!'
20 Forsoþe y am a begger & pore: þe lord is bisi of me.[2]
21 Thou art myn helpere & my defendere! my god, tarie þou not!
Antem: Lord, plese it to þe þat þou delyuere me! lord, loke þou forþ to helpe me!

psalm [41[3]]: Beatus qui intelligit.

1 **B**lessid is he þat vndurstondiþ on a nedi man & pore! þe lord schal delyuere him in þe yuel dai.
2 The lord kepe him, & quykene him, & make him blesful in þe lond! & bitake[4] not him in-to þe wille of hise enemyes!
3 The lord bere help to him on þe bed of his sorewe! þou hast ofte turned al his bedstree[5] in his siknesse.
4 I seide: 'lord, haue þou merci on me! hele þou my soule, for y synnede aȝenes þee!'
5 Myn enemyes seiden yuelis to me: 'whanne schal he die, & his name schal perische?
6 'And if he entride for to se, he spak veyn þingis: his herte gaderide wickidnesse.
He ȝede wiþ-out forþ; and spak to þe same ende.'[6]
7 Alle myn enemyes bacbitiden pryueli aȝenes me; aȝenes me þei þouȝten yuelis to me.
8 Thei ordeyneden an yuel word aȝenes me: 'wheþer he þat slepiþ schal not ley to,[7] þat he rise aȝen.'
9 For whi, þe man of my pees, in whom y hopide, he þat ete my looues, made greet disseit[8] on me.

[1–1] Euge, Euge! [2] sollicitus est mei [3] 40 Vulgate. [4] tradat [5] universum stratum [6] et loquebatur [7] non adjiciet [8] supplantationem

V. *The Office for the Dead.*—2. *Dirige (Matins* 3rd *Nocturn).* 67

10 But þou, lord, haue merci on me, & reise me aȝen! & y schal ȝelde¹ to hem.
11 In þis y knewe þat [þou] woldest² me: for myn enemy schal not haue ioie on me.
12 Forsoþe þou hast take me up for innocense; & hast confermyd me in þi siȝt wiþ-outen ende.³
13 Blessid be þe lord god of israel, fro þe world, & in to þe world,⁴ be it don! be it don!
   Antem: Lord, hele þou my soule! for y haue synned to þee.

psalm [42⁵]: **Quemadmodum.**

1 As an hert de[siriþ]⁶ to þe wellis of watris, so þou, god, my soule desiriþ to þee.
2 Mi soule þirstide to god, þat is a quyk welle:⁷ whanne schal y come, & appere bifore þe face of my god?
3 Mi teeris weren looues⁸ to me, bi dai & nyȝt, while it is seid to me ech dai: 'where is þi god?'
4 I biþouȝte of þese þingis, & y schedde out⁹ in me my soule; for y schal passe in-to þe place of þis wondurful tabernacle, til to þe hous of god,
5 In þe vois of ful out-ioiyng and of knouleching, is þe sown of þe etere.¹⁰
6 Mi soule, whi art þou sorie? & whi disturblest þou me?
7 Hope þou in god, for ȝit y schal knouleche¹¹ to him; he is þe helþe of my chere, [8] & my god.
    Mi soule is disturblid at my silf; þerfor y schal be myndeful of him, fro þe lond of iordan, & fro þe litil hil of hermonyim.
9 Depþe clepiþ depþe, in þe vois of þi wyndowis.¹²
    Alle þin hiȝe þingis & þi wawis passiden ouer me.
10 The lord sente his merci in þe dai, & his song [bi] niȝt.¹³
    At me is a preier to þe god of my liyf; [11] y schal seie to god: þou art my taker-up.¹⁴
    Whi forȝitest þou me? and whi go y soreuful, while þe enemy turmentiþ me?
12 While my boones ben brokun to gidere, myn enemyes þat trublen me dispisiden me,

¹ retribuam   ² MS. þat woldest.   voluisti   ³ in aeternum   ⁴ saeculum
   ⁵ 41 Vulgate.   ⁶ desiderat   ⁷ ad Deum fortem vivum   ⁸ panes
⁹ effudi   ¹⁰ sonus epulantis   ¹¹ confitebor   ¹² cataractarum   ¹³ nocte
                         ¹⁴ susceptor

13 While þei seien to me bi alle daies : ' where is þi god? '
14 Mi soule, whi art þou sorie? & whi disturblist þou me?
15 Hope þou in god, for ȝit y schal knouleche¹ to him; he is þe
   helþe of my chere, & my god.
   Antem: Mi soule þirstide to god, þat is a quyk welle !² whanne
   schal y come & appere bifore þe face of þe lord?
   Vȝ Lord, graunte þou hem endeles reste;
   [Rȝ] And euerlastynge liȝt, liȝtne to hem!
   Pater noster: Oure fadir [&c.].

   leccio vijᵃ : **Spiritus meus.** [Job xvii. 1—3, 11—15.]

1 Mi spirit schal be maad feble³; my daies schulen be maad
   schort; & oneli þe sepulcre is left to me. [2] y haue not
   synned; and ȝit myn iȝe dwelliþ in bittirnessis. [3] lord,
   deliuere þou me, & sette þou me bisidis þee; and þe hond of
   whom euere þou wolt,⁴ fiȝte aȝenes me ! [11] Mi daies ben
   passid.⁵ my þouȝtis ben scaterid, turmentynge⁶ myn herte.
   [12] þei han turned þe niȝt in-to dai; and efte aftir derknessis, y hope liȝt.⁷ [13] if y susteyne, helle is myn hous ;
   & y haue araied⁸ my bed in derknessis. [14] I seide to
   rotenesse : ' þou art my fadir '; & to wormes, ' ȝe ben my
   modir & my sister '; [15] þerfore, where is now myn abid-
   ynge, & my pacience? my lord god, þou it ert !
   Rȝ þe drede of deeþ trubliþ me euery dai, þe while y synne &
   repente me not, for in helle is no redempcion. haue merci
   of me, god, & saue þou me !
   Vȝ God, in þi name make me saaf, & in þi vertu delyuere þou me !
   [Repeet] Ffor in helle is no redempcion, haue merci of me, god,
   & saue þou me !

   leccio viij : **pelli mee.** [Job xix. 20—27.]

20 Whanne my fleisch was wastid, my boon cleuyde to my
   skyn, & oneli lippis ben left aboute my teeþ. [21] haue
   ȝe merci on me, haue ȝe merci on me; nameli, ȝe my
   frendis ! for þe hond of þe lord haþ touchid me. [22] whi
   pursue ȝe me as god doiþ, & ben fillid wiþ my fleschis⁹ ?

---

¹ confitebor   ² fortem   ³ attenuabitur   ⁴ cujusvis manus
⁵ transierunt   ⁶ torquentes   ⁷ spero lucem   ⁸ stravi
⁹ et carnibus meis saturamini

[23] who mai graunte me þat my wordis be writun? who mai graunte me þat þei be writun in a bok, [24] wiþ an yrun poyntel, eþer[1] wiþ a plate of leed, eþer wiþ a chisel be grauun in a flynt? [25] ffor y wot þat myn aȝenbier lyueþ; & in þe laste dai y schal rise fro þe erþe, [26] & eft y schal be cumpassid wiþ my[2] skyn; & in my flesch y schal se god my saueour. [27] whom y my silf schal se, & myn iȝen schulen biholde, beynge[1] not anoþir: þis is myn hope, & kept in my bosum.

R̃ Lord, graunte þou hem endeles reste! & euerlastynge liȝt, liȝtne to hem!

Ṽ Lord, þat reisidist stynkynge laȝer fro his graue, graunte hem reste!

[Repeet] And euerlastynge liȝt, liȝtne to hem!

leccio ix[a]: [Job x. 18—22.]
Quare de vulua, & cetera.

18 Whi brouȝtest þou me forþ fro þe wombe? wolde god þat y hadde be wastid,[3] þat noon iȝe hadde seie me! [19] þanne had y be as þouȝ y hadde not be; fro þe wombe ybore to þe graue. [20] wheþer þe fewenesse of my daies schal not be endid in schort tyme? lord! suffre[4] þou me, þat y weile a litil while my sorewe, [21] or y wende hennes, þat y turne not aȝen,[5] to þe derk lond, & keuerid wiþ þe derknesse of deeþ; [22] þe lond of wrecchidnesse and of derknesse, where þe schadewe of deeþ, & noon ordre, but euerlasting [g]risnesse dwelliþ inne.[6]

R̃ Lord, delyuere þou me fro endeles deeþ, in þat dredful dai, whanne heuenes & erþe schulen be moued; whanne þou schalt come to deme þe world bi fier!

Ṽ Þilke dai is a dai of wraþþe, & of chalenge, & of wrecchidnesse; a greet dai, & a ful bitter, Whanne heuene & erþe schulen be moued.

[Ṽ] Þerfore what schal y þanne, most wrechidful, þenke? what schal y seie, or what schal y do, whanne y schal schewe forþ no goodnesse to-fore so greet a iuge, Whanne þou schalt come to deme þe world bi fier?

---

[1] et   [2] MS. my my   [3] consumptus   [4] dimitte ergo
[5] antiquam vadam, et non revertar   [6] horror inhabitat

V̷ Now, crist, we axen þee, we biseche þee, haue merci on vs! þou þat come to aȝenbie hem þat weren lost, nyle[1] þou dampne hem þat þou hast bouȝt,

Whanne þou schalt come to iuge þe world bi fier!

V̷ Brennynge soulis wepen wiþ-outen ende; þei wepen wiþ-outen ende, walkynge bi derknessis; and ech of hem seien, wo! wo! wo! hou greet ben þese derknessis!

[Whanne þou schalt come to iuge þe world bi fier!]

V̷ God, makere-of-nouȝt of alle creaturis, þat formedist me of þe erþe, and wondurliche wiþ þin owne blood hast bouȝt us, þouȝ my bodi rotte now, þou schalt make it rise out of þe sepulcre in þe dai of doom. heere þou me! here þou me! þat þou comaunde my soule to be put in þe bosum of abraham, þe patriark,

Whanne þou schalt come to iuge þe world bi fier!

R̷[2] Lord, delyuere þou me fro þe peynes of helle,—þou þat brak þe ȝatis of bras, & visitidist helle, and ȝaf liȝt to hem [þat] þei myȝten se, þat weren in peynes of derknessis,

[V̷] Criynge & seynge, 'oure aȝenbier! þou art come to vs; þou þat brak þe ȝatis of bras & visitidest helle, & ȝaf liȝt to hem þat þei myȝten se, þat weren in þe peynes of derknessis!'

IN LAUDIBUS.

psalm [51[3]]: **Misere[re] mei, deus, secundum.**

1 God, haue þou merci on me, bi[4] þi greet merci! And bi þe mychelnesse of þi merciful doyngis,[5] do þou awey my wickidnes!

2 More[6] wasche þou me fro my wickidnesse; & clense þou me fro my synne!

3 For y knouleche my wickidnesse; & my synne is euer aȝenes me.

4 I haue synned to þee aloon, & y haue don yuel bifore þee; þat þou be iustified in þi wordis, & ouercome whanne þou art demed.

5 For, lo, y was conseyued in wickidnessis; & my moder conseyued me in synnes.

---

[1] Be unwilling, *Noli*.   [2] MS. gives V̷   [3] 50 Vulgate.   [4] secundum
[5] miserationum   [6] Amplius

V. *The Office for the Dead.*—3. *Dirige (Lauds).*

6 For, lo, þou louedist treuþe; þou hast schewid to me vnserteyn þingis & pryue þingis of þi wisdom.

7 Lord, bi-sprynge þou¹ me wiþ isope, & y schal be clensid; wasche þou me, & y schal be maad whit more þan snow.

8 ȝyue þou ioie & gladnesse to myn heryng; & boones maad meke schulen ful out make ioie.²

9 Turne awey þi face fro my synnes, & do awey alle my wickidnessis!

10 God, make þou a clene herte in me; make þou newe³ a riȝtful spirit in myn entrailes!

11 Caste þou not me awey fro þi face; & take þou not me a-wey fro me þin holi spirit!

12 ȝyue þou to me þe gladnesse of ȝin helþe; & conferme þou me wiȝ þe principal⁴ spirit!

13 I schal teche wickid men þi weies; & vnfeiþful men schulen be conuertid to þee.

14 God, þe god of myn helþe! delyuere þou me fro bloodis; & my tunge schal ioiefulli synge þi riȝtfulnesse.

15 Lord, opene þou my lippis! & my mouþ schal telle þi preisyng.

16 For if þou haddist wolde sacrifice, y hadde ȝoue: treuli þou schalt not delite in brente sacrifices.

17 Sacrifice to god is a spirit trublid: god! þou schalt not dispise a contrit herte and meke.

18 Lord! do þou benyngneli in þi good wille to sion; þat þe wallis of ierusalem be bildid.

19 Than þou schalt take plesauntli þe⁵ sacrifice of riȝtfulnesse, offringis & brent sacrifices; þanne þei schulen putte calues on þin auter.

Antem: Boones maad meke, schulen glade to þe lord.

psalm [65⁶]: **Te decet ympnus.**

1 GOd! heriyng⁷ bicomeþ þee in sion; & a vow schal be ȝoldun to þee in ierusalem.⁸

2 Here þou my preier! ech man⁹ schal come to þee.

3 The wordis of wickid men hadden þe maistry¹⁰ ouer us; & þou schalt do merci to oure wickidnessis.

4 Blessid is he whom þou hast chose & hast take! he schal dwelle in þi forȝerdis.¹¹

---

¹ Asperges   ² exultabunt ossa humiliata   ³ innova   ⁴ principali
⁵ MS. þe þe   ⁶ 64 Vulgate.   ⁷ hymnus   ⁸ Jerusalem   ⁹ omnis caro
¹⁰ praevaluerunt   ¹¹ atriis

We schulen be fillid wiþ þe goodis of þin hous; þi temple is holi, [5] wondurful in equyte.

God oure helpe, here þou us! þou art hope of alle coostis[1] of erþe, & in þe see afer.

6 And þou makest-redi[2] hillis in þi vertu, and art gird wiþ power; [7] which[3] disturblist þe depþe of þe see, þe soun of þe wawis þer-of.

Folkis schulen be disturblid, [8] and þei þat dwellen in þe endis[4] schulen drede of þi signes; þou schalt delite þe outgoyngis of þe morntide & euentid.

9 Thou hast visitid þe lond, & hast gretli fillid[5] it; þou hast multiplied to make it riche.[6]

10 The flood[7] of god was fillid wiþ watris; þou makest redi þe mete of hem; for þe makyng redi þer-of is so.

11 Thou, fillynge greetli þe stremes þer-of, multiplie þe fruytis þer-of! þe lond bryngynge forþ fruytis, schal be glade in þe goteris[8] of it.

12 Thou schalt blesse þe coroun of þe ȝeer of þi good wille; & þi feldis schulen be fillid wiþ plente of fruytis.[9]

13 The faire þingis[10] of desert schulen wexe fatte; & litil hillis schulen be cumpassid with ful out-ioiyng.

14 The weþeris[11] of scheep ben cloþid, & valeis schulen be plenteuouse of whete; þei schulen crie, & soþeli þei schulen seie heriyng.[12]

Antem: Lord, here þou my preier! ech man schal come to þee.

psalm [63[13]]: **Deus, deus meus!**

1 GOd, my god! y wake to þee ful erli.[14]

2 Mi soule þirstide to þee; my flesch þirstide to þee ful many fold!

In a lond forsakun, wiþ-out weie, & wiþout watir, [3] so y apperide to þee in hooli,[15] þat y schulde se þi vertu & þi glorie.

4 For[16] þi merci is betere þan lyues, my lippis schulen herie þee.

5 So y schal blesse þee in my liyf; & in þi name y schal reise myn hondis.

6 Mi soule be fillid [wiþ] innere fatnesse & outermere fatnes[17]; & my mouþ schal herie wiþ lippis of fu[l] out-ioiyng.[18]

---

[1] finium [2] Praeparans [3] Qui [4] qui habitant terminos
[5] inebriasti [6] locupletare eam [7] Flumen [8] stillicidiis [9] ubertate
[10] speciosa [11] arietes [12] hymnum [13] 62 Vulgate. [14] de luce
[15] in sancto [16] Quoniam [17] adipe et pinguedine [18] labiis exultationis

V. *The Office for the Dead.*—3. *Dirige (Lauds).*

7 So y hadde mynde of þee on my bed; in moruntidis y schal þenke of þee; [8] for[1] þou were myn helpere;

And in þe keuering of þi wyngis y schal make ful out ioie. [9] my soule cleuede aftir þee; þi riȝt hond took me vp.

10 Forsoþe þei souȝten in veyn my liyf: þei schulen entre in-to þe lower þingis of erþe; [11] þei schulen be bitakun in-to þe hondis of swerd; þei schulen be maad þe partis of foxis.

12 But þe king schal be glad in god; & alle men schulen be preisid þat sweren in him, for þe mouþ of hem þat speken wickid þingis is stoppid.

[Ps. 67[2]: **Deus misereatur.**]

1 God, haue merci on us & blesse us! liȝtne he his chere on us, & haue merci on us!

2 That we knowe þi weie on erþe, þin helpe in alle folkis!

3 God, puplis knouleche to þee; alle puplis knouleche to þee.

4 Heþene men, be glade & make fulli ioie; for þou demest puplis in equyte, & dressist heþen men in erþe.

5 God, puplis knouleche to þee; alle puplis knouleche to þee; [6] þe erþe ȝaf his fruyt.

God, oure god, blesse us! [7] god blesse us; & alle þe coostis of erþe drede hym!

Antem: Lord, þi riȝt hond haþ take me vp.

psalm: **Ego dixi.** [Isaiah xxxviii. 10—20.]

10 I seide: in þe myddil of my daies y schal go to þe ȝatis of helle.

I souȝte þe residue of my ȝeeris. [11] y seide: y schal not se þe lord in þe lond of lyueris.

12 Mi generacioun is takun awey, & is foldid to-gidere fro me, as þe tabernacle of scheepherdis is foldid to-gidere.

Mi liyf is kit doun as of a webbe[3]: he kittide doun me, þe while y was wouun ȝit.[4]

Fro þe moruntid til to þe euentid þou schalt ende me. [13] as a lioun, so he altobrake[5] alle my bones:

Fro þe morntide til to þe euentid þou schalt ende me. [14] as þe brid of a swalewe, so y schal crie; y schal biþenke[6] as a culuer.

---

[1] Quia [2] 66 Vulgate. [3] texente [4] dum adhuc ordirer, succidit me
[5] contrivit [6] meditabor

V. The Office for the Dead.—3. Dirige (Lauds).

Myn iȝen, biholdynge an hiȝ, ben maad feble. lord! y suffre violence; answere þou for me! [15] what schal [I] seie,[1] eþer what schal answere to me, whanne he haþ do?

I schal biþenke[2] to þee alle my ȝeeris in þe bitternesse of my soule.

16 Lord! if me lyueþ so, & þe liyf of my spirit is in siche þingis, þou schalt chastise me & schalt quykene[3] me. [17] lo, my bitternesse is moost bitter in pees.

Forsoþe þou hast delyuerid my soule, þat it perischide not; þou hast caste awey, bihynde þi bak, alle my synnes.

18 For not helle schal knouleche[4] to þee; neþer deeþ schal herie þee: þei þat gon doun in to þe lake schulen not abide[5] þi treuþe.

19 A lyuynge man, a lyuynge, he schal knouleche[4] to þee, as &[6] y to dai: þe fadir schal make knowun þi treuþe to sones.

20 Lord, make þou me saf! & we schulen synge oure salmes in alle þe daies of oure liyf in þe hous of þe lord.

Antem: Ffrom þe ȝate of helle, Lord delyuere her soulis!

psalm [148]: **Laudate dominum de celis, & cetera.**

1 Ȝe of heuenes, herie þe lord! herie ȝe him in hiȝ þingis![7]
2 Alle hise aungelis, herie ȝe him! alle hise vertues, herie ȝe him!
3 Sunne & moone, herie ȝe him! alle sterris & liȝt, herie ȝe him!
4 Heuenes,[8] herie ȝe him! & þe watris þat ben aboue heuenes, [5] herie þe name of þe lord!

For he seide, & þingis weren maad; he comaundide, & þingis weren maad of nouȝt.[9]

6 He ordeynede þo þingis in-to þe world, & in to þe world of world,[10] he settide a comaundement, & it schal not passe.

7 Ȝe of erþe, herie þe lord! dragouns & alle depþis of watris[11];
8 Fier, hail, snow, iys; spiritis of tempestis þat don his word;
9 Mounteynes, and alle litle hillis; trees berynge fruyt, & alle cedris;
10 Wielde bestis, & alle tame bestis; serpentis, & feþerid briddis;
11 The kingis of erþe, & alle puplis; þe princis, & alle iugis of erþe;
12 Ȝonge men & virgyns, elde men wiþ ȝongere, herie þe name of þe lord! for þe name of him aloon is enhaunsid.

His knouleching[12] be on heuene & erþe! [13] & he haþ enhaunsid þe horn of his puple.

---

[1] Quid dicam [2] Recogitabo [3] corripies me, et vivificabis [4] confitebitur [5] expectabunt [6] sicut et [7] in excelsis [8] Coeli coelorum [9] et creata sunt [10] in aeternum, et in saeculum saeculi [11] abyssi [12] confessio ejus

An ympne be to alle hise seyntis; to þe children of israel; to a puple neiȝynge to hym!

[Ps. 149]: **Cantate domino.**

1 Synge ȝe to þe lord a newe songe! his heriyng be in þe chirche of seyntis!
2 Israel, be glade in him þat made him! & þe douȝtris of sion, make ful out ioie[1] in her kyng!
3 Herie þei his name in a queer![2] seie þei salm to him in a tympan and sautre!
4 For þe lord is wel plesid in his puple; & he haþ reisid mylde men in-to helpe.[3]
5 Seyntis schulen make ful out-ioie in glorie; þei schulen be glade in her beddis.
6 The ful out-ioiyngis of god in þe þrote of hem, & swerdis scharpe in ech side in þe hondis of hem, [7] to do vengeaunce in naciouns, blamyngis in puplis;
8 To bynde þe kyngis of hem in stockis, & þe noble men of hem in irun manyclis;
9 That þei make in hem doom writun: þis is glorie to alle hise seyntis.

[Ps. 150: **Laudate dominum.**]

1 Herie ȝe þe lord in hise seyntis! herie ȝe him in þe firmament of his vertu!
2 Herie ȝe him in hise vertues! herie ȝe him bi[4] þe multitude of his[5] gretnesse!
3 Herie ȝe him in þe sown of trumpe! herie ȝe him in sautre & harpe![6]
4 Herie ȝe him in tympan & queer! herie ȝe him in stryngis & orgun!
5 Herie ȝe him in cymbalis sownynge wel! herie ȝe him in cymbalis of iubilacioun! [6] ech spirit, herie þe lord!

Antem: Ech spirit herie þe lord!
V⁊ Endeles reste, ȝyue hem, lord!
[℞] And euerlastynge liȝt, liȝtne to hem!

psalm: **Benedictus dominus deus israel!** [Luke i. 68—79.]

68 Blessid be þe lord god of israel! for he haþ visitid & maad redempcion of his puple;

[1] exultent   [2] choro   [3] salutem   [4] secundum   [5] MS. of his of his
[6] cithara

69 And he haþ rerid to us an horun of helþe, in þe hous of dauiþ his child:
70 As he spak bi þe mouþ of hise hooli profetis, þat weren fro þe world¹;
71 Heelþe² fró oure enemyes, & fro þe hond of alle men þat hatiden us:
72 T[o] do³ merci wiþ oure fadris, & to haue mynde of his holi testament;
73 In þe greet ooþ⁴ þat he swore to abraham oure fadir, to ȝyue him silf to vs,
74 That we wiþ-outen drede, delyuerid fro þe hond of oure enemyes, serue⁵ to him,
75 In holynesse & riȝtwisnesse bifore him, in alle oure daies.
76 And þou, child, schalt be clepid þe profete of þe hiȝest; for þou schalt go bifore þe face of þe lord, to make redi hise weies;
77 To ȝyue science of helþe⁶ to his puple, in-to remyssioun of her synnes.
78 Bi þe inwardnesse⁷ of þe mercy of oure god, in þe which he, sprynginge vp fro an hiȝ, haþ visitid us;
79 To ȝyue liȝt to hem þat sitten in derknessis & in schadewe of deeþ; to dresse oure feet in-to þe weie of pees.

Antem: I am aȝenrisyng & liyf; he þat bileueþ in me, þouȝ he be deed, he schal lyue; & euery man þat lyueþ & bileueþ in me, schal not die wiþ-outen ende.

Lord, haue merci on vs!
Crist, haue merci on vs!
Lord, haue merci on us!
Pater noster. Oure fadir [&c.].

psalm [30⁸]: **Exaltabo⁹ te, domine!**

1 Lord, y schal enhaunse þee; for þou hast up-take¹⁰ me; & þou delitidist not myn enemyes on me.¹¹
2 Mi lord god! y criede to þee; & þou madist me hool.
3 Lord, þou leddist out my soule fro helle; þou sauedist me fro hem þat gon doun in-to þe lake.
4 Ȝe seyntis of þe lord, synge¹² to þe lord; & knouleche ȝe to þe mynde¹³ of his holynesse.

¹ a saeculo ² salutem ³ ad faciendam ⁴ Jusjurandum
⁵ serviamus ⁶ scientiam salutis ⁷ viscera ⁸ 29 Vulgate.
⁹ MS. Exultabo ¹⁰ suscepisti ¹¹ super me
¹² Psallite ¹³ memoriae

V. *The Office for the Dead.*—3. *Dirige (Lauds).*

5 For ire is in his indignacioun; & liyf is in his wille.
  Weping schal dwelle¹ at euentid; & gladnesse at þe moruntide.
6 Forsoþe, y seide in my plente: 'y schal not be moued wiþ-outen ende.'²
  Lord, in þi wille þou hast ȝoue vertu [to] my fairnesse.
7 Thou turnedist awey þi face fro me, & y am maad disturblid.
8 Lord, y schal crie to þee; & y schal preie to my god.
9 What profit³ is in my blood, while y go doun in-to corrupcioun?
10 Wher⁴ dust schal knouleche to þee; eþer schal telle þi treuþe?
11 The lord herde, & hadde merci on me; þe lorde is maad myn helper.
12 Thou hast turned my weilyng in-to ioie to me; þou hast to-rent my sak, & hast cumpassid me wiþ gladnesse.
13 That my glorie synge to þee, & y be not compunct.⁵ my lord god! y schal knouleche⁶ to þee wiþ-outen ende.

[V⁊] **Requiem eternam**: Endeles reste, ȝyue hem, lord,
[R⁊] And euerlastinge liȝt, liȝtne to hem!
[V⁊] From þe ȝate of helle,
[R⁊] Lord, delyuere her soulis!
[V⁊] I bileue to se þe goodis of þe lord
[R⁊] in þe lond of lyuynge men.
[V⁊] Lord, here þou my preier,
[R⁊] & my cry come to þee!

Orisoun: Inclina, domine, aurem tuam!

Lord, bowe þou þin eere to oure preieris, wiþ whiche we bisechen lowliche þi merci, þat þou sette þe soulis of þi seruauntis,—boþe of men & wymmen þat þou hast comaundid to passe out of þis world,—in þe cuntre of pees & of liȝt; & comaunde þat þei be felowis of þin halewene, bi crist oure lord! amen!

ffor fadir & modir: deus, qui patrem & matrem.

God, þat hast comaundid [us] to worschipe fadir & modir, haue merci of þe soulis of my fadir & of my modir, & forȝyue hem alle her synnes, & make vs to lyue wiþ hem in þe blis with-outen ende. amen!

---

¹ demorabitur ² in aeternum ³ utilitas ⁴ Numquid
⁵ non compungar ⁶ confitebor

ffor a cors present: deus, cui proprium.

God, to whom it is proprid to haue merci & to spare euer more, loweliche we biseche þee þat þe soule of þi seruaunt which þou hast comaundid to-dai to passe out of þis world, be not take in-to þe hondis of oure enemy; ne forȝite it not in-to þe ende, but comaunde it to be takun vp of holi aungels, & to be lad in-to þe cuntre of liyf; so, for þat he hopide & bileuede in þee, late him disserue to be euer glad in þe cumpony of þin halewene. amen!

ffor a soule in mynde dai: Deus indulgenciarum.

Lord god of forȝyuenesse, graunte þou to þe soule of þi seruaunt, who[s] ȝeris mynde we make to-dai, a secte of refresching, blisse of reste, and cle[r]nesse of liȝt. amen!

here endiþ dirige.

VI. *Commendations.*

AND HERE BEGYNNEN COMENDACIONS.

[p*salm* 119[1]]: **Beati immaculati!**

1. Blessid ben men in þe weie wiþ-outen wem,[2] þat gon[3] in þe lawe of þe lord.
2. Blessid ben þei þat seken hise witnessyngis, seken hym in al herte!
3. For þei þat worchen wickidnesse, ȝeden not in hise weies.
4. Thou hast comaundid, þat þin heestis be kept gretli.[4]
5. I wolde þat my weies be dressid[5] to kepe þi iustifiyngis!
6. Thanne y schal not be schent, whanne y schal biholde parfitli[6] in alle þin heestis.
7. I schal knouleche to þee in þe dressyng[7] of herte, in þat þat[8] y lernede þe domes of þi riȝtfulnesse.
8. I schal kepe þi iustifiyngis; forsake þou not me in ech side!

p*salm*: **In quo corigit.**

9. In what þing amendiþ a ȝonge wexinge[9] man his weie? in kepynge þi wordis.
10. In al myn herte y souȝte þee; pute þou not me awey fro þin hestis!
11. In myn herte y hidde þi spechis, þat y do not synne aȝenes þee.
12. Lord, þou art blessid! teche þou me þi iustifiyngis!
13. In my lippis y haue pronounsid alle þe domes of þi mouþ.
14. I delitide in þe weie of þi witnessyngis, as in alle richessis.
15. I schal be occupied in þin hestis, & y schal biholde[10] þi weies.
16. I schal biþenke[11] in þi iustifiyngis; y schal not forȝite þi wordis.

[p*salm*: **Retribue seruo tuo.**]

17. Ȝelde[12] to þi seruaunt! quykene þou me! & y schal kepe þi wordis.
18. Liȝtne þou myn iȝen; & y schal biholde meruelis of þi lawe.
19. I am a comelyng[13] in erþe; hide þou not þin hestis fro me!
20. Mi soule couertide[14] to[15] desire þi iustifiyngis, in al tyme.
21. Thou blamedist þe proude; þei ben cursid þat bowen a-wey[16] fro þin hestis.

[1] 118 Vulgate.   [2] immaculati in via   [3] ambulant   [4] nimis
[5] dirigantur   [6] perspexero   [7] Confitebor tibi in directione   [8] quod
[9] adolescentior   [10] considerabo   [11] meditabor   [12] Retribue
[13] incola   [14] concupivit   [15] MS. to to   [16] declinant

VI. Commendations.

22 Do þou awey fro me schenschip¹ & dispisyng, for y souȝte þi witnessyngis.
23 For whi, princes saten & spaken aȝenes me; but þi seruaunt was occupied in þi iustifiyngis.
24 For whi, & þi witnessyngis is my þenking²; & my counsel is þi iustifiyngis.

psalm: **Adhesit pauimento anima mea.**

25 Mi soule cleuyde to þe pawment: quykene þou me, bi³ þi word!
26 I telde out⁴ my weies, & þou herdist me; teche þou me þi iustifiyngis!
27 Lerne þou me þe weie of þi iustifiyngis; and y schal be occupied in þi meruelis.
28 Mi soule nappide for anoie⁵: conferme þou me in þi wordis!
29 Remoue þou fro me þe weie of wickidnesse; & in þi lawe haue þou merci on me!
30 I chees þe weie of treuþe; y forȝate not þi domes.
31 Lord, y cleuyde to þi witnessyngis; nyle þou⁶ schende me!
32 I ran þe weie of þi comaundementis, whanne þou alargidist myn herte.

psalm: **Legem pone michi, domine.**

33 Lord, sette þou to me a lawe in þe weie of þi iustifyingis; & y schal seke it euere.
34 Ȝyue þou vndurstonding to me, & y schal seke þi lawe; & y schal kepe it in al myn herte.
35 Lede me forþ in þe paþ of þin hestis; for y wolde it.
36 Bowe doun⁷ myn herte in-to þi witnessyngis, & not in-to auarice.
37 Turne þou awey myn iȝen, þat þo sen not vanyte; quykene þou me in þi weie!
38 Ordeyne þi speche to þi seruaunt in þi drede.
39 Kitte a-wey my schenschip which y supposide; for þi domes ben myrie.⁸
40 Lo, y coueitide þi comaundementis; quykene þou me in þin equite!

---

¹ opprobrium   ² meditatio   ³ secundum   ⁴ enuntiavi
⁵ Dormitavit... prae taedio   ⁶ noli   ⁷ Inclina
⁸ Amputa opprobrium meum, quod suspicatus sum; quia judicia tua jucunda.

VI. *Commendations.*

Et ueniat super me.

41 And, lord, þi merci come on me! þin heelþe come, bi[1] þi speche!

42 And y schal answere a word to men seiynge schenschipe[2] to me; for y hopide in þi wordis.

43 And take þou not a-wey fro my mouþ þe word of treuþe outerli, for y hopide aboue[3] in þi domes.

44 And y schal kepe þi lawe euere, in-to þe world, & in-to þe world of world.

45 And y ȝede in largenesse[4]; for y souȝte þi comaundementis.

46 And y spak of þi witnessyngis in þe siȝt of kingis; & y was not schent.

47 And y biþouȝte[5] in þin heestis, whiche y louede.

48 And y reiside myn hondis to þi comaundementis, whiche y louede; & y schal be excercisid in þi iustifiyngis.

psalm: Memor esto verbi tui.

49 Lord, haue þou mynde on þi word to þi seruaunt, in which word þou hast ȝoue hope to me.

50 This confortide me in my lownesse,[6] for þi word quykenyde me.

51 Proude men diden wickidli bi alle þingis; but y bowide not awey[7] fro þi lawe.

52 Lord, y was myndeful on þi domes, fro þe world[8]; & y was confortid.

53 Failyng[9] helde me, for synneris forsakinge þi lawe.

54 Thi iustifiyngis weren delitable to me to be sungun,[10] in the place of my pilgrymage.

55 Lord, y hadde mynde on þi name bi nyȝt, & y kepte þi lawe.

56 This þing was maad to me, for y souȝte þi iustifiyngis.

Porcio mea domine.

57 Lord, my part, y seide, to ke[pe][11] þi lawe.

58 I bisouȝte þi face in al myn herte; haue þou merci on me bi þi speche[12]!

59 I biþouȝte[13] my weies, & y turnyde my feet in-to þi witnessyngis.

60 I am redi, & y am not disturblid, to kepe[14] þi comaundementis.

---

[1] secundum [2] exprobrantibus [3] supersperavi
[4] ambulabam in latitudine [5] meditabar [6] humilitate [7] declinavi
[8] a saeculo [9] Defectio [10] cantabiles [11] custodire
[12] secundum eloquium tuum [13] Cogitavi [14] ut custodiam

VI. Commendations.

61 The cordis of synneris han biclippid me; & y haue not forʒite þi lawe.
62 At mydniʒt y roos to knouleche to þee, on þe domes of þi iustifiyngis.
63 I am parcener of alle þat dreden þee, and kepen þin hestis.
64 Lord, þe erþe is ful of þi merci; teche þou me þi iustifiyngis.

Bonitatem fecisti cum.

65 Lord, þou hast do goodnesse wiþ þi seruaunt, bi[1] þi word.
66 Teche þou me goodnesse & lore, eþer chastysyng and kunnyng[2]; for y bileuyde to þin hestis.
67 Bifore þat [y][3] was maad meke, y trespasside; þerfor y kepte þi speche.
68 Thou art good; & in þi goodnesse teche þou me þi iustifiyngis!
69 The wickidnesse of hem þat ben proude is multiplied on me; but in al myn herte y schal seke þin hestis.
70 The herte of hem is cruddid as mylk; but y biþouʒte[4] þi lawe.
71 It is good to me þat þou hast maad me meke, þat y lerne þi iustifiyngis.
72 The lawe of þi mouþ is betere to me, þan þousyndis of gold & of siluer.

Manus tue fecerunt.

73 Thyne hondis maden me & formeden me; ʒyue þou vndurstonding to me, þat y lerne[5] þin hestis.
74 Thei þat dreden þee, schulen se me, & schulen be glad; for y hopide more[6] on þi wordis.
75 Lord, y knewe þat þi domes ben equyte; & in þi treuþe þou hast maad me meke.
76 Thi merci be maad þat it saue[7] me, bi[8] þi speche to þi seruaunt.
77 Thi merciful doyngis come to me, & y schal lyue; for þi lawe is my þenkyng.[9]
78 Thei þat ben proude be schent, for vniustli þei diden wickidnesse aʒenes me; but y schal be occupied in þin hestis.
79 Thei þat dreden þee, be turned to me, & þei þat knowen þi witnessyngis.
80 Myn herte be maad vnwemmed in þi iustifiyngis, þat y be not schent.

---

[1] secundum [2] Bonitatem, et disciplinam, et scientiam [3] ego
[4] meditatus sum [5] et discam [6] superspernvi [7] consoletur
[8] secundum [9] meditatio

VI. Commendations.

psalm: Defecit salutare tuum.

81 Mi soule failide in-to þin helþe[1]; & y hopide more on þi word.
82 Myn iȝen failide in-to speche, seiynge, ' whanne schalt þou conforte me?
83 For y am maad as a bowge[2] in frost; & y haue not forȝite þi iustifiyngis.'
84 Hou many ben þe daies of þi seruaunt? whanne schalt þou make doom of hem þat pursuen me?
85 Wickid men telden to me iangelyngis[3]; but not as þi lawe.
86 Alle þi comaundementis ben treuþe. wickid men han pursued me; helpe þou me!
87 Almest þei endiden me in erþe; but y forsook not þi comaundementis.
88 Bi þi merci, quykene þou me; & y schal kepe þe witnessyngis of þi mouþ.

In eternum, domine, verbum tuum.

89 Lord! þi word dwelliþ in heuene wiþ-outen ende.
90 Thi treuþe dwelliþ in generacioun & in-to generacioun: þou hast foundid þe erþe, & it dwelliþ.
91 The dai lasteþ contynueli bi þin ordenaunce, for alle þingis seruen to þee.
92 No but þat[4] þi lawe was my þenking; þanne perauenture y hadde perischid in my lowenesse.[5]
93 Wiþ-outen ende y schal not forȝite þi iustifiyngis, for in þo þou hast quykened me.
94 I am þin; make þou me saaf; for y haue souȝt þi iustifiyngis.
95 Synneris aboden me for to lese[6] me: y vndurstood þi witnessyngis.
96 I siȝ þe ende of al ende[7]: þi comaundement is ful large.

Quomodo dilexi legem tuam!

97 Lord! hou louede y þi lawe! al dai it is my þenkyng.
98 Aboue myn enemyes, þou madist me prudent bi þi comaundement; for it is to me wiþ-outen ende.
99 I vndurstood aboue alle men techinge me; for þi witnessyngis is my þenking.
100 I vndurstood aboue elde men; for y souȝte þi comaundementis.

---

[1] Defecit in salutare tuum [2] uter [3] fabulationes
[4] Nisi quod [5] humilitate [6] expectaverunt ... ut perderent
[7] Omnis consummationis

101 I forbede my feet fro al yuel weie; þat y kepe þi wordis.
102 I bowide¹ not fro þi domes; for þou hast set lawe to me.
103 Thi spechis ben ful swete² to my chekis; aboue hony to my mouþ.
104 I vndurstood of³ þin hestis; þerfor y hatide al þe weie of wickidnesse.

Lucerna pedibus.

105 Thi word is a lanterne to my feet, & liȝt to my paþþis.
106 I swoor, & purposide stidefastli,⁴ to kepe þe domes of þi riȝtfulnesse.
107 I am maad low bi alle þingis, lord; quykene þou me bi þi word!
108 Lord, make þou wel plesynge þe wilful þingis⁵ of my mouþ; & teche þou me þi domes!
109 Mi soule is euere in myn hondis; & y forȝate not þi lawe.
110 Synneris settiden a snare to me; & y erride not fro þi comaundementis.
111 I purchaside þi witnessyngis bi eritage wiþouten ende⁶; for þo ben þe ful ioiynge of myn herte.
112 I bowide myn herte to do þi iustifiyngis, wiþ-outen ende, for ȝeldinɡ.⁷

Iniquos odio habui.

113 I hatide wickid men; & y louede þi lawe.
114 Thou art myn helpere & my taker up; & y hopide more⁸ on þi word.
115 Ȝe wickid men, bowe awey⁹ fro me; & y schal seke þe comaundementis of my god.
116 Uptake þou me bi¹⁰ þi word, & y schal lyue; & schende þou not me fro myn abiding.¹¹
117 Helpe þou me, & y schal be saaf; & y schal biþenke¹² euere in þi iustifiyngis.
118 Thou hast forsake¹³ alle men goynge awey fro þi domes; for þe þouȝt of hem is vniust.
119 I arettide alle þe synneris of erþe brekeris of lawe¹⁴; þerfor y louede þi witnessingis.
120 Naile¹⁵ þou my fleischis wiþ þi drede; for y dredde of þi domes.

¹ declinavi ² Quam dulcia... ³ a ⁴ statui ⁵ Voluntaria
⁶ in aeternum ⁷ propter retributionem ⁸ supersperavi ⁹ declinate
¹⁰ secundum ¹¹ ab expectatione mea ¹² meditabor ¹³ Sprevisti
¹⁴ Praevaricantes reputavi... ¹⁵ Confige

VI. *Commendations.*

ffeci iudicium.

121 I dide doom & ri3tfulnesse: bitake þou not me to hem þat falseli calengen[1] me!

122 Take vp þi seruaunt in[2] to goodnesse; þei þat ben proude, calenge[3] not me!

123 Myn i3e[n][4] failiden in-to þin helþe, & in-to þe speche of þi ri3tfulnesse.

124 Do þou wiþ þi seruaunt bi[5] þi merci; & teche þou me þi iustifiyngis!

125 I am þi seruaunt; 3yue þou vndurstondinge to me, þat y kunne þi witnessyngis.

126 Lord! it is tyme to do: þei han distried þi lawe.

127 Therfor y louede þi comaundementis, more þan gold & topasion.

128 Therfor y was dressid[6] to alle þin heestis; y hatide al wickid weye.

Mirabilia testimonia tua, domine!

129 Lord, þi witnessyngis ben wondurful! þerfor my soule sou3te þo.

130 Declaryng of þi lawe li3tneþ, & 3yueþ vndurstonding to meke men.[7]

131 I openyde my mouþ, & drowe[8] þe spirit, for y desiride þi comaundementis.

132 Biholde þou on me, & haue merci on me, bi[9] þe doom of hem þat louen þi name.

133 Dresse[10] þou my goyngis bi[9] þi speche, þat al vnri3tfulnesse haue not lordschip on me.

134 A3enbie þou me fro þe false calengis[11] of men, þat y kepe þin hestis.

135 Li3tne þi face on þi seruaunt; & teche þou me þi iustifiyngis!

136 Myn i3en ledden forþ þe outgoyngis[12] of watris; for þei kepten not þi lawe.

Iustus es, domine!

137 Lord, þou art iust, & þi doom is ri3tful!

138 Thou hast comaundid ri3tfulnesse, þi witnessyngis; & þi treuþe gretli to be kept.[13]

---

[1] calumniantibus   [2] MS. in in   [3] calumnientur   [4] Oculi mei
[5] secundum   [6] dirigebar   [7] parvulis   [8] attraxi   [9] secundum
[10] dirige   [11] a calumniis   [12] Exitus ... deduxerunt
[13] veritatem tuam nimis

139 Thi feruent loue¹ made me to be meltid; for myn enemyes forʒaten þi wordis.
140 Thi speche is gre[t]li set a fier²; & þi seruaunt louede it.
141 I am ʒonge &. dispisid; y forʒat not þi iustifiyngis.
142 Lord, þi riʒtfulnesse is riʒtfulnesse wiþ-outen ende; & þi lawe is treuþe !
143 Tribulacion & aunguysche founden me; þin hestis is my þenkyng.³
144 Thi witnessyngis is equyte wiþ-outen ende⁴ : ʒyue þou vndurstonding to me, & y schal lyue.

Clamaui in toto corde.

145 I criede in al myn herte, 'lord, here þou me !' y schal seke þi iustifiyngis.
146 I criede to þee, 'make þou me saaf, þat y kepe þi comaundementis !
147 I bifore cam⁵ in ripenesse, & y criede; y hopide aboue⁶ on þi wordis.
148 Myn iʒen bifore camen to þee ful eerli, þat y schulde biþenke⁷ þi spechis.
149 Lord, here þou my vois, bi⁸ þi merci; & quykene þou me bi⁸ þi doom !
150 Thei þat pursuen,⁹ neiʒeden to wickidnesse : forsoþe þei ben maad fer fro þi lawe.
151 Lord ! þou art nyʒ; & alle þi weies ben treuþe.
152 In þe bigynnyng y knewe of þi witnessyngis; for þou hast foundid þo wiþ-outen ende.¹⁰

psalm: Vide humilitatem.

153 Se þou my mekenesse, and delyuere þou me; for y forʒate not þi lawe.
154 Deme þou my doom, and aʒenbie þou me; quykene þou me for¹¹ þi speche !
155 Helpe is fer fro synneris; for þei souʒten not þi iustifiyngis.
156 Lord, [þi] mercies¹² ben manye; quykene þou me bi⁸ þi doom.
157 Thei ben many þat pursuen me, & don tribulacioun to me : y bowide¹³ not awey fro þi witnessyngis.

---

¹ zelus meus ² Ignitum ... vehementer ³ meditatio ⁴ in aeternum
⁵ Praeveni ⁶ quia ... supersperavi ⁷ meditarer ⁸ secundum
⁹ persequentes me ¹⁰ in aeternum ¹¹ propter ¹² Misericordiae tuae
¹³ declinavi

VI. Commendations.

158 I siȝ brekers of þe lawe, & y was meltid, for þei kepten not þi spechis.
159 Lord, se þou for[1] y louede þi comaundementis; quykene þou me in þi merci!
160 The bigynnynge of þi wordis is treuþe; alle þe domes of þi riȝtfulnesse ben wiþ-outen ende.

psalm: Principes persecuti me.

161 Princis pursueden me wiþ-outen cause[2]; & myn herte dredde of þi wordis.
162 I schal be glade on þi spechis, as he þat fyndiþ many spuylis.[3]
163 I hatide & wlatide[4] wickidnesse; forsoþe[5] y louede þi lawe.
164 I seide heriyngis to þee seuene siþis in þe dai, on þe domes of þi riȝtfulnesse.
165 Miche pees is to hem þat louen þi lawe; & no sclaundre[6] is to hem.
166 Lord, y abode þin helþe[7]; & y louede þin hestis.
167 Mi soule kepte þi witnessyngis; & y louede þo gretli.[8]
168 I kepte þi comaundementis & þi witnessyngis; for alle my weies ben in þi siȝt.

Intret[9] deprecacio.

169 Lord, my bisechyng come nyȝ in þi siȝt! bi[10] þi speche, ȝyue þou vndurstondyng to me!
170 Myn axyng entre in þi siȝt! bi[11] þi speche, delyuere þou me!
171 Mi lipis schulen telle out[12] an ympne, whanne þou hast tauȝt me þi iustifiyngis.
172 Mi tunge schal pronounce þi speche; for whi,[13] alle þi comaundementis ben equyte.
173 Thyn hon[d][14] be maad þat it saue me; for y haue chose þin hestis.
174 Lord, y coueitide þin heelþe; & þi lawe is my þenking.
175 Mi soule schal lyue, & schal herie þee; & þi domes schulen helpe me.
176 I erride as a schep þat perischide: lord, seke þi seruaunt! for y forȝate not þi comaundementis.

[1] quoniam [2] persecuti sunt me gratis [3] spolia
[4] odio habui, et abominatus sum [5] autem [6] scandalum
[7] Expectabam salutare tuum [8] vehementer [9] Appropinquet [10] juxta
[11] secundum [12] Eructabunt [13] quia [14] manus tua

VI. Commendations.

[V̸] Endeles [reste] ȝyue hem, lord;
[R̸] And euerlastynge liȝt, liȝtne to hem!
Lord, haue merci of us!
Crist, haue merci of us!
lord, haue merci of us!
Pater noster: Oure fadir [&c.].

psalm [139¹]: Domine, probasti me.

1 Lord! þou hast proued me, & hast knowe me; þou hast knowe my sittyng & my risyng aȝen.
Thou hast vndurstonde my þouȝtis fro fer; [2] þou hast enquerid my paþ & my coord.²
And þou hast bifor seien³ alle my weies; [3] for no word is in my tunge.
Lo, lord, þou hast knowe alle þingis; [4] þe laste þingis & elde. þou hast formed me, & hast set þin hond on me.
5 Thi kunnyng is maad wondurful of me; it is confortid, & y schal not mowe⁴ to it.
6 Whidur schal y go fro þi spirit? & whidur schal y flee fro þi face?
7 If y schal stie to heuene, þou art þere; if y schal go doun to helle, þou art present.
8 If y schal take my feþeris ful eerli, & schal dwelle in þe laste partis⁵ of þe see,
9 And soþeli⁶ þidur þin hond schal lede me forþ, & þi riȝt hond schal holde me.
10 And y seide, 'in hap,⁷ derknessis schulen defoule⁸ me; & þe nyȝt is my liȝtnyng in my delicis.
11 For whi, derknessis schulen not be maad derk fro þee; & þe nyȝt schal be liȝtned as þe. dai; as þe derknessis þer-of, so & þe liȝt þer[of].⁹
12 For þou haddest in possessioun my reynes; þou tokest me vp fro þe wombe of my modir.
13 I schal knouleche to þee; for þou art magnefied dredfuli¹⁰: þi werkis ben wondurful; & my soule schal knowe ful myche.
14 Mi boon, which þou madist in pryuyte, is not hid fro þee; & my substaunce in þe lower parties of erþe.

---

¹ 138 Vulgate. ² funiculum ³ praevidisti ⁴ non potero
⁵ in extremis ⁶ etenim ⁷ Forsitan ⁸ conculcabunt
⁹ ita et lumen ejus ¹⁰ terribiliter

VI. Commendations.

15 Myn iȝen siȝen myn vnparfit þing[1]; & alle men schulen be writun in þi book, [16] þat is in þi kunnyng. daies schulen be formed; & no man is in þo.

17 Forsoþe, god, þi frendis ben mad honourable ful myche to me; þe princehede of hem is confortid ful myche.

18 I schal noumbre hem, & þei schulen be multiplied aboue grauel.[2] y roos up, & ȝit y am wiþ þee.

19 For[3] þou, god, schalt sle synneris: ȝe manquelleris, bowe awey[4] fro me!

20 For þei seien in þouȝt, 'take þei her citees in vanyte.'

21 Lord! where y hatide not hem[5] þat haten þee? & y failide—þat is, mornede gretli[6]—on þi enemyes.

22 Bi parfit hatrede, y hatide hem; þei weren maad enemyes to me.

23 God, preue þou me, & knowe þou myn herte! axe þou me, & knowe þou my paþþis!

24 And se þou if þe weie of wickidnesse is in me; & lede þou me forþ in euerlastynge liyf!

V7 Endeles reste, ȝyue hem, lord;

[R7] And euerlastynge liȝt, liȝtne to hem!

[V7] From þe ȝate of helle,

[R7] Lord, delyuere her soulis!

[V7] I bileue to see þe goodis of þe lord,

[R7] In þe lond of lyuynge men.

[V7] Reste þei in pees!

[R7] Amen!

Orisoun: **Tibi, domine, comendamus.**

Lord! to þee we bitaken þe soul[is] of þi seruauntis, boþe men & wymmen; so þei þat ben deed to þe world, mowen lyue to þee. & alle þe synnes þat þei han don bi freelte of worldli lyuynge, þou, lord, waische hem awey, bi þe forȝyuenesse of þi moost merciful pitee, bi crist oure lord. amen!

Here enden comendaciouns [and the Mediæval Prayer-book proper].

---

[1] Imperfectum meum   [2] arenam   [3] Si   [4] declinate   [5] nonne qui oderunt
[6] et ... tabescebam

[*For No.* 109, *Original Series, E. E. T. Soc., The Prymer, Part II.*]

A FEW NOTES ON THE PRYMER.

BY H. LITTLEHALES.

(*Reprinted from* "*The Tablet,*" *August* 22, 1896.)

THE following article attempts to add one or two notes to those texts and volumes already published on the subject of the Prymer, or Prayer-book of the lay people before the Reformation. This Prayer-book contains the Hours of the Blessed Virgin, the Seven Penitential Psalms, the Fifteen Gradual Psalms, the Litany, the Office for the Dead and Commendations. To these indispensable devotions others of varying nature were often appended.

A Certain Misconception Respecting the Contents of the Prymer.—In searching the ordinary dictionary for an explanation of the term "Prymer" we shall probably find either no mention of the book at all or, if dealt with, it will sometimes be described as containing, in addition to its actual contents, the Pater Noster, Ave Maria, Creed and Ten Commandments. Now the Prymer—I am referring to manuscript copies alone—rarely contained the Pater Noster or Hail Mary as separate devotions; still more rarely did it contain the Creed in any form, and, perhaps, in no case the Ten Commandments (we are excepting the printed versions), a fact which may easily be verified by an examination of any catalogue of these manuscripts or the books themselves.

The Office for the Dead Distinct from the Burial Service.—In a valuable catalogue of manuscripts recently issued, we find the Office for the Dead invariably described as the "Burial Service," a mistake which occurs, I think, throughout. Both the Office for the Dead, as well as that for Burial will be found in the common mediæval service book known as the Manual (or Book of Services for baptism, wedding, burial, &c.). Certain devotions are common both to the

Office for the Dead and that for Burial, but the greater part of each varies very distinctly from the other. The Office for the Dead may be said in the absence of any corpse, but the Burial Office, as its name implies, is for one certain purpose alone. Both Offices have been published in the invaluable *York Manual*, issued by the Surtees Society, and may there be readily compared.

A Prymer Lost on Tower Hill.—The first volume of Mr. Gairdner's edition of the *Paston Letters* contains the following passage in a letter written from London in 1451: "Sir T. T. lost hes primer at the Tour Hill and sent his man to seche (look for) it, and a good felaw wyshed hit in Norfolk so he wold fetch hit there." (*Paston Letters*, January 2, 1451.)

A Reference to the Use of the Prymer.—The following extract is from the will made in 1466 by Robert Gregory, citizen and mercer of London. He bequeaths certain property to his son John: "And all' so my best prymer' to sey his seruice thereon." (Somerset House Wills, Godyn, lf. 117.)

Parish Churches Possessed Prymers amongst their Service Books before the Reformation.—In one of the volumes on the Prymer not long since published, it was pointed out that amongst the service books possessed by a certain parish church in Canterbury were two Prymers, the inventory in which the items occur having been drawn up some years before the Reformation.

We know, now, by the following valuable extract, for which we are indebted to the kindness of Dr. Furnivall, that the case of the Kentish church is not unique; and this being so, we have good reason for believing that parish churches, before the Reformation, frequently contained one or more copies of the Prymer. Our extract, taken from the Inventory of the property of an Essex church, and made in the autumn of the year 1297, on the occasion of a visitation of the church, is as follows: "Erdele (Ardley, Yerdley) Item vnum primarium cum septem psalmis, et XV., et Placebo et Dirige." (Camden Society's *Visitations of Churches belonging to St. Paul's Cathedral*, pp. 49, 50.)

The Name Known in the 13th Century.—The above extract is also of exceptional value inasmuch as it is the earliest reference to the Prymer which, up to the present time, has come to light.

Possible Use of the Prymer in a Parish Church.—In the work on the Prymer, to which reference has just been made, it was suggested that the explanation for the presence of a Prymer at the Canterbury church may possibly lie in a belief that the book was not for use, but merely formed part of the property of the church given by pious parishioners for the purpose of eventual sale by the churchwardens, the proceeds to go to the sustentation of the church fabric and services.

Without in any way contradicting this theory, it may not, perhaps, be uninteresting to advance another, perhaps equally credible, though neither can be considered, at present, to be in any sense established.

We know the modern idea believing books in the Middle Ages to have been of especial rarity and value, and the ability to read them confined almost exclusively to the clergy, though until comparatively lately very widely accepted, is now very far from being generally received. Is it possible, then, that service books and prymers were at times used as books from which children and choristers were sometimes taught? Certainly the two following extracts seem to lend some support to such a theory: "Item III. old legendys for childryn to learn on." (Inventory printed in *Boys' History of Sandwich,* p. 376.)

In the second extract, the child mentioned has previously been specially referred to as a "little clergeon" or chorister.

> This litel child, his litel book lerninge,
> As he sat in the scole at his prymer,
> He Alma redemptoris herde singe,
> As children learned hir antiphoner.
> —(Chaucer's *Tale of the Prioress,* Skeat's edition.)

Princess Margaret's Prymer.—In the Library at Chatsworth is a Prymer of more than common interest; the book, according to a comparative modern inscription on its fly leaf, having been given by Henry VII. to his daughter, Margaret, by whom it was afterwards given to the Archbishop of St. Andrews. In two places unoccupied by the text of the volume occur the following inscriptions in the handwriting of the King: "Remembre your kynde and louyng fader in your good prayers, HENRY R." (lf. 14). "Pray for your louyng fader that gave you this booke and gave you att all tymes gooddes blessyng and myne, HENRY R." (lf. 32 b.).

The book contains the full text of the Prymer, with additional matter; is a Latin version, and retains two unmutilated illuminations representing the murder of St. Thomas of Canterbury. It is a Sarum book. On the last page but one is written: "My good lorde of saynt tandrews I pray you pray for me that gaufe yow thys bwuk yowrs too my powr, Margaret."

According to an inscription on the last page, the book was for many years in the possession of a magistrate of Bruges. The binding retains the original sides of stamped leather inscribed four times: "Dona nobis pa . . . ."

The manufacturer's authorised representative in the EU for product safety is Oxford University Press España S.A. of el Parque Empresarial San Fernando de Henares, Avenida de Castilla, 2 – 28830 Madrid (www.oup.es/en or product. safety@oup.com). OUP España S.A. also acts as importer into Spain of products made by the manufacturer.

www.ingramcontent.com/pod-product-compliance
Ingram Content Group UK Ltd.
Pitfield, Milton Keynes, MK11 3LW, UK
UKHW022151230426
12049UKWH00003BA/41